MW00332812

ASIA SHOCK

ALSO BY PATRICK GALLOWAY
Stray Dogs & Lone Wolves: The Samurai Film Handbook

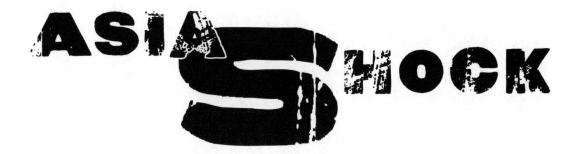

ASIA SHOCK

*Horror and Dark Cinema
from Japan, Korea,
Hong Kong, and Thailand*

by Patrick Galloway

Illustrations by Greg Lofrano

Stone Bridge Press • Berkeley, California

Published by
Stone Bridge Press
P.O. Box 8208
Berkeley, CA 94707
tel 510-524-8732 • sbp@stonebridge.com • www.stonebridge.com

Text © 2006 Patrick Galloway. Illustrations © 2006 Greg Lofrano.

Front-cover photograph © 2003 SHOW EAST. All rights reserved.

Cover and text design by Linda Ronan.

All rights reserved.

No part of this book may be reproduced in any form
without permission from the publisher.

Printed in the United States of America.

2010 2009 2008 2007 2006   10 9 8 7 6 5 4 3 2 1

LIBRARY OF CONGRESS CATALOGING-IN-PUBLICATION DATA
Galloway, Patrick.
   Asia shock: horror and dark cinema from Japan, Korea, Hong Kong, and
Thailand / Patrick Galloway; illustrations by Greg Lofrano.
      p. cm.
      Includes bibliographical references and index.
      ISBN-10: 1-933330-12-0
      ISBN-13: 978-1-933330-12-9 (pbk.)
      1. Horror films—Asia—History and criticism. 2. Fantasy films—Asia—
History and criticism. I. Title.
      PN1995.9.H6G35 2006
      791.43'6164095—dc22

2006028264

TABLE OF CONTENTS

WORD # FOREWORD FORE

Ever since I can remember, I've loved the dead. Not literally, you understand, but conceptually. From an early age, my imagination and curiosity have run to the morbid, the depraved, to desperate acts with guns and knives, to people in the woods with plastic bags and shovels, to dark secrets behind the boathouse, to things unearthed that play havoc with the living—that sort of thing. As a teenager I read *The Exorcist*, *The Omen*, *The Amityville Horror*, Poe, Lovecraft, and King, and I wrote my own twisted little tales. And, of course, horror films were a perennial pleasure. Years later, when I discovered Asian film, I found not only a lively tradition of macabre cinema (particularly in Japan), but one far more extreme and outrageous than anything I'd experienced before. Rivers of blood! Mountains of corpses! There seemed to be no limits placed on the Asian filmmaker's vision, no boundaries in terms of topic or depiction. Everything imaginable was on the chopping block, so to speak. How gratifying to find two things I loved, morbid tales and Asian cinema, coming together so beautifully. This book is an expression of my appreciation for the Asian films and filmmakers who opened my eyes to what horror is really all about.

I am forever grateful for the insight and editorial advice of Shirley Galloway, without whose love I'd be pushing up daisies and this book wouldn't exist. Mighty thanks to Peter Goodman, Greg Dicum, Greg Blote, Greg Lofrano (that's a lot of Gregs!), Seiichi Sasaki, and Ric Menello.

I should also introduce Daigon, the official mascot of *Asia Shock*.

© GREG LOFRANO

"Let the madness begin!"

Daigon is a demon warrior and, for the purposes of this book, Patron Saint of Extreme Asian Cinema. He'll be popping up occasionally in these pages, mostly to give his own brand of "thumbs up" or "thumbs down" in the many capsule reviews that accompany the longer critical pieces.

Asia Shock represents a personal journey. It was not my intention to write an exhaustive discussion of Asian dark cinema and this is certainly no all-inclusive omnibus. My aim was to look at a lot of films and write about what I considered the standouts, films that had more to offer than just blood, films that explored the grotesque rather than the merely gross. It is my hope that I've come up with some good insights and shed some light—but not too much light. The darkness hates the light. . . .

Patrick Galloway

1 DARK CINEMA

This book is an exploration of what I've termed "dark cinema." Dark cinema is a meta-genre that embraces the macabre and disturbing, shocking and profane, dire and devastating extremes of the contemporary film experience. Dark cinema encompasses the horror genre, but extends to exploitation film, black comedy, psychological thrillers, and police procedurals (the kind that investigate a string of abominable crimes), as well as certain types of art house fare. The common denominator? The *darkness.* In my scheme, dark essentially equals death, and there's no escaping the cold shadow of that scythe-toting, bony-finger-beckoning cowled one—it extends over all the films on offer in *Asia Shock,* a region of dark corners, nightmares, cruelty, insanity, imprisonment, murder, and revenge. There's also a good deal of gore, ghosts, curses, cannibalism, voodoo, disease, zombies, demons, necrophilia, rape, psychosis, all manner of torture, and bulging bin bags of body parts. Along the way you'll encounter human pork buns, a haunted cell phone, the odd corpse in a wall, a bit of tongue amputation, a cursed videotape, someone hung from hooks, and the occasional unpleasant medical experiment. Fasten your seatbelts, folks. . . .

But there's more to this dark journey than just a horror show; wipe away the blood and you'll find an awful lot of very good films here. My criteria for choosing movies for *Asia Shock* was twofold: (1) The films had to have a certain unnerving quality, to be sure, but (2) they had to be *good.* I don't particularly care for schlock, and have no interest in writing an in-depth meditation on something that doesn't merit it. Therefore

9

all of the films discussed here (with the exception of a few sidebars) are well-mounted, well-executed, worthwhile affairs made by talented people who genuinely have something to offer. There is a quality to each film, a luminescence cutting through the miasma of depravity and dementia—the shining light of sublimely shocking art! And because the perfect fusion of art and atrocity is a rare thing, you can be sure that I screened many a film that didn't qualify for this book. I sought out only the best, and for every film included here there are three or four that didn't measure up. So, far from some all-inclusive, omnibus effort, *Asia Shock* represents a look at dark cinema that is selective, or, if you prefer, *subjective;* I understand nobody's going to agree with me on every one of these films and I'm sure I'll hear all about the films I left out or shouldn't have included in the first place. But if you're a fan of dark film or Asian cinema (or both), there should be enough here to satisfy your intellectual curiosity, as well as your thirst for blood.

In the meantime, let's set out on our tenebrous trek. We've got a collection of films that are as shocking as they are superb (and vice versa), but there's a third quality that sets these magnificent movies apart: they're all from Asia. We've got movies from Japan, South Korea, China (Hong Kong, really), and Thailand. Whether you come to these films from a genuine interest in the national cultures of the various countries or are merely seeking some perceived "exoticism," you'll soon find your interest has led you to some exceptional entertainment.

I should state at the outset that the distribution is far from equitable. Roughly half the films are Japanese and only a handful are from Thailand. This is due to various factors, including availability of titles, relative development of respective national cinemas, and personal taste. In the case of Thailand, I'm sure there are many more films that would have merited inclusion but for the paucity of subtitled prints; the exploding yet still-emergent Thai film industry has yet to penetrate world markets, making it tough for us in the West to see these great films. As it is, getting your hands on the Thai films reviewed here is trickier than it should be (although this will surely change in the future). As for Japan, forget about it—there was no way Japanese cinema wasn't going to dominate this book. Japan has a long and illustrious film history rivaling that of Hollywood, and when it comes to dark cinema, nobody does it like the Japanese. Hong Kong cinema boasts a distinguished history and massive output as well, but less so in the realm of dark film; time and again I screened Hong Kong films, only to find the dark aspects superseded by comedic or action elements (although that's not to say I didn't find some absolute corkers). And then there's Korean film. As of this writing, South Korea is experiencing a cinematic Golden Age, and it is my sincere pleasure to celebrate its astounding contributions in these pages. I should add that the Korean films reviewed here don't pull any punches; like the psychic equivalent of a busted rib, they'll stay with you, reminding you of your recent trauma with every turn, every breath.

Nobody Does It Darker

Why is a Hong Kong film about a man who murders a family infinitely more harrowing than its nearest American counterpart? What makes a psychotic Korean hitchhiker so much more terrifying than the freakiest Hollywood hitcher? And are those Japanese kids really playing soccer with *a human head?* While Hollywood only talks about eating someone's liver with some fava beans, the Asian version will actually *serve it up.* Or worse. Consider the various human brain dishes in *Another Heaven* (Japan), the fetus dumplings of *Three . . . Extremes* (Hong Kong), or the live octopus in *Oldboy* (South Korea)—when you really sit down and dig into dark Asian cinema, comparing what's on the menu with Western fare, there's no escaping the conclusion that the Asian stuff is far more intense. *Asia Shock* is a celebration of this filmic fact, imbued as it is with a general theme of *vive le difference!*

But why should it be so? What is it about Asian dark cinema that makes it so deeply dark, so intrinsically transgressive? There are many possible answers to this question, a few of which are discussed below. Like points on a map charting the dark waters, they will help us navigate the murky depths and enhance our understanding and enjoyment of these marvelously morbid movies.

RELIGION

Let's face it, growing up in the United States puts a bit of the puritanical in everybody. The spirit of those dour pilgrims lives on in the heart of America, a land where repression and denial play a part in daily life. Certain provocative or unpleasant but nevertheless essential truths regarding the human experience just aren't on the table here, due in no small part to the historical (and contemporary) influence of religion. Traditional Christianity simply won't tolerate certain types of exploration in thought, deed, or art; the resultant baffles and filters are so inculcated in our popular culture that it isn't until you watch a film from a country without such conventions that you begin to see what, perhaps, you didn't even know you were missing! Dark Asian

KOROSHIYA ICHI

© PRENOM/OMEGA

Kakihara from *Ichi the Killer*

films are a good wake-up call in this regard, coming as they do from a more transcendent, pragmatic philosophical tradition. Never mind monotheism, Asian religious traditions extend to pantheism, polytheism, even atheism. Instead of a short life followed by an eternity in heaven or hell, how about everything is alive and will be forever (viz. animism and reincarnation)? Such an approach, incorporating a generalized awareness of the eternal nature of the world, would tend to make for a more relaxed attitude toward, say, flights of the imagination in art, literature, and film. In Japan, such imaginative excursions in film, manga, and anime serve as a necessary pressure valve for young and old alike. Ever notice how you never hear about Japanese serial killers? What's the old joke? An American despairs, kills twelve people; a Japanese despairs, kills himself (ho, ho).

What can account for this greater imaginative freedom in Asian cultures? In a nation like the United States, where fundamentalist perceptions are not uncommon—not just religious fundamentalism, but a generalized, simplistic, black/white, good/evil approach to many aspects of society—*to imagine* something almost equates to *doing* it. Consider the Catholic concept of the three stages of sin (i.e., by thought, word, and deed). Without these kinds of cultural restraints, journeys of the imagination, in which even deep-seated fears and nightmares can be explored without restriction, can lead to a sense of freedom and catharsis. Whereas an American may claim that a "sick" horror film introduces sick ideas into a viewer's mind and is bad for society, an Asian filmgoer may be less concerned with such issues and more likely to enjoy it for the flight of dark fancy that it is.

All this is not to say that folks on the Asian side of the Pacific Rim are all carefree and unrepressed, meditating on the Tao, and smiling all day; people are people and Eastern man has his problems just like Western man. And, of course, there has always been a lively belief in the tortures of Hell in Japanese and Chinese culture (an eventuality never mentioned by the Buddha, by the way). Nevertheless, the absence of an overarching puritanical religious tradition in Japan, Korea, China, and Thailand plays a definite role in the resultant attitudes toward (and depictions of) life and death expressed in their respective national cinemas. This allows for a greater (and at times more extreme) range of material.

THE SUPERNATURAL

While Western man's motto is, "There's no such thing as ghosts," in Asia the story is somewhat different. The idea of ghosts is still a going concern in Chinese culture, for example, based on centuries of tradition and providing a culturally flexible model for all sorts of non-human beings (for example, the pejorative term for Caucasians in Cantonese is *gwai-lo*, literally "ghost person"). The Chinese *gwai* ranges from the familiar fading phantom to a seemingly flesh and blood individual. In Japanese folklore, a *yokai* (ghost) can make love with you or just as soon rip your ears off, such is their potential for physicality. Often, though, they'll use illusion, haunting and taunting you into a terrified rage, then overshadow a family member, thus forcing you in your distraught state to slay the ones you love (this is a favorite method of revenge). In Thailand there is the Pob, or "liver-hungry ghost," a hideous old hag with long, sharp nails for getting at that delicious organ meat you keep concealed in your midriff.

The physical prowess of Asian ghosts makes for a more intense supernatural thriller, movie-wise. In the West we're so used to the idea of spooky yet essentially ineffectual specters that when one actually becomes destructive on the physical plane, we say "Oooh, a *poltergeist!*"—whereas the Pob is too busy ripping your innards out to care about moving stuff around in your house. You see the difference? The relative physical presence of the ghost correlates with its cultural presence; Western ghosts are ethereal floaters because our collective belief in them is weak, but the Asian ghost is powerful and strong, willing and able to take you on. You can see how this raises the stakes in film; often the living are not merely haunted by ghosts, they're *murdered* by them.

But whether the ghost physically assaults you, influences another to do you in, or simply scares you to death, there will be no time wasted, no tiresome longueurs puzzling over the phenomena like you might get in a Hollywood picture. A generalized ghost-belief in the audience means the filmmaker can hit the ground running without having to make the investigative or scientific case for spook activity (unless the film consciously incorporates Western influences as in films like *Inner Senses* and *The Eye*).

HISTORY

It's no secret that as powerful and influential as America is, we've got a culture that is in many ways insulated, ignorant, and immature. This is due in part to our history, a rather short one when compared to that of Europe and, to a greater extent, Asia. A culture is like an individual in that the longer it lives and the more it sees, the less shocked it's likely to become by the horrendous realities of life. That's why if *Se7en* had been made in Japan, Korea, or China, you'd have seen Gwyneth Paltrow's head in that box; the Asian filmmaker recognizes what a powerful cinematic payoff such a shot would be and, considering the subject matter, wouldn't pull such a solid punch so late in the game. Watching dark or extreme Asian cinema, one is often struck by the frankness and almost down-to-earth quality of the screen violence; ancient, seen-it-all cultures are less likely to flinch at the cruel, disturbing, yet all-too-familiar aspects of human behavior. Consider the murder of a child. I can tell you from experience that killing kids on screen isn't the taboo in Asian film that it is in the United States. These cultures have seen a lot over the centuries (how many children died in the endless wars, famines, and plagues of Chinese history? How many were incinerated in Hiroshima and Nagasaki?). These cultures don't have the whole Cult of the Child thing as we do here in the States. In Asian films, kids don't always make it.

I appreciate the honesty; history is filled with countless brutal murders of women, children, the old, and the infirm, so why pretend this isn't part of the human experience? Screen violence in American film, while decried by moralizers, is in fact fairly tame; whether the filmmaker cuts away at the crucial moment or renders the proceedings cartoonish with video-game verisimilitude, the cumulative experience of the filmgoer doesn't come close to the visceral impact of a Category III Hong Kong picture or a Toei Studios exploitation flick from the '70s, Japan's golden age of film atrocity. Seeing these films for the first time, one will experience feelings ranging from shock and awe to something akin to liberation. It's as if certain dark cinematic truths have been kept locked away by an over-protective parent and, suddenly, a film from a foreign land with a millennium or two of history has blown open the door. It's a form of culture shock that can, if you're ready for it, be good for your soul.

Catharsis and Ambiguity

I realize until now I've been dwelling on the more extreme aspects of dark Asian cinema, but it isn't all weeping and wailing and mourning and gnashing of teeth. In choosing titles for *Asia Shock,* I have tried to provide a spectrum of film experience ranging from the obvious to the obscure—in effect, from the jarringly cathartic to the tantalizingly ambiguous. Let's look more closely at this latter quality.

A hundred years ago, the word "inscrutable" was commonly used to describe members of the populations of "The Orient"; the word has since been banished from enlightened parlance (as has "The Orient"), but the fact remains that Eastern Man is not, on average, as forthcoming with what's on his mind as his Western counterpart. This is by no means a bad thing. Indeed such reserve, when applied to literature and drama, can lend a stately, refined, and somewhat mysterious distance to the artistic endeavor. Japanese horror films are an inheritor of this elliptical narrative tradition, often exhibiting a willful ambiguity, challenging audiences to come up with solutions to puzzles left unsolved. Sometimes it's just a matter of a light touch, of not straining to dot every "i" and cross every "t" plot-wise, as is more the case in American horror cinema (compare Hideo Nakata's original *The Ring* to its Hollywood remake for a good example of this dichotomy).

Leaving things unsaid or obscure is an integral component in Japanese culture, so common that there's a term for it in everyday speech, *aimai.* For this reason, Japanese audiences are more likely to accept a certain degree of ambiguity in film and not immediately interpret it as a flaw or plot problem. This is not to excuse plain old narrative sloppiness; Asian filmmakers make their share of stinkers just like anybody else. But when indirectness and obscuration are consciously incorporated into the director's palette and used in just the right measure, they can render subtle, beautiful, and surprisingly effective results. This uniquely Asian brand of artful ambiguity, when done right, stimulates post-screening discussion and debate, inspires people to create websites to explore the film more fully, and most often rewards repeat viewings. I tend to find that, provided it's well made, the most perplexing Asian film will eventually unravel itself upon return visits. I see films like *Suicide Club* and *Another Heaven* as challenging yet ultimately decipherable enigmas, yielding up their treasures to those willing to dig.

At the other end of the scale we find films that explore deprav-

"Listen carefully and I will explain all about *Battle Royale!*"

ity and darkness in no uncertain terms, providing (if you're up to the sensory and emotional onslaught) unexpected moments of cathartic release. For example, I'm not particularly drawn to torture; I don't practice it, don't approve of it politically, and never really considered it a dramatic element worthy of basing a whole film on. Then I saw *The Joy of Torture*. Having witnessed all the terrible things that go down in that film (see review), when the cruel ones finally got their comeuppance, I felt a rush of vicarious vengeance like no other. We all know what it's like to be oppressed, bullied, tormented, but when those feelings are pushed to the breaking point in a film like *The Joy of Torture,* the catharsis that follows is nothing short of revelatory. It's akin to the "good cry" of the tearjerker or the belly laugh of an uproarious comedy. It's *release*. And in this way, dark cinema can be seen as a helpful, even therapeutic, pastime for members of modern, technological societies with all their attendant stress and humiliation (be they East or West).

National Cinema

The year 1997 was a watershed for Asian cinema. Financial crises, the Hong Kong handover, and a groundswell of exciting new films from

Thailand and Korea made 1997 a turning point in the history of Far Eastern film culture. To get some perspective, let's take a look at the various national cinemas discussed in *Asia Shock.*

JAPAN

Japan's film industry is as old and innovative as the twentieth century, but unfortunately most of its output during the first half of that period was destroyed during World War II. The post-war period, particularly after the withdrawal of the U.S. occupation forces in 1953, saw a flowering of Japanese cinema, featuring the continuing work of pre-war auteurs such as Ozu and Mizoguchi, and striking, vital films from newcomers like Akira Kurosawa and Masaki Kobayashi. This Golden Age extended through the '50s and '60s, the latter decade also marked by the rise of the Japanese New Wave and directors like Nagisa Oshima, Masahiro Shinoda, Hiroshi Teshigahara, and Yasuzo Masumura. The '70s saw a decline at the box office, causing increasingly desperate studio executives (particularly at Toei Studios) to turn to extreme sex and violence to attract moviegoers. This trend resulted in a copious flow of still-shocking exploitation films, with more than a few masterpieces from Toei shockmeisters Teruo Ishii and Norifumi Suzuki. The '80s and '90s were less remarkable decades in Japan's cinema history (with the exception of films by Takashi Miike, Sabu, Shinya Tsukamoto, and "Beat" Takeshi Kitano). Then the turn of the millennium brought an explosion of fresh and frightening supernatural horror films known collectively as J-horror. The J-horror boom reinvigorated the Japanese film industry and influenced other countries in the region, particularly South Korea. The impact of J-horror is currently being felt in the United States with a continuing string of Hollywood remakes of J-horror classics like *The Ring* and *Ju-on.*

SOUTH KOREA

In terms of cinema, South Korea is one of the new kids on the block, a brilliant kid, restless and wild and tough as nails. The twentieth century wasn't a fun time for Korea. Following the less-than-kindly rule of the Japanese from 1910 to 1945, the beleaguered country was plunged into civil war from 1950 to 1953, with each half of the divided nation subsequently controlled by military dictatorships. You could say it hasn't been a real good run for the artist class. Even after political reforms were instituted in South Korea in the late '80s, the film industry was still corporate-sponsored and generally conservative in its output. But the Asian financial crisis of 1997 changed all that. Big corporations pulled out of the movie biz, private investors came in, and a new at-

A Snake of June

© KAIJU THEATER

mosphere of creative freedom and artistic daring nurtured the birth of a new wave of phenomenal South Korean films. Directors like Kim Ki-duk and Park Chan-wook re-envisioned Korean cinema as a vibrant and visceral medium for exploring themes ranging from the political to the universal. In films of explosive visual style and emotional impact, these filmmakers and their contemporaries express the pent-up energy and rage of a century of repression. South Korean films have also scored big at the box office, their take increasing yearly since 1997 against other foreign imports. Ever on the hunt for product to remake, Hollywood has come a-calling, buying up the rights to dozens of Korean hits, the Americanized versions of which will be appearing soon at a cineplex near you.

HONG KONG

For decades, Hong Kong was the Hollywood of Asia, a regional powerhouse second only to Bollywood (Mumbai, India) in output. Hong Kong's status as a British colony (from 1842), coupled with its use of Cantonese (as opposed to Mandarin), set it on a separate course from mainland Chinese cinema from the advent of talkies in the early '30s. The schism was complete by the end of World War II and the ascension of Chairman Mao in 1949. During the '50s and '60s, Hong Kong cinema produced films based on Cantonese opera, martial arts pictures (such as the Wong Fei Hung series), *wuxia* (fantasy sword films), and home dramas. The early '70s saw Cantonese film faltering, but the formation of the Golden Harvest production company by two ex-Shaw Bros. executives turned things around, kickstarting the '70s kung fu explosion with pictures starring Bruce Lee and Jackie Chan. Hong Kong cinema peaked during the '80s and early '90s, coming to dominate the region with a massive output of hugely entertaining films covering action, comedy, drama, martial arts, and wuxia (often blenderizing them in the process). In 1988, a ratings system was established and the early '90s saw the proliferation of "Category III" pictures, lurid films featuring softcore pornography and gruesome horror/true crime. Then came 1997 and the handover of Hong Kong to China, a circumstance that changed the feel and fecundity of the city's film output forever. However, this is not to take away from uproarious post-handover comedies from Stephen Chow (*Shaolin Soccer, Kung Fu Hustle*) or slick cop actioners like the Infernal Affairs series.

THAILAND

The decline of Hong Kong cinema meant opportunities for other emergent national cinemas; Thailand (along with South Korea) was a direct beneficiary of this socio-political development. The year 1997 saw the release of two groundbreaking Thai pictures, Pen-ek Ratanaruang's *Fun Bar Karaoke* and Nonzee Nimibutr's *Dang Bireley and the Young Gangsters*. These movies broke Thai film big on the world stage, resuscitating it from years of decline and establishing their directors (both formerly in advertising) as industry players and stylistic innovators. The two filmmakers' reputations were further cemented by Ratanaruang's *6ixtynin9* and *Last Life in the Universe* and Nimibutr's *Nang Nak* and *Jan Dara*. Other important names on the Thai film scene include Hong Kong-born brothers Oxide and Danny Pang (*Bangkok Dangerous, The Eye*); Wisit Sasanatieng (*Tears of the Black Tiger*); Apichatpong Weerasethakul (*Mysterious Object at Noon, Tropical Malady*); and Prachya Pinkaew and Tony Jaa, director and star, respectively, of worldwide Muay Thai phenomenon *Ong Bak*. Also increasing the visibility of new Thai film was the first annual Bangkok International Art Film Festival in 1997. Older, established film genres like the historical epic got a shot in the arm as well from the Thai film resurgence with the releases of *Bang Rajan, Angulimala*, and *Suriyothai* (the latter directed by real-life royal Prince Chatreechalerm Yugala and executive produced by Francis Ford Coppola). A decade on, innovation has begun to wane, but Thailand remains a strong and vibrant force on the Asian film scene.

A Word on Romanization

The process of rendering words written in different symbol systems into our own familiar twenty-six letters is called romanization. Romanization is a tricky business, what with the inevitable variations on how it's done. Sure, there are standard methodologies for the way Asian words and proper names are written in roman letters, but sometimes there is more than one standard. Other times the person doing it (say some-

© GOLDEN SCENE/DAIEI

Pulse

one writing subtitles) is just making it up as he goes along. Needless to say, a pan-Asian survey such as *Asia Shock* offers numerous romanization choices and so, in the interest of full disclosure, I offer my romanization scheme:

- Japanese names are written Western-style, with given name first followed by surname.
- All other names are written in the name order particular to their own culture. In the case of Chinese names, which often have a Western given name appended to the front, the surname actually appears in the middle of the name (i.e., Anthony Wong Chau Sang, Wong is the surname). I use this form in cast lists, but I default to the Western name in the text (i.e., Anthony Wong).
- For Korean name spellings I standardized according to the Han Cinema Korean Movie and Drama Database (http://www.hancinema. net). For Chinese names, I observed the form used by Hong Kong Cinemagic (http:// www.hkcinemagic.com).

As for movie character names, I followed the spelling used in the subtitles. This can lead to romanization inconsistencies (and drive my publisher to distraction), but I feel it's important to preserve the link between the book and the film experience. The idea is that if you're watching a film and pick up this book, the name of a given character on the screen should match the name in the book.

Seeing the Films

It's my guess that if you're reading this book, you have at least a passing interest in seeing the films discussed here (if you haven't already) and the good news is you can—some authors like to write at length about obscure, rarely glimpsed films, but not me. If I can't see the thing, what's the point? So the good news is you can see all the films in *Asia Shock*, via either rental or purchase. Some of the titles you may have to buy to see, and I'll explain why, but first let's discuss rental options.

RENTAL

The rental scene is getting better for Asian film fans. I sometimes hit the local Hollywood Video and am always gratified by the ever-growing selection of Asian titles I see there, far more than I'd normally expect from such a corporate outlet. This tells me that Asian film is a hot market and getting hotter. My friends who patronize Blockbuster report similar progress. However, you're only going to get so much from such places, and you're certainly not going to find all the movies reviewed in this book. If you live in a big town, there's sure to be a place that specializes in foreign and art house films; brave the traffic and make that pilgrimage. Or not—use an online rental service like GreenCine (http://www.greencine.com). They have every unusual film you can think of (or if not, they'll get it for you). So with all these options you're all set to rent all the films in *Asia Shock*, right? Wrong.

DVD REGION ENCODING

As you may know, the world has been divvied up by the entertainment and consumer-electronics industries into global regions that determine who gets to watch what DVD. If you dare to buy a DVD from another part of the world, chances are your player won't play it due to an infuriating and consumer-unfriendly practice called "region encoding." Here's the breakdown:

Region 1—United States, Canada
Region 2—Japan, Western Europe, South Africa, Middle East, Greenland
Region 3—South Korea, Taiwan, Hong Kong, parts of Southeast Asia
Region 4—Australia, New Zealand, Latin America (including Mexico)

Region 5—Eastern Europe, Russia, India, Africa
Region 6—China
Region 7—Reserved for unspecified special use
Region 8—Reserved for cruise ships, airlines, etc.

If you live in the United States, chances are you bought your DVD player in the United States and that player will only play DVDs encoded for Region 1. This practice was instituted ostensibly to coordinate theatrical and DVD releases of films so a guy in England (where Hollywood films come out a few months later than in the U.S.) couldn't buy the DVD of a movie just hitting theaters there. But this logic falls apart when you realize they do the same thing with console video games. No, it's really all about price-fixing and making sure that DVD vendors can gouge consumers by charging more in some regions than in others. Americans in particular pay far more for DVDs than folks in other parts of the world. So where does that leave us? Less selection, higher prices. Doesn't seem right, does it?

That's why I recommend owning a region-free DVD player. If you're tech savvy, you may be able to modify your existing machine (just remove one chip), but there are other advantages to having a region-free player, such as PAL to NTSC conversion (a feature on many models). And rest assured that owning a region-free DVD player is not illegal. Region encodings are a matter of trade agreements, not regulation or national law, and buying a player that circumvents them is perfectly alright (no matter what the guy at Circuit City tells you). Best of all, your options for film viewing become truly global; you'll be able to see any film from anywhere on the planet, often for a lot less than you're used to paying. My region-free Malata 520 has more than paid for itself in savings from overseas orders. Of course, there are always those big-ticket Japanese disks that you kick down for because there's no other option. But at least you can see 'em!

All this is a rather roundabout way of saying that some of the films in *Asia Shock* will require a region-free player to watch. I can't tell you which ones because I honestly don't know what will be available in what region by the time you read this. In the past I've tried to offer availability ratings for films, but things are changing so fast these days that it's just not worth the inevitable inaccuracies that accumulate as time goes on. Just since starting this book, half a dozen titles I had to buy in other regions have been released in Region 1 (some have even been released theatrically in the United States, like *Pulse* and *Three . . . Extremes*). Who'd have thought we'd ever see a Region 1 disk of Hong Kong voodoo flick *The Eternal Evil of Asia?* Now every citizen of the

United States and Canada will have the chance to see Elvis Tsui's immortal performance as a man whose head is transformed into a giant penis. The times, they are a-changin.'

PURCHASE

If you're like me, you're an obsessive sort who wants to own these freaky films, to collect them, display them, cherish them, and force your friends to watch them! Again, some films you're just not going to find on Amazon. When the going gets tough, I go here:

Amazon UK—http://www.amazon.co.uk
> Yes, it's Amazon in the UK, and you'll find things here that are unavailable on the American site. Even items that are available on both sites can be eye-openingly cheaper here (but it's all Region 2, so get that region-free player, already!).

CD Japan—http://www.cdjapan.co.jp
> The real deal: a Japanese company selling Japanese disks out of Japan. Be forewarned, though, it ain't cheap. But I've found stuff here I could find nowhere else.

EThaiCD—http://www.ethaicd.com
> This is a great source for all things Thai. I found films here after much searching elsewhere.

Yes Asia—http://www.yesasia.com
Sensasian.com—http://www.sensasian.com
> Yes Asia and Sensasian are good for filling in the gaps. In addition to movies and music, you can find books, toys, and collectibles to feed that otaku urge!

Bear in mind you won't be able to enjoy the cornucopia of fabulous films available from these vendors without a region-free player. In addition to these resources, there are always third-party vendors, entrepreneurs who acquire rare foreign titles, make copies, add subtitles, and voilà! Even *more* films to obsess on.

I mentioned earlier that you may have to buy some of the films in this book to see them. This is because of the region encoding—big chains aren't going to rent anything but Region 1. This goes for online rental outfits like GreenCine and Netflix, as well. There are places online that rent DVDs for other regions, but I haven't used them so I can't make a recommendation.

It all starts here. Family is the miasma from which we all must emerge, a bubbling cauldron of neuroses, abuse, and recrimination where we stew for the formative years of our young lives, a period from which few emerge unscathed. And yet our own family traumas are nothing compared to the horrors of those who populate the following films. As we shall see, some family members will fall upon one another like feral beasts, while others work together to achieve their own dark ends. A father will have trouble with his dead mistress, a son will kill the rivals of his yakuza daddy, various mothers will wreak vengeance from beyond the grave, and two brave sisters will challenge the darkness that surrounds them. Blood indeed is thicker than water. . . .

Visitor Q

What do filmmakers Jean Renoir, Pier Paolo Pasolini, Paul Mazursky, and Takashi Miike all have in common? They've all made films (with varying degrees of success) concerning a mysterious houseguest and the profound effect he has on the various inhabitants of the household. In Renoir's *Boudu, Saved from Drowning* (1932), the visitor comes in the form of a scruffy old Paris tramp who, subsequent to being plucked from the waters of the Seine, sets about trashing his rescuer's home and seducing his wife and maid. In Pasolini's *Teorema* (1968), the stranger

2001

Japan

84 min.

DIRECTOR: Takashi Miike

CAST: Kenichi Endo,
Shungiku Uchida,
Fujiko, Jun Muto,
Kazushi Watanabe,
Shoko Nakahara

(Terence Stamp), who is either Jesus or Satan (or just a suave young bloke) winds up sleeping with an entire family (mom, dad, brother, sister, and the maid) before leaving them to self-destruct in the barren wasteland of their bourgeois existence. Mazursky's *Down and Out in Beverly Hills* (1986) appears to be a synthesis of both *Teorema* and *Boudu* (minus Pasolini's homosexual agenda) set against the pink and teal backdrop of opulent '80s Los Angeles.

Miike for his part does things a little bit differently: His visitor does not seduce anyone (not literally, at least) and outside of delivering the odd massive rock blow to the head (dad, sis) and getting up to a bit of tit squeezing (mom), he's actually a rather well-behaved, unobtrusive guest. His hosts, on the other hand, are a mess, without a doubt the most dysfunctional family in movie history. No worries, though; like his cinematic forebears, Mr. Q's sojourn will transform this wretched group, leaving a deep and lasting impression on all concerned.

And speaking of lasting impressions, good God, Keiko Yamazaki (Shungiku Uchida) is covered with them: deep lacerations, the result of brutal beatings meted out by her son Takuya (Jun Muto) with a rug-beater (he has a whole collection in his closet). "Please, not the face!" she screams as he launches into one of his sadistic assaults. It's a cycle of abuse, really; Takuya's been taking his own beatings from a group of school bullies who also enjoy humiliating him by forcing him to defecate by the side of the road and, when he can't, urinating on him. He isn't even safe in his home; the bullies come around each night, shouting taunts, busting his windows, and shooting all manner of fireworks into his room. So mom takes the brunt. To get away from it all, she retires to her room and avails herself of the persuasive charms of a little sweet China White. But her heroin habit costs money, so off she goes each morning to turn a few tricks for johns who dig her slashed-up skin and cute little limp.

Kiyoshi Yamazaki (baggy-eyed Kenichi Endo in a career-peak performance) is Keiko's husband and Takuya's dad. He's a television news reporter who's recently fallen from favor; an interview with some Tokyo street punks went awry and caused a scandal (they shoved his microphone up his ass . . . on camera). Now he's trying to find a gripping social issue-type story he can use to regain his status in the industry. However, he seems incapable of looking any farther than his own children for the story. First he chooses teenage prostitution (a real-life social problem in Japan) and interviews his daughter Miki (Fujiko), who's recently moved out and turned pro. His plan backfires during the interview as his daughter seduces him, instantly transforming the taped interview into an incest porno. Then Kiyoshi turns to his son's victimization at the hands of school bullies (another big issue in Japanese society), but instead of getting involved or helping his son in any way, he voyeuristically videotapes the boy's abuse and degradation from afar. Soon the bullies are launching an all-out fireworks attack on the Yamazaki household, filling it with whizzing colored lights and explosions like a mini-war scene, as the family and Visitor Q are having dinner. Kiyoshi tapes everyone at the table and the general chaos around them, shouting narration:

> Can you see this? This is my home. My home! Did you see that? The big strong bullies are here. This is my wife! She's a lovely little wife! Dinner was delicious. [The camera falls on Q] This is . . . I don't know who this is, we're not acquainted. Watch! It's amazing, truly amazing! What a scene, it's unbelievable . . . How am I supposed to feel? I don't know how a father should feel! But I know my family is being destroyed!

Kiyoshi has a girlfriend named Asako (Shoko Nakahara), a pretty reporter to whom he's been pitching his ideas. He wants to get her involved in his bullying story, but as they sit in his car watching his son being done over, Asako becomes disgusted and storms off, telling Kiyoshi what he can do with his "story" and their relationship. This sends Dad over the edge. He attacks Asako, rips off her clothes and rapes her in a ditch. Suddenly he notices that he's accidentally strangled her to death and gets Q to help get her back to his house. Once there, in the greenhouse out back, he tells Q, "Alright, we'll cut her in small pieces

Ju-on: The Grudge (Japan, 2003) You'd be hard pressed to find a Japanese family more dysfunctional than *Visitor Q*'s Yamazaki family, but the Saekis of *Ju-on: The Grudge* are certainly in the running. For one thing, they're all murderous ghosts, made so by dad in a jealous rage: He carved up wife Kayako, little son Toshio, even the cat! Now whoever sets foot in their house shortly succumbs to their infernal rage. As of this writing, the Ju-on saga spans five films: two straight-to-video installments from 2000 (the first starring Chiaki Kuriyama from *Battle Royale* and *Shikoku*), then two theatrical versions (*Ju-on: The Grudge* and *Ju-on: The Grudge 2*, both 2003), and finally the inevitable U.S. remake, *The Grudge* (2004). A sequel to the latter is in the works and, with a rumored *second* Japanese sequel, who knows where it will end? Director Takashi Shimizu (who developed the original story for a workshop conducted by Kiyoshi Kurosawa) directed every installment and so impressed Sam Raimi that the American horror auteur hired Shimizu to helm the Ghost House Pictures 2004 version starring Sarah Michelle Gellar, creating that rarest of things: a decent Hollywood remake. But for this writer's money, *Ju-on: The Grudge* is still the one to watch.

and put them in a plastic bag. Keep [video]taping until she's in the trash." Kiyoshi marks the important dismemberment spots on Asako's nude body, but this gets him turned on again: "Some things are truly strange," he muses. Then: "Come on, let's do it. I don't care if you are a corpse. Corpses are fine with me." *In flagrante*, he reaches down: "The mysteries of life are amazing! A corpse can get wet!" A moment later, a dark discovery: "It's not a mystery of life, it's shit!" (In this moment of unparalleled cinematic perversity, Yamazaki's existential epiphany echoes that of Theater of Cruelty founder Antonin Artaud, who put it this way: "Where there is the stink of shit, there is the smell of being.")

Visitor Q was shot on digital video, the final installment of the six-part, direct-to-video Love Cinema series for Japanese distributor CineRocket. Shooting in DV gives *Visitor Q* a sharp, clean look that blends seamlessly with Kiyoshi's own obsessive "coverage," and lends the whole proceeding a documentary flavor. Documentaries tend to put us in the midst of the action, inviting us to examine and evaluate what we are seeing on the screen; such a technique heightens the absurdity of the various over-the-top situations in this film, leading to laughter. How uncomfortable this laughter is will come down to the personal makeup of the individual viewer.

Takashi Miike shot *Visitor Q* in one week for $70,000. Like the rest of the Love Cinema series, it got an obligatory "theatrical release" in a little suburban theater outside Tokyo (to help legitimize it in marketing materials), but was never intended for anything more than retail product. Miike, no stranger to V-cinema (the straight-to-video market), thrives on obstacles and tight budgets, sublimating the attendant stress and aggravation of the shoot back into the film itself. Miike's genius lies in incorporating spontaneity and found objects, in what accident does to artifice seconds out of the ring. "For me, film is something to bump into by accident. I like the feeling of chance encounters" (Patrick Macias, *Tokyoscope*, p. 217). His is the ideal personality for a prolific workaholic churning out mind-blowing movies at breakneck speed on miniscule budgets.

Shungiku Uchida, who plays the mother, Keiko, in *Visitor Q*, made a unique personal contribution to the film that perfectly illustrates Miike's penchant for utilizing available resources. Uchida had given birth just before shooting began and was lactating copiously. This quickly became a central feature and theme of the story. In the film, Q squeezes Keiko's breasts and milk unexpectedly begins to squirt from her nipples, shooting everywhere, including, symbolically, on a photo of her estranged daughter. The breast-milk-as-maternal-love symbolism is sustained throughout the film; once she begins lactating, Keiko is renewed, revitalized, in touch with her strong, nurturing mother-self. She stands up to her son (with a knife), reconnects with her husband, rediscovers the joys of domesticity, and smiles a lot.

Uchida turns in a subtle yet moving performance made all the more compelling considering her background. Uchida is a writer and manga artist whose bestseller, *Father Fucker,* relates a semi-autobiographical account of her own experiences with incest and abuse. Imagine the emotional memories stirred up by the scene where Keiko recognizes her own daughter's vaginal scent on her husband's penis. It's the kind of dramatic moment method actors dream of.

For all its outrageousness and depravity, *Visitor Q* is essentially a story about family, a daring entry in the "home drama" genre, and, in the end, it upholds traditional Japanese family values. The fundamental unit of Japanese society is the *uchi,* meaning "house" or "household," a word containing the implicit notion of interiority, of that which is intrinsically *inside* (as opposed to the people and things outside the uchi). Chaos within the uchi is a symptom and also a cause of instability in the society, a concept not lost on filmmakers like Miike, whose *Visitor Q* can be seen as a comment on the economic and social decline of Japan in the '90s. Therefore, to restore harmony in the uchi (albeit via dismemberment, multiple homicide, and the odd blow to the head) is to restore order in the nation of Japan and thus provide a public service. Hats off to Takashi Miike, shock cinema auteur and savior of the nation.

The Quiet Family • Choyonghan kajok

1998
South Korea
105 min.

DIRECTOR: Kim Ji-woon
CAST: Song Kang-ho, Park In-hwan, Na Mun-hee, Choi Min-sik, Lee Yeon-sung, Go Ho-kyung, Lee Ki-yeong, Ji Su-won, Jeong Woong-in, Ki Joo-bong

Black comedy should be two things: exceedingly morbid and ball-bouncingly funny. *The Quiet Family* is both in *spades* (and talking of spades, there are plenty around for digging shallow graves). Black comedies really don't get much better than this for plot, comedic timing, casting, ensemble acting, pacing, editing, and soundtrack. In fact, this is a perfect film to show someone you wish to turn on to dark Asian cinema (provided they have the prerequisite sick sense of humor).

The eponymous family, the Kangs, are a grim lot. Father (Park In-hwan) is stern and morose; Mother (Na Mun-hee) is bitter and short-tempered; seventeen-year-old Mi-na (Go Ho-kyung) is the youngest—introspective, cynical, and bored; Mi-su (Lee Yeon-sung), her sister, is lazy, vain, and lonely for a man; Uncle Chang-ku (Choi Min-sik) is lonely, too, and something of a loser, as is only-son Yeong-min (Song Kang-ho), who also has a criminal record and a proclivity for

© ILSIN PICTURES

Family secrets abound in *The Quiet Family*

peeping. The Kang family has opened a mountain lodge and business is the shits. Nobody comes to their little guesthouse, and as the tension mounts, tempers are wearing thin—Dad is kicking the dog, Uncle Chang is strangling Mi-na, etc. Is there a curse on the place? Perhaps. Early in the film a crazy old lady from the village assails the lodge and various family members, screaming, "The head dripping with blood was hidden here! Now why is it up there? Damn you!" She scowls up at something only she can see near the rooftop. "Get the hell away from there! Fools! You've got a damn ugly one (hock tooey)!" Later, at supper, Mi-na and Uncle Chang amuse themselves attempting to imitate the old hag's singular hocking and spitting technique, much to the consternation of Mi-su and Father.

Finally, a guest arrives, a wretched middle-aged man whom the family initially takes for a vagrant (popular character actor Ki Joo-bong). He checks in, orders a few beers, makes a weird speech to Yeong-min about loneliness, and that's the last time anyone sees him alive as he offs himself later that night. What's a family to do? He's left no note or will, his wallet is missing (all eyes on Yeong-min)—it looks suspicious as hell. Plus, if word of the death were to get out, it would further damage the already dismal business at the lodge. There's nothing for it, decides Father, so he, Mom, Uncle Chang, and Yeong-min grab shovels and a plastic tarp and dig a hole—that's that. Unfortunately, this isn't the last suicide they'll have to cover up; a pale young couple check in, engage in one final, candle-lit union (secretly observed by Yeong-min) and in the morning are both found dead of an overdose. During the burial, how-

© ILSIN PICTURES

The Quiet Family welcomes you with open ... graves

ever, the male corpse comes screaming back to life and in the ensuing
panic Father inadvertently finishes
the job with a short, sharp shovel to
the head.

Things proceed from bad to
worse. Every time it seems like the
Kangs finally have things under
control, another catastrophe occurs.
The new road they've been waiting
for to improve business becomes a
threat when Father realizes that the
ensuing excavation will disturb the
freshly dug graves. When Mi-su is
assaulted by a guest (Jeong Woong-
in), Yeong-min head-butts him,
sending him careening off a cliff.
Murder plots, exhumations, police
investigations, a hit man, a captive, North Korean spies, and a corpse-
revealing storm all dog the efforts of the hapless Kangs. Will they ever
find peace?

The Quiet Family is an instant classic, and a remarkable debut by
director Kim Ji-woon. The comedy is tight, subtle, and right on the
money, keying on the intimacy and antagonism of the family dynamic.
The film is strewn with perfect moments, little bits of family-based comedic business that pay off because of their universality. There's Mom
spying a bit of missed blood on the woodwork and spit-cleaning it with
her fingers. Here's Dad, beaming with pride as he commends his son
for his fine grave-digging abilities. And here's Brother, basking in the
glow of his father's respect, asking if anyone has anything else to bury,
a kimchee pot perhaps?

As Laurence Olivier said in Anthony Shaffer's immortal *Sleuth*,
"There's nothing like a little mayhem to cheer one up!" and a little mayhem is just what the Kangs need to reinvigorate their sense of togeth-
erness and family bonding. In this way, *The Quiet Family* can be compared
to Takashi Miike's *Visitor Q;* both films concern families made closer by
the exigencies resulting from random violence and a preponderance
of dead bodies. It's not surprising, therefore, that Miike decided to do
a remake of *The Quiet Family*, the infamous musical *The Happiness of the
Katakuris*. I saw *The Happiness of the Katakuris* first, but after seeing *The
Quiet Family*, I can safely say that, once again, the original is better than
the remake. (There are only two remakes I'm aware of that are better

than the originals: *Little Shop of Horrors* and *The Thing*.) In retrospect, it seems Miike knew he had a tall order on his hands remaking such an excellent, pitch-black comedy. So, in typical Miike style, he went over the top—*way* over the top. He cast aging Japanese rock star Kiyoshiro Imawano in the role of the cliff-hanging (and falling) cad. He reconfigured the family, adding a small child and a grandpa, and cast film legend Tetsuro Tamba in the latter role. For the father, he got Kenji Sawada who, back in 1981, portrayed the Christian martyr-turned-demon-ghost Shiro Tokisada Amakusa in *Samurai Reincarnation* (1981). Miike turned the suicidal couple into a sumo wrestler and his underage date (who die of heart failure and suffocation, respectively). He added sappy songs, zombie dance numbers, even a claymation sequence featuring a uvula-devouring cherub. But for all its razzle-dazzle, *Happiness* fails to live up to the economical storytelling, fine performances, and spot-on timing of *The Quiet Family*.

The cast of *The Quiet Family* features two actors who became superstars throughout Asia a couple of years later: Choi Min-sik and Song Kang-ho. Choi, known for more somber and/or threatening characters, was cast against type as the loveable loser Uncle Chang. Any fan of his subsequent performances in *Shiri* or *Failan* will be shocked to see him cower and cry as he receives a beating from his considerably older brother. Elsewhere, we find him mooning sheepishly over a female lodger, or falling asleep reading kid's manga. He's also got a bit of an oral fixation, continuously chewing on one thing or another. Choi and Song do a lot of acting together as well, displaying a natural chemistry and ease with one another that enhances the laughs. When Uncle Chang discovers Yeong-min peeping at a copulating couple, he pinches the voyeur's ear in a finger-and-thumb vice grip and drags him away with the kind of intimacy and anger you only get from family.

Song Kang-ho is, in this reviewer's opinion, the funniest thing about *The Quiet Family*. His facial takes and high-pitched whine come from a naturalism he developed during his early-'90s stint in an improvisational theater group led by Kee Kuk-seo. Kee's group focused on instinct and method to reach emotional states. This experience seems to have been the perfect proving ground for Song, whose appeal lies in his genuineness on screen, along with a kind of affable approachability. These qualities made him the perfect partner for the charismatic Han Suk-kyu in the career-making blockbuster *Shiri* (1999) and lent depth to his portrayal of a complex-yet-courageous North Korean officer in the border zone psychological thriller *Joint Security Area* (2000). All this is not to say that Song is unable to play less savory characters; his turn in *No. 3* (1997) as a brutal assassin and fledgling gang leader was what first brought him to the attention of audiences and filmmakers. In 2002, he starred in the first film of Park Chan-wook's Revenge Trilogy, *Sympathy for Mr. Vengeance*, as a father whose daughter dies during a botched kidnapping; drained of all emotions but hatred, he employs a number of gruesome strategies in his revenge against the kidnappers.

The Quiet Family was the directorial debut of filmmaker Kim Ji-woon, an impressive first stab (he also wrote the script). Kim would later pursue the twin elements of humor and the macabre in separate films. His follow-up to *The Quiet Family, The Foul King* (2000), is a comedy about a timid bank teller (Song Kang-ho) who pursues a career as a Z-list professional wrestler. The film was a big hit and proved Song could open a picture. *A Tale of Two Sisters,* 2003's modern horror masterpiece, proved that Kim could jettison the laughs and do just fine with a somber story of insanity and the supernatural.

One can't discuss the deliriously manic atmosphere of *The Quiet Family* without talking a little about the unusual songs on the soundtrack. As the opening credits roll over moving camera shots of the inn's interior, we hear the Spanish horns of what appears to be Herb Alpert's "Lonely Bull" before suddenly kicking into the hip-hop groove of Delinquent Habits' "Tres Delinquentes," a musical cue that all is not what it seems. Later, during running-around and freaking-out moments, the comedic tension is heightened by the jumpy rhythms of The Stray Cats' "Wild Saxophone" and "Ubangi Stomp." Other seemingly odd yet right-on-the-money artist choices include Nilsson, Love and Rockets, The Box Tops, and, in a final WTF turn, The Partridge Family performing "I Think I Love You" under the end credits. This last choice was likely inspired by the faux-ironic retro-'70s craze of the late '90s, as well as offering up a squeaky-clean contrast (the Partridges) to the dour denizens of the doomed lodge (the Kangs).

If you're looking for a different kind of comedy experience, I'd highly recommend *The Quiet Family.* If you're not scared of blood, dead bodies, or subtitles, you're sure to enjoy this glinting little black gem of a film.

Fudoh: The New Generation • Gokudo sengokushi: Fudo

Takashi Miike has made so many shocking pictures that I could fill this book with his movies if I were so inclined. However, like many highly prolific film figures, his output has been a bit checkered, narrowing the field considerably. Even so, it's difficult to pick just a handful of his movies to discuss; the man has made quite a number of remarkable

1996

Japan

100 min.

DIRECTOR: Takashi Miike

CAST: Shosuke Tanihara, Kenji Takano, Marie Jinno, Tamaki Kenmochi, Toru Minegishi, Miho Nomoto, Satoshi Niizuma, Riki Takeuchi

films. My criteria were mind-bending content, presentational panache, strength of filmcraft, and cohesion. This last quality is vital; many a Miike film is marred by the lack of it. Ironically, for a filmmaker who claims he thrives on chaos and production problems for inspiration, the films he's adapted from more structured material such as novels and manga tend to be his best.

Of the subset of Miike films I've seen, *Fudoh: The New Generation* stands out, a Hitoshi Tanimura manga-driven epic of teen yakuza, kiddie assassins, giants, hermaphrodites, high school anal hijinks, mullets, decapitations, vaginal blow darts, filicide, fratricide, patricide, and one mean kimchee-obsessed Korean hit man. Ladies and gentlemen, I give you the main characters:

- Riki Fudoh (Shosuke Tanihara): High school honor student by day, badass yakuza boss by night, Riki runs Nakasu, the entertainment district of Fukuoka, Kyushu(southern Japan). He's mean with a samurai sword, has an outsized switchblade in his cell phone, and sports a blood tattoo of a fearsome diety on his back. The blood is that of his dead brother (more on that later). Riki commands a crack team of underage operatives that include . . .

- Akira Aizone (Kenji Takano): This swaggering, long-haired gargantua is a transfer student, new to Nakasu Commercial High School. He likes to ride his motorcycle, ruin prostitutes with his "huge eggplant dick" (as one irate brothel employee calls it), and can brush men aside as though they were matchsticks. He's soon kicking ass and taking names for Riki.

- Mika (Miho Nomoto): Riki's classmate and sometime girlfriend

Audition (Japan, 1999) The *other* Miike shock masterpiece (alongside *Fudoh* and *Ichi the Killer*), *Audition*, would have received a longer entry in this book but for the fact it hinges on a harrowing and horrendous denouement that would be criminal to reveal. In fact, *Audition* is one of those dishes that's best served cold; you should come to it knowing nothing, just letting the story unfold, drawing you in, slowly, inexorably, diabolically pulling you down into a swirling, suffocating vortex of unspeakable . . . oops, almost blew it.

No, I must say as little as possible about this film; if you've seen it, a nod and a wink will suffice, and if you haven't, by all means do. It will leave an indelible mark on your psyche that no amount of psychiatric scrubbing will ever shift. It stars punk rocker-turned-actor Ryo Ishibashi as the middle-aged male lead and beautiful ex-Benetton model Eihi Shiina as the object of his affection. Also on hand in small roles are beloved thesps Renji Ishibashi and Ren Osugi. The script was adapted by Daisuke Tengan (son of distinguished director Shohei Imamura) from a Ryu Murakami novel, and Miike directs with remarkable focus and restraint. The perfect date movie.

Take a wild ride with Riki Takeuchi

Mika has a talent for shooting darts from her nether regions. Her zipper-fitted panties allow her to do her act in nightclubs (popping balloons, etc.) without revealing what else she's packing down there . . .

- Touko Zenzai (Tamaki Kenmochi): Pretty Touko is another classmate/secret weapon of Riki's. Her innocent looks allow her to get up close to her target before dosing him with poisoned coffee or blowing him away with an assault rifle.
- Iwao Fudoh (Toru Minegishi): Riki's fiendish father. He beheaded his eldest son Ryu to solidify his position in the Kyushu Nioh Group when Riki was just a nipper (young Riki secretly witnessed the gruesome incident). Riki loved his brother deeply (it's Ryu's blood in Riki's tattoo) and though Iwao moves from strength to strength due to Riki's behind-the-scenes assassinations, one wonders how Riki really feels about old dad.
- Daigen Nohma (Riki Takeuchi): He's the Fifth Grand Successor of the Yasha Gang based in Kobe. More than just a yakuza boss, though, he's an evil Machiavel, attempting through his influence to instigate a war between North Korea and the United States. While his fearsome aspect is lessened somewhat by a mullet-headed, Nehru-jacketed look and retinue in purple livery, he's nevertheless the villain to watch.
- Jun Minoru (Marie Jinno): A sexy substitute English teacher in black leather micro-mini (like we all had, remember?). She's filling in for Mr. Arita, whose head Riki's gang's been using for a soccer ball. She insinuates herself into Riki's life, but what's she really after?
- Akihiro Gondo (Satoshi Niizuma): Iwao Fudoh's Korean son and Riki's half brother. Gondo is a kimchee-obsessed killer who winds up getting a gig as the new gym teacher at Nakasu Commercial High School. He doesn't seem to spend much time in the gym, but that's not to say he doesn't interact with the students . . .

Fudoh: The New Generation is mounted with a dour, no-nonsense tone, elevating scenes of violence that might otherwise turn chuckle-

V-cinema sensation Riki Takeuchi

some if treated less seriously. When a poisoned yakuza boss vomits gallons of blood or a school-girl assassin declares, "Your blood is the purifying water" before mowing down a roomful of gangsters, it's no laughing matter. Also ennobling the proceedings is fine cinematography by Hideo Yamamoto, who lensed other Miike standout films *Audition* (1999), *Ichi the Killer*, and *Visitor Q* (both 2001), as well as Beat Takeshi's *Fireworks* (1997), and Takashi Shimizu's Hollywood remake of his own *Ju-On*, 2004's *The Grudge*.

Everyone in *Fudoh: The New Generation* turns in a solid, if po-faced performance. Satoshi Niizuma, here playing Gondo, is in real life as tough as he looks on film. A professional kick-boxer before trying his hand at acting, he eventually tired of working before the camera and became a high-level *yojimbo* (bodyguard). Riki Takeuchi (Nohma) is a V-cinema institution, having made some 200 features in the last twenty years. You've no doubt seen his wild eyes and trademark sneer glaring at you from a rack at your local corporate video rental outlet; having saturated Japan, Takeuchi has since oozed into U.S. markets with titles like *Yakuza Demon* (2003), *Blood* (1998), Miike's *Dead or Alive* (1999) and *Dead or Alive 2* (2000), and the Tokyo Mafia series.

Fudoh: The New Generation was the film that put Takashi Miike on the map in the United States and it isn't hard to see why. Smoldering rage, eruptions of shock gore, hot girl on boy/girl sex, all wrapped up nice and pretty with slick production values and a serious dramatic tone. All in all, still one of Miike's best.

A Tale of Two Sisters • *Janghwa, Hongryeon*

You might think *A Tale of Two Sisters* yet another K-horror knockoff, complete with terrifying, long-haired lady ghost, a couple of teenage girls, and a spooky old house. But you'd be wrong. Sure, those elements are present, but there's much more to this horror/psychological thriller hybrid, based on a traditional Korean folktale, "Janghwa Heungryeon-

2003
South Korea
115 min.
DIRECTOR: Kim Ji-woon
CAST: Lim Su-jeong,
Mun Geun-yeong,
Yeom Jeong-ah, Kim
Kap-su

jeon." The problem posed for anyone trying to promote or discuss *A Tale of Two Sisters* (like me) is that what really knocks you out is a series of twists and revelations that would be spoiled by a detailed story description. Still, what can be discussed is tantalizing enough to capture the curious and enthrall the thrill-seeker.

A Tale of Two Sisters begins *in medias res* and stays that way for a good portion of the film. We are continuously confronted by hints and intimations of things that happened before our arrival, and director Kim Ji-woon uses the resulting confusion to dramatic effect. The story concerns a deeply dysfunctional family. Father (Kim Kap-su) is emotionally exhausted, burnt out by some episode or series of events within the family that has left him little more than a weary, gray-haired presence. Elder sister Su-mi (Lim Su-jeong) is sullen, depressed, and more than a little hostile toward everyone except her little sister, Su-yeon (Mun Geun-yeong), who receives all her love and protective affection. Stepmother (Yeom Jeong-ah) is a shrill, taut wire of a woman from her first scene, as she emerges from a shadowy hallway like a wraith, showering the two girls with a flood of chatter at once officious and menacing. Su-yeon, fawn-like and fragile, is clearly terrified of her and, again, we are led by subtle dialog cues and facial expressions to assume some abuse in the past.

And then there is the house. In all good spook stories concerning a haunted dwelling, the place itself is a character, sometimes even the main character. In *A Tale of Two Sisters*, it plays a strong supporting role, a dark, brooding Victorian pile contained within the austere perpendicular lines of a Korean country house. Ornate glasswork, antique wall sconces, Persian rugs, lots of greenery, William Morris wallpaper, and patterned *everything*—all of it in perpetual semi-darkness. The combination of murky lighting and busy, old-fashioned interior design creates a muted yet powerful assault on the senses, conjuring up an atmosphere more reminiscent of a nineteenth-century English ghost story than a modern Korean one.

Things are kept elliptical, but we gather that the girls have been away somewhere and are supposedly "better" now. Where were they? A hospital, a retreat, an asylum? What was the cause of their departure? What was wrong with them? One thing's for sure, all is not well, and the girls' return seems to be creating more problems for everyone. Dad is making secret phone calls to someone, saying, "Things don't look so good right now. It wouldn't help much if you came." Who the hell is he talking to? Such is the director's talent, however, that these questions don't leave us frustrated or angry. Through expert manipulation of lens and light, color and sound, as well as methodical pacing (à la Kobayashi or Kubrick), Kim infuses each scene with a floating, dreamy quality; so deft is his touch that it's as if he's tapping into our subconscious willingness to accept the strangeness of dreams. Once we are in this quasi-hypnotic state, we are at Kim's mercy and utterly vulnerable to the nasty shocks he'll administer later.

Kim Ji-woon has learned his J-horror lessons well, and added his own uniquely Korean spin. For example, when Su-mi encounters the traditional vengeful ghost, the apparition has a suitably disturbing, crooked body posture (a broken neck, perhaps?), and approaches Su-mi with a slow, creepy crawl. Then suddenly the she-ghost jumps on Su-mi's bed, stands over her, and behold: blood and a baby's arm come crawling down the phantom's leg. This last bit is what I consider the Korean aspect, that extra push over the cliff. Elsewhere the evil stepmother has her own run-ins with a couple of ghosts in the kitchen, one an inert figure slumping at the table like something from Kiyoshi Kurosawa's *Pulse*, the other a gloopy girl under the sink (the sink girl's *gotcha* move is sure to make you jump!). Other attractions include a big, lumpy sack dripping blood, and a mysterious linen cabinet that Su-yeon won't go near—the very sight of the thing terrifies her. When we eventually learn why, the revelation is more heartbreaking than horrific.

The theme of madness plays a large part in *A Tale of Two Sisters*. One or more characters in the film are playing with something far short of a full deck, which makes for some fascinating and unexpected reveals toward the end. But it's not for mere narrative trickery that the element of mental instability is introduced as a component of the story. Insanity plays a subservient role to the larger theme of loss. Death and insanity comprise the two most devastating forms of interpersonal loss. In death, the loved one is gone forever; in insanity, the loved one remains, but whatever it was that made him/her beloved has become distant and bizarre, rendering the individual a corrupted version of the original or, worse, a stranger. The death and insanity in *A Tale of Two Sisters* sets off a chain reaction in the family, ultimately destroying it. The family unit is all-important in Korean culture, and through its destruction, the film achieves its greatest impact. On the surface, *A Tale of Two Sisters* is a horror film, but at its core it is a profound tragedy.

A Tale of Two Sisters opened in South Korean theaters on June 13, 2003, and was an immediate smash success. It knocked *The Matrix Reloaded* out of the top box office slot and quickly became a phenomenon, spawning numerous fan websites and chat room discussions dedicated to unraveling the film's mind-bending plot twists. For the role of Su-mi, director Kim Ji-woon had initially slated *My Sassy Girl*'s Jeon Ji-hyun, with Lim Su-jeong lined up to play little sister Su-yeon. However, the lovely Miss Jeon complained that the film was too scary and turned down the role to appear in the significantly less scary *Univited* (2003). At this point, Kim gave Lim Su-jeong another look and decided to bump her from little sister to big sister. Smart move: Lim won the Korean Blue Dragon Film Award for Best New Actress for her performance. Mun Geun-yeong, who plays little sister Su-yeon, has also become a popular actress since appearing in the film. "And she's not just popular," gushes a Korean newspaper columnist, "but also critically acclaimed. Critics do not hesitate to call her the future movie scene queen, which is now void of big-time actresses" (Park Jeong-ho, Chun Su-jin, http://joon-gangdaily.joins.com).

So check out *A Tale of Two Sisters*. It isn't hard to find. I found it in a Hollywood Video outlet (it doesn't get much easier than that). And pay no attention to the upcoming (as of this writing) Dreamworks remake. None of these Hollywood remakes come close to the original, so do yourself a favor, go for the real thing.

The Ghosts of Yotsuya • Yotsuya kaidan
The Ghost of Yotsuya • Tokaido Yotsuya kaidan
Illusion of Blood • Yotsuya kaidan

Tokaido Yotsuya kaidan (usually translated *The Ghost of Yotsuya*) is a traditional Kabuki play right up there with *Macbeth* for theatrical and cultural significance, as well as supernatural chills, vaulting ambition, cruelty, treachery, and revenge. The play, penned by Namboku Tsuruya IV, has been a hit since its first performance in 1825 at the Nakamuraza theater in Edo (now Tokyo). Needless to say, film versions have proliferated over the years, resulting in a plethora of great renditions—too many, in fact, for me to choose just one. I've managed to narrow it down to three standout versions, each unique and important in its own way.

Let's start out with a quick rundown of the characters, as well as who shows up in which of the three films:

	1956	1959	1966
Iemon, ronin	•	•	•
Iwa, Iemon's wife	•	•	•
Sode, Iwa's sister	•	•	•
Samon, Iwa's father	•	•	•

The Ghosts of Yotsuya

Japan

1956

86 min.

DIRECTOR: Masaki Mouri

CAST: Tomisaburo Wakayama, Chieko Souma, Haruo Tanaka, Choko Iida, Shigeru Ogura, Michiko Ozawa

The Ghost of Yotsuya

Japan

1959

76 min.

DIRECTOR: Nobuo Nakagawa

CAST: Shigeru Amachi, Katsuko Wakasugi, Syuntaro Emi, Noriko Kitazawa, Junko Ikeuchi, Jun Otomo

Illusion of Blood

Japan

1966

105 min.

DIRECTOR: Shiro Toyoda

CAST: Tatsuya Nakadai, Mariko Okada, Junko Ikeuchi, Kanzaburo Nakamura, Mayumi Ozora, Yasushi Nagata, Eitaro Ozawa, Masao Mishima, Keiko Awaji

Character			
Naosuke,* Iemon's associate	•	•	•
Takuetsu, Masseur/servant	•	•	•
Ume, Iemon's fiancée	•	•	•
Ito , Ume's father	•	•	•
Yomoshichi,* Sode's fiancé		•	•
Maki, Ume's nurse			•
Kohei, Iemon's servant			
Maki, Iemon's mother		•	

*Naosuke's mother makes a brief appearance in the 1959 version, as does Yomoshichi's father in the 1966 version, but neither is an active character in the story.

The original play has Iemon as a complete and utter bastard, a contemptuous, cruel, self-centered, social-climbing murderer with an explosive temper and a very short fuse. That's right, he's the villain. His wife, Iwa, is sweet and kind, an innocent, loving woman and ideal wife to the undeserving Iemon, himself a ronin fallen on hard times, forced to make umbrellas for a living. Iwa doesn't realize that she wouldn't be Iemon's wife at all had her husband not used his sword to end Samon's objections to their marriage; Iemon, feigning innocence, vowed revenge on Samon's killer. Now, two years later, with a baby, no prospects, and a wife he's tired of, Iemon is restless and weighing his options.

Enter Ume, a rich young lady who wants very much to be Iemon's wife. Her parents are completely supportive, going so far as to give Iwa a disfiguring poison in the guise of a healthful tincture to help make up Iemon's mind to leave her (he's still attached to Iwa in his way). Being the villain, Iemon goes along with the plan, even setting up his servant, a masseur named Takuetsu, to seduce Iwa, thus providing him a pretext for divorce (or worse). But the poison takes effect before Takuetsu can get his groove on. Horrified at Iwa's transformation, the shamed masseur finally tells her everything. Distraught over her appearance (a massive, discolored sore breaks out across the entire right side of her face), Iwa tries to comb her hair, only to have it come out in bloody tufts on her comb, leaving her partially bald. The poor woman eventually falls on a sword and dies, but her vengeful spirit isn't finished with Iemon. . . .

There's also a subplot in which Naosuke, a commoner from the same fief as Iemon, courts Sode, now working in a brothel. He's in love, but his dreams are shattered with the appearance of Yomoshichi. Right around the time Iemon is dispatching his father-in-law, Naosuke makes quick work of Yomoshichi. Or does he? One thing's for sure, each murderer knows of the other's crime, the shared knowledge forming a bond between the two men. Naosuke declares the same vendetta-for-his-own-

© SHIN TOHO

Nobuo Nakagawa's *The Ghost of Yotsuya*

crime as Iemon, using it as a way to hang on to Sode. The only problem is, she won't sleep with him until he takes his revenge on Yomoshichi's killer. Oops! It seems the best laid plans don't always get you laid.

You might assume that of the three film adaptations reviewed here the older ones would be more loyal to the original Kabuki play. However, just the opposite is the case. The most faithful version is 1966's *Illusion of Blood* with Tatsuya Nakadai as Iemon; his villainous ronin is by far the cruelest (in keeping with the play) and the core cast of characters has been preserved (some are dropped in the other film versions). This is not to denigrate the quality of the earlier films; they are likely based on time-honored variations on the original story (or else the screenwriters were trying something new). Nakadai's Iemon is shrewd, calculating, heartless; far from the hothead in the other two films, his murder of Samon (Yashushi Nagata) is carried off with sophistication and sangfroid—he baits Samon into making the first move, then casually strikes him down. This scene follows up on an earlier declaration he'd made to a sword merchant admiring his genuine Osafune blade: "With this I'll get back at all those that let me down."

Tomisaburo Wakayama's Iemon, in the black-and-white 1956 Shin Toho version, is more immature, a self-pitying mama's boy. When he flies into a rage, it is petulant, flailing. You can actually hear him choking on his own vitriol, the sound coming out in an animalistic glottal fricative. In this film, Iemon's mother, Maki (Choko Iida), is the supreme Machiavel, planning Iemon's marriage to Ume, suggesting the murder of Iwa, even supplying the poison (here deadly as well as disfiguring). "It's a cruel world," Maki tells her son. "You have to be cruel to get ahead in it." With a mom like this, no wonder Iemon's such a nasty piece of work! Like all mama's boys, Wakayama does what mother says and goes through with the requisite heinous villainy, although he's ultimately remorseful, and even meets his end crying out, "Iwa, forgive me!" This early performance from Wakayama is a treat for fans of the notorious Lone Wolf and Cub series, in which the martial arts master appeared much later in his career. Here he's young, relatively thin, full of piss and vinegar, and, as always, pouring every ounce of himself into his role.

Shigeru Amachi, in Nobuo Nakagawa's renowned 1959 interpretation, is steely and proud, his chief concern that of rank. As a ronin, he is a man of no status, and his rankless state rankles him no end. His Iemon is all about ambition, although he, like Wakayama, dies with Iwa's name on his lips (an effort in both films to humanize the character somewhat). Amachi smolders in the role of Iemon, his narrowed eyes forever glinting with rage barely contained beneath the sober composure of the samurai. Those familiar with director Nakagawa's celebrated horror masterpiece, *Jigoku* (1960), will find a very different Amachi here, far from that film's cursed protagonist, yet sharing the same tortured quality (Amachi's own dramatic specialty). Where the Wakayama version had Iemon's mother providing the soul-destroying, Lady Macbeth-like bad influence (with Naosuke bringing up the rear), here it's all Naosuke; a patent medicine peddler, he's the one who suggests doing away with Iwa and procures the pitiless potion. But in the end, it is Iemon who does the evil deed, and it is he who shall bear the retribution of the vengeful Iwa's ghost.

And what of Iwa, our titular specter? Is she in death as menacing and vengeful as she was benevolent and forgiving in life, the discorporate essence of righteous indignation? Oh, yes. And that hideous facial deformity works for her as well. She gets haunting help from Takuetsu (or Kohei, depending on which version you're watching—it was Kohei in the play), also murdered by Iemon, the two subsequently nailed to either side of a large, wooden shutter and dumped in the river. This gruesome, dual-sided crucified corpse configuration is a handy device for scaring the wits out the audience, the shutter rising as it does from the water later on (the well-known *toitagaeshi* or "door transformation" sequence), allowing the ghosts to confront the terrified Iemon. But Iwa doesn't spend all her time nailed to a piece of wood. Oh no, she enjoys a freedom of movement and range of powers that allow her to effectively wreak havoc on the minds and aspirations of Yaosuke and Iemon, destroying them utterly. One great bit from the original play (reenacted in *Illusion of Blood*) has her cold, dead hand reaching from a tub of washing to grab Naosuke's leg. Like many Asian ghosts, Iwa works largely with

Nobuo Nakagawa (1905–84) Commonly considered the first master of Japanese horror, director Nobuo Nakagawa began his career in silent film. Throughout his long and prolific career (ninety-seven films in all) he covered a wide range of genres and worked with many of the great names in Japanese cinema. Literary adaptations, comedies, home dramas, period pieces, film noir, social awareness pictures—there was nothing Nakagawa couldn't pull off with his own unique and creative style. He worked with a young Tomisaburo Wakayama in *Dandy Sahichi Detective Story—Six Famous Beauties* (1956), Yunosuke Ito in the home drama *Kaachan* (1961), and sword-wielding sister Junko Miyazono as "Quick-draw" Okatsu in *Okatsu the Avenger* (1969). But it is his horror films of the '50s and '60s for which he is best remembered, including *The Mansion of the Ghost Cat* (1958), *The Lady Vampire* (1959), *The Ghost of Yotsuya* (1959), and *Hell* (1960).

© SHIN TOHO

Katsuko Wakasugi as Iwa in *The Ghost of Yotsuya*

hallucinations, causing Naosuke to see snakes (quite a lot in the Nakagawa version) and wrapping her own apparition around Iemon's new wife, Ume, so that when Iemon reaches for his sword, well, you get the idea.

All three Iwas, Chieko Souma (1956), Katsuko Wakasugi (1959), and Mariko Okada (1966) are top-notch and, as with their respective Iemons, it's impossible to pick the superior performance. It's an example of the power of a timeless literary masterpiece like *Tokaido Yotsuya Kaidan* that it can accommodate any number of outstanding and varying productions. Those who have seen Hiroshi Inagaki's Samurai Trilogy (1954–56), starring Toshiro Mifune as seventeenth-century swordsman Musashi Miyamoto, may recognize Mariko Okada as one of Musashi's love interests, the wayward Akemi (although a dozen years older here, Okada is still looking good).

Depending on which movie you see, you may find that all the female characters names begin with an "O," making them Oiwa, Osode, Oume, etc. This is due to the application of an honorific, O–. Like –san, –chan, or –sama, honorifics can denote affection, respect, or obeisance. During the Tokugawa period (during which the play was written and set), honorifics were employed far more extensively than they are today in modern Japan.

There are many other film versions of *Tokaido Yotsuya Kaidan*, but the three discussed here are particularly recommended places to start, or continue, your enjoyment of this timeless kabuki classic.

Nang Nak

NG NAK NANG

1999

Thailand

100 min.

DIRECTOR: Nonzee Nimibutr

CAST: Intira Jaroenpura, Winai Kraibutr

Nang Nak is one part love story, one part Buddhist parable, and two parts supernatural shocker, played out in a tropical jungle setting of primeval beauty and grandeur. Story-wise, it shares elements with the first vignette in Masaki Kobayashi's *Kwaidan,* as well as the ending of Kenji Mizoguchi's *Ugetsu,* two films based on folkloric ghost tales from a country at the opposite end of the Asian Pacific rim, Japan. The story of Mae Nak Phrakhanong, upon which the film is based, is itself a frightening Thai folktale dating back to the mid-nineteenth century, leading one to believe that this old story, about a faithful wife who remains devoted to her husband even after death, has been kicking around Asia for untold centuries, a truly pan-Asian ghost story.

Nak (Intira Jaroenpura) and Mak (Winai Kraibutr) are newlyweds living in a jungle village. They are very much in love and young Nak already has a bun in the oven. Unfortunately, Mak is called away to fight the Burmese in the Chiang Toon War (this isn't explained, but you can tell by the way Nak is sobbing, as Mak is rowed away by his friend Prig, that he's headed toward some deadly unpleasantness). Soon enough we see the front-line carnage, all manner of twisted corpses and pieces thereof. Mak staggers through the gory scene searching for Prig, whom he soon finds, just in time to watch him die of a gushing neck wound. Mak soon receives his own near-fatal wound, and a worried Nak appeals to her local priest, the old, tattooed Master of Mahabud temple. She asks the priest if he can lessen Mak's bad luck. "I'll make merits to redeem him from his karma," the priest assures her.

Sure enough, Mak pulls through, due largely to the ministrations of High Dignitary Buddhacharn Somdej To, the Master of Rakang Temple in Bangkok. The High Dignitary is *the man,* a benevolent yet powerful presence whose appearance, like a one-man Buddhist cavalry, always saves the day. Mak's recovery is not free from spells of horrific delirium, however; he is tormented by an undead Prig and waves of zombie soldiers in flames calling out his name. Mak's febrile dementia is cross-cut with scenes of Nak suffering the rigors of a particularly difficult birth, attended by an imperious and vaguely questionable old midwife. Nak's final scene ends on a scream, unresolved.

A year later, Mak is all healed and itching to leave Rakang Temple. The High Dignitary suggests that Mak enter the monastery to ease his bad fortune, but Mak declines the offer, thinking only of getting back to Nak. The High Dignitary gives him some timeless Buddhist advice,

Entrance to the Nang Nak
shrine, Bangkok, Thailand

© PAT GALLOWAY

which also figures significantly in the remainder of the story: "From
now on, whatever may happen, remain calm and be aware that everything goes by way of karma. Never set yourself on attachments. It
will only bring you misery." On the way home, rowing alone down
the river, Mak sees komodo dragons, smashed boats, and a dilapidated
shrine, all portending some evil fate. At last he reaches the village dock
where Nak has been waiting, babe in arms. Their tearful reunion is a
blessed event . . . or is it cursed?

Nang Nak is the kind of film that rewards repeat viewings. Decep-
tively simple, the film is filled with quick edits that convey plot cuesvia
encoded shots of animals and nature imagery. The first time around,
one is knocked out by the stunning natural beauty of rural Thailand.
Images of misty rivers, sunlight filtering down through dense foliage,
tropical flora and fauna, staggering sunsets, and scenes of village life all
converge on the mind of the Western viewer, creating an effect at once
intoxicating and hypnotic. It's easy to see how one might miss culture-
specific or slyly ambiguous shots woven intricately into the fabric of the
story. In one sequence we see a montage of sun and clouds, snakes and
rain and a frog on a lily pad intercut with a crab and a fish struggling
in mud, and shots of ants that build into a swarm. It is natural beauty
infused with the unease of looming death; the crab, the fish, and the

ants conflict with the serenity of the other scenes. This points to the larger truth that the jungle, by nature so teeming with life, is likewise the scene of inexorable death and decay.

Also easy to miss on a first viewing of *Nang Nak* are subtle clues to Nak's true nature after Mak's return. We are told by a narrator at the outset that Nak "was a true and perfect wife, highly loyal to her husband. Even death could not halt her love and loyalty. Her loving soul wandered, awaiting her husband and a return to living together." Yet in the telling of the tale, director Nonzee Nimibutr keeps things deliberately ambiguous, choosing to let the realization of Nak's ghostly status filter in slowly, fooling us (as Mak is fooled) into thinking that perhaps she isn't a ghost after all. But there are clues. Upon Mak's return, we find Nak giving her man a haircut as Mak relates his horrendous misadventures (his wound, the fact that he survived on chilies, salt, and the occasional yam, etc.). Although the household seems clean and neat, Nak finishes the haircut by showing Mak his reflection in a filthy mirror. It's odd. Why not clean the thing? Only later do we realize that the whole house is in fact dirty and dilapidated but Mak doesn't see it because Nak, in her benevolent way, has bewitched him. Only the mirror, the object that reflects his own vision, cannot be disguised. Later in the same scene, Mak asks Nak why she carries the baby, a newborn, everywhere she goes. Yet Mak's been gone a year, so the baby couldn't be a newborn. Unless. . . .

The clues become more blatant when Nak starts appearing behind Mak out of nowhere. Also, the front steps of the house are rotten, yet they never break when Nak steps on them. Hmm. Oh, and the house is infested with rats. Old friend Um finally tells Mak straight out that he's living with ghosts, but Mak refuses to accept it, becoming enraged and threatening Um. Later the old priest from Mahabud Temple comes around the house to tell Mak about Nak. Mak offers the priest areca palm and betel leaves, but it's really just some dusty old bowls and a dead rat! As they talk, Mak points to his "baby" in a cobwebby, empty hammock. He still refuses to accept the truth, and the priest leaves, but dispenses this advice: "If you want to see the truth, concentrate. Keep the Buddha in mind. Bend to the front and look between your legs. The truth will reveal itself to you." What he means is to look behind you through your knees, that somehow seeing things upside-down in this fashion will break the ghost's spell. Mak tries it and sees his house clearly: it is rotten with nasty gray weeds, the storage area beneath the house strewn with old bones. He sees a piece of fruit fall through the floorboards and Nak's arm preternaturally stretching down to pick it up (one of the high points in the traditional folktale).

Front of the Nang Nak
shrine, Bangkok, Thailand

© PAT GALLOWAY

The whole "upside-down" issue in *Nang Nak* is intriguing. Not only
does looking at things upside-down reveal the truth for Mak, but later,
when the now-terrified husband takes refuge in Mahabud Temple, Nak
appears standing on the ceiling. Perhaps it is the only way she can manifest in the holy temple. Or, maybe, since Mak is no longer enchanted
by her, upside-down is the only way she can appear to *him*. Intriguing,
as well, is the ambiguity regarding Nak's supposed dark side. Yes, people
in the village are dying mysteriously and it's easy to blame Nak, as everyone does. However, we don't actually see her killing anyone and
Nak herself protests her innocence to a group of angry young men as
they burn her house down. Is it her doing when the wind comes up and
blows the flaming material all over them, burning them alive? Is it her
fault when old Urb, the midwife who stole Nak's wedding ring, dies of
indeterminate causes and is eaten by komodo dragons? (A deliciously
gruesome sequence, that.) Again, Nimibutr has left this question open.
It may have been to appease the thousands of Thai people who revere
Mae Nak as a deity (her full name is Mae Nak Phrakhanong, Phrakhanong being the province of her birth; Nang means "lady," hence "Lady
Nak"). The Mae Nak shrine in Bangkok is a popular destination for
tourists and locals alike, where the faithful make their oblations and the
superstitious can buy lottery tickets (Mae Nak bestows good luck). The

shrine is filled with diapers and toys (offerings to Dang, Nak's baby), as well as garlands, fresh fruit, candles, incense, perfume, and a TV (always on) before Nak's statue so she can watch whenever she likes. No, I'm not making this up. Also, because Nak's suffering was caused initially by Mak's conscription, she is the patron saint of draft-dodgers, AWOL soldiers, and those hoping for a discharge. Pregnant women, however, are not encouraged to visit her shrine for obvious reasons.

The striking visual impact of *Nang Nak* is due in large part to the talents of cinematographer Nattawut Kittikhun, who also lensed the Thai cult western *Tears of the Black Tiger* (2000, directed by Wisit Sasanatieng and produced by Nonzee Nimibutr) and Sutape Tunnirut's *Angulimala* (2003), the historical saga of a psychotic Hindu Brahmin who liberates his fellow men from the suffering of life by killing them. Director Nimibutr, a leader of the Thai New Wave, has moved on since *Nang Nak* to become a mover and shaker, writing, directing, and/or producing a whole slew of great pictures. *Nang Nak* was his second film as director, following *Dang Bireley and the Young Gangsters* (1997) and consequently followed by the sexy, censor-baiting *Jan Dara* (2001). Nimibutr served as producer on hit films *Bangkok Dangerous* (1999), *Bang Rajan* (2000), and *The Eye 2* (2004) among others.

Nang Nak was a huge success in Thailand upon its release in 1999. It broke all previous box office records (raking in a phenomenal $4.5 million in Bangkok alone), and remains one of the top grossing Thai films of all time. It even beat out James Cameron's *Titanic,* an amazing feat for a domestic release that only cost 12 million Thai baht (it went on to gross well over ten times that amount). The success of the picture is due in part to the universality of the story in Thai culture, but it's also a damn fine film that will appeal to anyone, even those who know nothing about Thailand and its folklore.

3

Whether a society be large or small, it is inevitably made up of two kinds of people: predator and prey. In this chapter, we'll spend time in human communities ranging from a fishing resort to a small rural town to a megalopolis. We'll see how dichotomies between types of communities, social class, and custom bring about unexpected (and often unexpectedly bloody) results. Some films explore the effect of urban existence on the individual, leading to extremes of alienation and suicidal depression. Others consider the aberrations of small, isolated communities. But no matter the size or configuration, one thing's for sure: people in groups can get up to some freaky shit.

The Isle • Sèom

2000
South Korea
100 min.

DIRECTOR: Kim Ki-duk

CAST: Seo Jeong, Kim Yoo-seok, Seo Won, Jang Hang-seon, Jo Jae-hyeon

If you never considered fishing a blood sport, you will after watching *The Isle*—I guarantee you'll never look at a fishhook the same way again. Director Kim Ki-duk's breakout film is not for the squeamish; during a press screening in 2000, an Italian journalist fainted dead away (yes, the scene involved fishhooks). Yet this is no exploitation film; we're squarely in the realm of art house here, with a host of haunting, lyrical images punctuated increasingly by moments of violence ranging from casual sadism to punishing brutality. Kim plays things low-key, with little dialog and a minimum of music, offering instead enigmatic yet absorbing characters and a setting of staggering natural beauty that creates its own uniquely hypnotic ambience.

The story takes place in and around a remote mountain lake. At the bank there's a house and a dock and in the water bob half a dozen tiny fishing huts on floats. The lake is often shrouded in mist, giving it an ethereal feel, and the imagery easily lends itself to existential metaphor. Each float is painted a different color, bright yellow, pastel green, electric lavender, etc. This is a place where men come to fish and party. It's run by a beautiful and mysterious woman (Seo Jeong) who owns the only boat and makes regular rounds to the floats, servicing the needs of the men: coffee, live bait, sex—it's a full-service establishment. She's earthy yet poised, catlike and doesn't talk much. In fact, we never hear her say a word, but we do see her making a phone call through a window, so she's not a mute. She's quite at home in the water and is by no means dependent on the boat, as are the men; with or without her boat, she easily traverses the distances between the floats while the men remain isolated from one another. Are you getting the symbolism?

Into the woman's life comes a man (Kim Yoo-seok), whom I'll call "the man." He has a small pet bird and takes the yellow float. Over time, the woman finds herself falling for the man. This is presented subtly, via small yet revealing moments, as the woman observes the man's behavior, as well as reactions to little things she does for him. She sees him weeping in his hut; she helps him catch a fish without his knowledge and smiles when he throws it back; she kills and skins a frog and feeds the meat to his bird. When he inquires about a toilet, she shows him the trapdoor in the float. He's a nice guy, but haunted and desperate; there's a dream sequence that points to a violent incident, indicating he's on the run. He also has a gun and tends to hold it to his head. What's remarkable is that there's very little in the way of traditional character development (like exposition or flashback), yet every action and nuance in the present builds character so efficiently that we soon have a very definite feel for these two individuals and are personally invested in what happens to them. It's a tribute to Kim's talent as a visual storyteller and most likely an influence on Park Chan-wook's 2002 feature *Sympathy for Mr. Vengeance* (also featuring a non-speaking central character).

Eventually the woman and the man begin to interact, she bringing him homemade comestibles, he making her little toys out of wire. At one point he ruins a gentle moment, making an awkward, quasi-rape attempt. Although her job involves prostituting herself, the woman is no whore, and, being kind of hung up on the guy to boot, is understandably upset by the incident. She makes her point by order-ing up a local floozy for the man. He doesn't avail himself of the prostitute's services, however, thus causing *her* to fall for him as well. The woman's jealousy of the prissy pro will eventually lead both her and the man down a dark road, but in the mean-time the cops arrive. As they make a float-to-float search, the man, lacking his gun (he dropped it in the lake earlier when the woman stopped his self-execution by stabbing him in the ass from beneath the float), makes the world's most ill-advised suicide attempt: spying some fishing hooks attached to lines, he decides to swallow them and then yank them back out. (This might be the scene that laid out that Italian journo. But maybe not—there are other heinous hook scenes later.) The thing is, he yanks, but the hooks stay put, lodged in the tissues of his throat. This allows the woman to hide him down the "toilet" when the cops arrive at the yellow float, and afterward liter-ally *fish* him back out. It's a pivotal image in the film, rife with variegated symbolism.

Kim Ki-duk was a painter in Paris before moving to film, and *The Isle* is a painterly work. Depending on your tempera-ment, the sheer beauty of Kim's aesthetic vision, played out with spot-on lighting and compositional choices, will either en-hance or defuse the contrasting nasty bits of cruelty and vio-lence. Perhaps it will do both. Being an animal lover, the first time I saw this film, I was appalled by the frog, dog, bird, and extreme fish abuse I saw in the film. Now, while I'm still against such practices in film, I nevertheless see what Kim was going for artistically. And I don't believe he was necessarily enjoying filming such scenes. As he told the *Guardian*, "We cooked all the fish we used in the film and ate them, expressing our apprecia-tion. I've done a lot of cruelty on animals in my films. And I will have a guilty conscience for the rest of my life" (Steve Rose, "I've Done a Lot of Cruelty to Animals," http://film.guardian. co.uk). Ultimately, it's like the water buffalo sacrifice scene at the end of *Apocalypse Now;* the animal's life is taken in the name of art. Better that than the daily casual killing of animals in anonymous industrial facilities. Kim remarks,

> In America you eat beef, pork, and kill all these ani-mals. And the people who eat these animals are not concerned with their slaughter. Animals are part of this cycle of consumption. It looks more cruel on-

screen, but I don't see the difference. And yes, there's a cultural difference, and maybe Americans will have a problem with it—but if they can just be more sensitive to what is acceptable in different countries I'd hope they wouldn't have too many issues with what's shown onscreen. (Andy McKeague, "An Interview with Kim Ki-Duk and Suh Jung on *The Isle*," http://dvd.monstersandcritics.com)

Kim Ki-duk is a unique presence in Korean as well as world cinema. A former marine, seminary student, and factory worker, the unschooled Kim eventually made his way to Paris in 1990, working as a freelance painter and discovering the medium of film. Following two years in France, he returned to Korea and started writing screenplays, winning awards and drawing attention sufficient to secure his directorial debut, 1996's *Crocodile*. Telling the story of a man who saves a woman from suicide only to subsequently rape and abuse her, *Crocodile* won few kudos from critics, but secured Kim a permanent slot at the Pusan International Film Festival (which opened the doors to the international film festival circuit for later films). Thereafter, Kim shot one or two films a year, but it wasn't until *The Isle* that he garnered worldwide attention. In recent years, he's toned things down a bit with films like *Spring, Summer, Autumn, Winter . . . and Spring* (2003, also set largely in a floating building on a lake) and the romantic victimless crime film *3-Iron* (2004).

One gratifying thing about Kim Ki-duk is how forthcoming he is. In interviews he is completely honest, never coy or egotistical. I leave you with a lengthy yet priceless quote that allows the man himself to explain the characters in his films:

The reason that in my movies there are people who do not talk is because something deeply wounded them. They had their trust in other human beings destroyed because of promises that were not kept. They were told things like 'I love you,' and the person who said it did not really mean it. Because of these disappointments they lost their faith and trust and stopped talking altogether. The violence that they turn to, I prefer to call a kind of body language. I would like to think of it as more of a physical expression rather than just negative violence. The scars and wounds which mark my figures are the signs of experiences which young people go through, in an age when they can not really respond to outside traumas. They cannot protect themselves against physical abuse, for example from their parents, or verbal abuse or when they see their parents fight. Or when you walk in the street and someone beats you up. When those kinds of things happen, you are helpless and you cannot do anything about it. These experiences remain as scars for those people. I personally had experiences like these. For instance, in the past, some kids who were younger than me but physically stronger beat me up. I could not defend myself. Also, in the marines, because some of the soldiers were in a higher rank they beat me up for no logical reason. In the process of having gone through experiences like this I ask myself, why does this have to be? These questions stayed with me until I became a director and now I express how I think and feel about these things. (Volker Hummel, *"Interview with Kim Ki-Duk,"* http://www.sensesofcinema.com)

Suicide Club • *Jisatsu saakuru*

Japan

2002

94 min.

DIRECTOR: Shion Sono

CAST: Ryo Ishibashi, Masatoshi Nagase, Saya Hagiwara, Yoko Kamon, Rolly

Think the abnormally high teen suicide rate in Japan is a result of crushing academic workloads, extreme bullying, and a stiflingly repressive culture? Think again. Actually, it's due to an ingenious and far-ranging conspiracy involving a psychotic glam rocker, kids making existential crank phone calls, rolls of human skin, a disused bowling alley worryingly dubbed The Pleasure Room, enigmatic yet prescient websites, a mystery girl known only as "The Bat," the lonely guy from *Audition,* Track 8 at Shinjuku Station, secret telephone keypad codes, horrible things done to people and animals in bags, and an adorable five-girl pop idol group called Dessert. Mass suicide is more complicated than you ever imagined in Shion Sono's deliriously audacious, uniquely demented *Suicide Club,* a vision of post-millennial Japan that delivers sardonic social commentary along with the screams and flying human offal.

It's difficult to know exactly where to start. The opening scene, in which fifty-four high school girls, all in black and white school uniforms, hold hands along Track 8, Shinjuku Station, and jump beneath the oncoming Tokyo express to the exuberant strains of a Celtic reel . . . everyone starts there. The ensuing geysers of gore, covering the appalled onlookers and flooding the platform, are indeed impressive, but what interests me more is the subsequent cut to a performance by Dessert, five girls with an average age of twelve-and-a-half, performing their inescapably catchy new hit, "Mail Me":

Suicide Club: The before photo at Shinjuku Station

Mail me
Hurry and hit the "send" key
Can't you see? I've waited patiently
Mail me
To my phone or PC
I'm ready to tell you that I'm standing by
Mail me
I want to let you know
As friends go, yours is the best hello
Mail me
I'm sure you never knew
How I feel about you, this is real
I need to hear from you right now or I'll die

Is filmmaker and screenwriter Shion Sono merely mocking the horror of the preceding scene with this bouncy, seemingly carefree pop song (a cover of Haruko Momoi's hit from 2000), or is there a deeper connection? Dessert (variously romanized throughout the picture as Dessert, Dessart, Desert, and Dessret) occupy an increasingly dominant position in *Suicide Club*, their influence on the story and the Japanese pop culture presented in it growing more ominous with each appearance. There seems to be a poison pill beneath the candy coating . . . however, there are plenty of patently horrific events to distract us from this slow-burn revelation, such as the fate of two nurses in a dark, spooky hospital, the sick-making contents of a white gym bag, and a website that displays only red and white dots.

It turns out the red dots represent girl suicides and the white dots boy suicides, the number of dots increasing with each new wave . . . but *before* the suicides occur. Huh? But how? Who? A girl calling herself The Bat contacts the police, getting the attention of the only two cops on the force who think there's something behind the suicides (all the other detectives pooh-pooh them, convinced it's just a "suicide fad"). But Kuroda (Ryo Ishibashi, the unfortunate widower in Miike's *Audition*) and Shibusawa (Masatoshi Nagase—remember him as the wannabe redneck in Jarmusch's *Mystery Train?*) follow the leads and are soon peering into a white gym bag found unattended on the platform at Track 8. It so happens that this bag, as well as an identical one found at the spooky hospital, contains a large, stinky roll of human skin. It

© TLA RELEASING

Genesis: "Welcome to the Suicide Club. You're guests of my pleasure room!"

looks like one of those rolled-up, flat hoses you see on a fire engine, except that it's raggedy and bloody, composed as it is of ten-centimeter-long strips stitched together end to end. Some segments have tattoos. The coroner assures Kuroda and Shibusawa that each piece is from a different person. Each roll has 100 or so pieces, so together with the roll in the other bag, that adds up to a lot of people walking around with a postcard-sized swatch missing from their epidermal covering. Actually, not all of them are walking around; the coroner removes a sheet from another table to reveal a massive pile of body parts retrieved from Shinjuku Station showing areas where skin strips have been removed. The plot *sickens.*

The next day, more trouble: A high school rooftop recreation area becomes the scene of tragedy when "let's all jump to our death" jokes among the students go too far. The ones who *really were* only joking stand quivering at the edge of the roof, staring down at the ones who weren't. During routine investigation, a cop notices an ear on a ledge; with a hearty "Here comes an ear!" he pokes it off to land in the gooey mess below. No white bag is found this time.

To make a long story short (I know, *too late*), things get weirder and weirder. The suicides accelerate, spreading to all ages and walks of life, as illustrated in a creepy montage: a sidewalk food vendor OD's on pills, a girl puts her head in an oven, a smiling mom in a kitchen blithely slices off her thumb, and somewhere in the mix, Dessert are hawking their new line of chocolate treats. Meanwhile, Kuroda comes home and doesn't notice his daughter walking around the house covered in blood. The Bat is kidnapped by a bunch of rocker dudes, and before long finds herself in an old bowling alley, greeted by a flamboyant, blond-haired, rhinestone-studded platform-wearing villain of Japanese extraction named Genesis. This glitterrific jeepster, clearly a lad insane, strikes a pose with purpose and says, "Welcome to the Suicide Club." He stomps on an animal in a bag, vogues again and adds, "You're guests of my pleasure room." He does some more sadistic shtick, then launches into an unexpected musical number, the haunting *Suicide Kiss:*

Scanch (Rolly's the big blonde, second right)

Time and time again
The sky is blue and yet it's strange
How people always seem to fall in love
An unfamiliar yellow dog
Keeps grinning as it tears us
From the ones we love

(Chorus)
Because the dead
Because the dead
Because the dead shine all night long

I want to die as beautifully
As Joan of Arc
Inside a Bresson film
Lesson one, apply the shaving cream
And smile as you then slowly
Slice away the heart

(Chorus)

Feel the warmth of the spring rain
As it gently moistens down a cheek
That's streaked with dried up tears
A guileless boy but five years old
Stares blankly in the face of death
While his heart is cut and torn away

(Chorus)

It's a glorious glam moment and a dark anthem worthy of inclusion in any set by Bolan, Bowie, or Alice. Genesis is played by '90s glam rock sensation Rolly (née Kazuo Teranishi), a singer/guitarist who's made ten albums with his band, Scanch, and another five solo (for more info, go to http://www.rollynet.com, but be warned—it's mostly in Japanese). His inclusion here as self-styled "Charles Manson of the Information Age" is a stroke of casting genius. Also great is Ryo Ishibashi as the world-weary cop and dad who finds himself in over his head, unable to cope with the truths he uncovers in the course of his investigation.

The theme of *Suicide Club* is enigmatic, upon first viewing almost bewilderingly so. However, it is entirely possible to make sense of this film. At its core lies an existential message, an ontological absolute that must be acknowledged for life to have any meaning. This is true of the characters in the film as well as those who see it. The mysterious force or influence that gradually permeates the society in the film, causing many to take their own lives (could it be Dessert's perky pop confections?), serves as a litmus test; those who are truly in touch with themselves will escape the urge toward self-destruction. Those that aren't, won't. Folks who lack any sense of introspection will likely miss this and consider *Suicide Club* just a sick film. Too bad, their loss. There's more to this uncompromising, one-of-a-kind shockfest than meets the eye.

The Eternal Evil of Asia • Nan yang shi da xie shu

1995
Hong Kong
89 min.

DIRECTOR: Cash Chin Man Kei

CAST: Ellen Chan Nga Lun, Benny Chan Kwok Bong, Elvis Tsui Kam Kong, Ben Ng Ngai Cheung, Bobby Au Yeung, Lily Chung Suk Wai, Chin Gwan, Lo Meng, Ng Sui Ting, Kingdom Yuen King Tan, Julie Lee Wah Yet

If you were about to complain that there aren't any voodoo flicks in this book, bite your tongue—*The Eternal Evil of Asia* has voodoo up the yin yang (and speaking of yin yang, there's a surly Taoist priest as well), plus sorcerer smack-downs, gaggles of ghosts, a whole heap o' hexes (illusion hex, mating hex, pin hex, invisible hex, love hex, etc.), an enchanted worm, a wiggly sword, a golden witch, possessions, an invisible rapist, and Elvis Tsui learning the true meaning of being a dickhead. This mind-blowing horror/sex/comedy is another example of the amazing Hong Kong hybrid, a movie that is as funny as it is gruesome and as sexy as it is funny.

Our story begins with Nam (Bobby Au), an asshole dad who's bullying his wife and son. OK, he's distraught, having just buried his parents, and the sight of his son blithely eating cup noodles and watching TV has set him off (he considers cup noodles unhealthy junk food). Then the phone rings.

FATHER: Son, we don't want to sleep in the coffins. We
           want to come back.
MOTHER: It's dark here, and we are bitten by insects.

Nam thinks it's a crank call, but a minute later moldering mom and dad are at the door. Dad's hungry and wants . . . you guessed it, cup noodles. Soon he and mom are force-feeding Nam the soggy ramen noodles (which turn into worms as they approach his mouth). Nam loses it, grabs a cleaver, and starts hacking away, only to find the bloody corpses of his wife and son on the kitchen floor. All this is cross-cut with shots of a mysterious stranger manipulating a doll with Nam's face. Soon friends arrive and Nam sees *them* as his parents. Before long he's haunted by them, his wife, his son, *and* his parents. Nam flips and jumps off the roof, landing in a lighting vendor's stall, impaled on seven fluorescent lights.

We gradually learn that Nam has recently traveled to Thailand where he earned the wrath of a powerful sorcerer. And he wasn't alone. Here's a breakdown of the guys that went with him as well as the other main characters in the film:

- Bon (Benny Chan): Cartoonist and official nice guy, Bon holds down the male integrity end of things, in contrast to his somewhat sleazy friends. On the trip to Thailand, he stays faithful to his fiancé while the other guys get their rocks off.
- Kent (Ng Sui Ting): He's a sales representative and regular guy. He was along for the fun in Thailand and had his share.
- Kong (Elvis Tsui): The loudmouthed jerk (every group of guys has one). Kong has no visible means of support and is something of a hothead, albeit a cowardly one. He'll pay a heavy price for his Thai holiday.
- May (Ellen Chan): Kong's sister and Bon's fiancé. May runs Carve Salon and doesn't believe in enchantment at first, but before long it will be up to her to save the day.
- Sister Mei (Lily Chung): A Thai-born Chinese business woman and secret white witch. She knows May from the salon and comes to her aid when the ghosts and curses start to pile up.
- Laimi (Ben Ng): The sorcerer. He initially befriends Bon, Nam, Kent, and Kong in Thailand, but things take a terrible turn when . . . oh, you'll see.
- Shui Mei (Chin Gwan): Laimi's sister. She falls heavily for Bon, but it's not meant to be—Laimi's love hex doesn't go as planned. . . .

The day after Nam's demise, May is cutting Sister Mei's hair and we get this exchange:

SISTER MEI: In Thailand, Malaysia, and Viet Nam, enchantment is very popular. If a wizard gets your stuff, say hair, fingernails, or your blood, he can easily enchant you . . . I won't dump my used napkins anywhere either.

MAY: To keep vampires from using them as teabags, right?

SISTER MEI: So disgusting! You'd better watch it, no man will marry you!

Later that night, Bon feels like having some fun with May, but is thwarted by Laimi, who puts a hex on his johnson, alternately disabling and restoring it to torment him. Later, Bon is visited by the ghost of Nam (complete with protruding, flickering fluorescent tubes). Nam warns Bon that Laimi is after him. Soon thereafter we get the flashback, detailing the events of the ill-fated Thai vacation.

A trip to a whorehouse, trouble with pimps, a flight into the bush, and soon our quirky quartet has taken refuge in a house with a lot of candles, a skull, and other spooky accoutrements. Laimi appears and informs the men that it's too dangerous to leave, that he's got an impending showdown with a pair of powerful wizards. "Damn, look at that dickhead," says Kong, "he's just bluffing." "You will become what you

---

***Red to Kill (Ruo Sha)* (Hong Kong, 1994)** This lurid little Category III shocker concerns a musclebound "sex lupine" (gotta love those Hong Kong subtitles) who has a thing about the color red. Chan (Ben Ng, in an Anthony Wong-caliber performance) supervises mentally challenged folks down at the Social Welfare Department's Sheltered Workshop and Hostel by day, and prowls the building, raping and strangling crimson-clad ladies by night. (The building also houses regular citizens, who initially blame the handicapped residents for the murders.) Into this unpleasantness comes the lovely Ming Ming (Lily Chung), a sweetly retarded girl who loves to dance and charms everyone in the place. Too bad she wears a red dress for her big dance recital. . . .

Red to Kill features excellent performances from Ben Ng and Lily Chung (who co-starred together in the following year's *The Eternal Evil of Asia*), as well as Money Lo as Ming Ming's long-suffering social worker. Director Billy Tang delivers the goods with an extreme yet even-handed style, using lighting and mise en scène to accent Ng's metamorphosis from bespectacled nice guy to all-out man/monster. Lily Chung's Oscar-worthy, Forest-Gump-style turn as Ming Ming is contrasted, however, by her eyeball-rolling, ridiculously grimacing supporting cast. Still, it's an intense, well-made Hong Kong thriller.

used to insult me," says Laimi, and before you can say "glans penis," Kong's head is transformed into an outsized version of the one in his pants. Let me pause here to say that this gag will be much funnier for the men in the audience than the women, but, as a guy, I found it one of the most hilarious things I'd ever seen. (Clearly Bobby Au, Benny Chan, and Ng Sui Ting thought so too, as they're obviously cracking up at the sight of Elvis Tsui's newly bald and flanged noggin.) As the four friends watch the battle between Laimi and necromancer couple Barran and Chusie (the latter played by Lulie Lee, the unfortunate waitress in *The Untold Story*), Kong gets scared and pisses himself . . . from up top! Later, as the green Barran and the buxom Chusie perform a mating hex, essentially flying through the air while copulating, thus somehow causing explosions on the ground, Kong gets excited and starts massaging his throat . . . fortunately nothing comes of it.

Laimi finally employs a living dead hex that forces Barran to behead Chusie and all is well. Laimi invites the guys back to his place where they meet his sister Shui Mei (who promptly falls for Bon). Laimi sympathizes and makes a love hex, but it's delivered not to Bon but to his buddies. They all proceed to have a big orgy with the comely Shui Mei, who thinks she's having it off with Bon.

Back in the present, Laimi's revenge eventually gets the better of him, turning him to the dark side, as it were. His sights are set on May, but many a hooker's blood will be shed in the service of his evil magic. Kong seeks the protection of a thuggish Taoist master (Lo Meng), with diminishing returns of success until he ends up looking like Pinhead from *Hellraiser*. Kent doesn't fare much better; possessed by a hungry ghost, he goes berserk at a restaurant and munches on a number of other diners as well as stripping his own left arm to the bone. Laimi also brings Bon to the edge of death; his only hope is May and the teachings of Sister Mei.

The Eternal Evil of Asia reunites Ben Ng and Lily Chung, who starred together in the previous year's dark shocker *Red to Kill* (see sidebar). But it's Elvis Tsui who really steals the show. A member of the 100+ Club (film appearances, that is), Tsui has been in great films like *The Seventh Curse* (1986), *Sex and Zen* (1991), *Royal Tramp* (1992), and *Storm Riders* (1998), just to scratch the surface. Here he plays an uncharacteristically poltroonish role to the hilt, making this writer long for more films featuring his irrepressible Kong.

When it comes to deliriously extreme horror/sex/comedy, you can't go far wrong with *The Eternal Evil of Asia*. You'll laugh, you'll scream, and you'll almost certainly get aroused, all in the same sitting. Like a massive turntable of exotic and varied dishes, this film will sate your appetite, whatever strange craving may possess you!

Sympathy for Mr. Vengeance • Boksuneun naui geot

2002

South Korea

121 min.

DIRECTOR: Park Chan-wook

CAST: Sin Ha-gyoon, Bae Doona, Song Kang-ho, Ryoo Seung-beom, Ki Joo-bong

I am Revenge: sent from the infernal kingdom,
To ease the gnawing vulture of thy mind,
By working wreakful vengeance on thy foes.
Come down, and welcome me to this world's light;
Confer with me of murder and of death:
There's not a hollow cave or lurking-place,
No vast obscurity or misty vale,
Where bloody murder or detested rape
Can couch for fear, but I will find them out;
And in their ears tell them my dreadful name,
Revenge, which makes the foul offender quake.
—*Titus Andronicus*, Act V, Scene II

It's not an exaggeration to say that *Sympathy for Mr. Vengeance* is a contemporary revenge tragedy that stands in a long and illustrious line running back through the great works of the Elizabethan age right to the feet of Seneca the Younger (4 B.C.–A.D. 65), the great-grandfather of this most bloody and harrowing of all dramatic forms. *Sympathy* is a dark and devastating tale. The Fates are cruel to its two protagonists, the deaf-mute Ryu (Sin Ha-gyoon) and the industrialist Park (Song Kang-ho), spinning their fortunes into tattered rags, heaping calamity upon calamity, crushing the men under the weight of unbearable grief and frustration. Along the way, others are swept up in the maelstrom of the revengers' rage, villain and innocent alike, only to be left in the aftermath like so many heaps of autumn leaves to await the crematory flame.

However, all is not weeping and gnashing of teeth. Park Chan-wook, the director of the film, utilizes an inventive, lyrical approach to his tragic tale. Refusing to flinch at extreme, not-for-the-squeamish scenes of violence, Park's deft, virtuoso touch in fact transforms such moments; in his hands, scenes of murder and mutilation become poignant, ironic meditations, providing an undercurrent of Buddhist transcendence. Such is the art of Park's approach that base acts of brutality and revenge become moving, compelling rather than merely repellant. Yes, *art* is happening here, but many will not grok with it, cloaked as it is in a blood-spattered raincoat of pure style. My advice: Keep an open mind and viddy well.

The story concerns a young man with dyed hair that drifts from teal to somewhere around a light green. His name is Ryu and he can neither hear nor speak. He works in a foundry and lives in a tenement. He has an invalid sister with kidney disease. Ryu isn't the sharpest tool in the shed, but he has a good heart and an unstoppable will. When he seeks out the services of some shady organ peddlers for a kidney for his sister, he winds up nude and alone with his own kidney missing. He becomes so desperate that he decides to follow the advice of his radical leftist girlfriend (another one long on gumption but short on brains, played by cute and spunky Bae Doona): they kidnap the daughter of wealthy Mr. Park, president of Iishin Electronics. Ryu, his sister, and his girlfriend are all very kind and loving to the little girl, which makes it all the more sad and pathetic when she accidentally drowns. This sends Park hurtling down the path of single-minded vengeance. Ryu, too, has his own revenge-based agenda, pursuing the wicked organ thieves who ruined his last chance to save his sister. If you're familiar with the dramatic conventions of revenge tragedy, you already know how this one's going to end.

More important than the story of *Sympathy for Mr. Vengeance*, however, is how the story is told. There are so many subtle touches, brilliant flourishes, deadpan nuances; the art of cinema involves telling a story without words, using pure image, and here, with a tale of a deaf mute and his taciturn revenger, words truly do not get in the way. Consider an image of four young men masturbating to the sounds of a woman's moans. The camera pans across to the next apartment to find Ryu's sister in fact groaning in agony. In one pan, Park has rendered a perfect visual representation of the often-slippery concept of "irony." The perversity of the moment is extended as the camera continues to pan, finally coming to rest on Ryu in the foreground, blithely slurping noodles in deaf ignorance of his wretched sister writhing behind him. This scene is mirrored later in the film, as the kidnapped girl flails ineffectually in a river, calling out to the oblivious Ryu, who stands, once again, with his back to her. The image is perfectly composed, illustrating his inaction while reinforcing his blamelessness in his inability to hear her final cries. This kind of scene thwarts the expectations and impulses of the audience. Who do we blame? Who is the bad guy? Who do we root for? There are no easy answers to these questions. With the exception of the organ thieves, everyone in the film is an ordinary person pushed by fate into extraordinary circumstances, forced to face themselves and each other in the unflattering light of the worst day of their lives.

Many techniques are used throughout the film to keep the audience somewhat off balance, slightly disoriented. One useful tool is the jump cut, or rather the narrative version of a jump cut, wherein a dramatic scene is cut short, leaving the audience hanging momentarily (or

Park Chan-wook

longer), only to be resolved in a subsequent or later scene. At times whole sections of dramatic action are jettisoned, such as the actual kidnapping of the little girl. We see Ryu and his girlfriend in their car, discussing the idea of taking the girl, then cut to them in a park, the girlfriend French skipping and singing a patriotic, anticommunist song (irony again), only to be joined by the little girl, who is now with them. The plot point is resolved and the storyline neatly streamlined in one fell swoop. Later, we find the girlfriend alone in her apartment. She gets up to answer the door—cut to her face, frightened and beaten. She is bound to a chair, looking up at Park who is now in her apartment and, worryingly, has set about assembling an apparatus that includes a car battery, some kind of console, and *jumper cables.* . . .

I've said it once before but it bears repeating: *Sympathy for Mr. Vengeance* realizes the cinematic principle of telling a story visually (i.e., "show, don't tell") with potent, complex imagery, often made up of seemingly mundane components—Park sitting inside his daughter's inflatable plastic play bubble telling the policeman on the phone of his plan to kill her kidnapper; Ryu standing at the back of an elevator full of policemen, secretly holding hands with his dead girlfriend; Park, tied to a pole, the black plastic bag over his head inflating and deflating with his every choked scream for help; Ryu's sister lying still in a bathtub, the water tinged with red. There are more such moments than it is practical to relate here. Suffice to say the film is endlessly innovative in the art of visual storytelling.

No discussion of *Sympathy for Mr. Vengeance* can overlook the performance of Song Kang-ho, an actor who, in the opinion of the film's director (and this reviewer), is nothing less than a national treasure. Song's range and complexity are rivaled only by Choi Min Sik, an actor with whom he starred in Kim Ji-woon's *The Quiet Family* (see *Quiet Family* and *Sympathy* back to back for a look at Song in roles so dissimilar, you might mistake him for two different actors). As Park, Song is controlled, focused, a quiet man who keeps his feelings inside. Yet these feelings do come out, such as when he observes his little girl's autopsy—his child is literally ripped apart before his eyes, as he is before ours. The camera stays on his face, which weeps, contorts, gains control, loses control, playing out a dark dance of emotion that almost narrates the gruesome actions of the coroners. At times the director deliberately keeps Park's grief from us, as if to protect him from our gaze; his initial breakdown by the riverside is shown mostly in a long shot from the opposite bank. His subsequent interview with a police detective in a van shows the detective questioning Park, but only Park's legs are visible in the shot. When he finally gets his hands on Ryu and manages to knock him out, Park is overwhelmed. Weeping, giddy, confused, he starts to murder his adversary in different ways, unable to make up his mind what to do. This moment in particular carries a definite ring of authenticity—the flood of emotion in such a circumstance would very likely be enough to flummox you, thwarting your resolve. However, Park is no melancholy Dane. . . .

Sympathy for Mr. Vengeance is the first installment in Park Chanwook's now-famous revenge trilogy, *Oldboy* and *Sympathy for Lady Vengeance* completing the set. Park himself penned a statement to address the maddening string of never-ending, repetitive questions about the trilogy that provides a unique insight to aspects of his work. (Note: *JSA—Joint Security Area* was Park's breakout film, made immediately before *Sympathy for Mr. Vengeance.* It is a tale of friendship and tragedy among a group of soldiers from opposite sides of a checkpoint in the demilitarized zone on the North/South border. It stars Lee Byeong Heon and Song Kang Ho.)

> *Sympathy for Mr. Vengeance,* the first of the Vengeance Trilogy, was born out of my desire to tackle class conflict within South Korea after doing *JSA,* which tackled conflict of division between North Korea versus South Korea. I wanted to focus on the two greatest problems that weigh on the minds of Koreans . . . *JSA* had gun fights, big sets, many characters, and had complicated structure with a touch of romanticism. Thus, I approached *Sympathy for Mr. Vengeance* with more a minimalistic approach with a simple, calm and dry feel. I wanted to cut down on the dialogue so I made one of the main characters mute. Then I became sick of that so *Oldboy* turned out the way it did. (Kung Fu Cult Cinema, http://www.kfccinema.com, July 14, 2005)

So there it is. I hope you'll seek out *Sympathy for Mr. Vengeance* (if you haven't already) and discover that beneath the bloodshed and chaos, it is in the end that most treasured and wonderful of things: a great movie.

Pulse • Kairo

2001

Japan

119 min.

DIRECTOR: Kiyoshi
Kurosawa

CAST: Kumiko Aso,
Haruhiko Kato,
Koyuki Kato,
Masatoshi Matsuo,
Kurume Arisaka,
Kenji Mizuhashi, Shinji
Takeda

Who are they? Are they really alive? How are they different from ghosts? In fact, ghosts and people are the same whether they're dead or alive.

The young lady, Harue Karasawa (Koyuki Kato) is referring to shadowy figures that haunt the monitors of half a dozen computers. It is a pivotal scene from *Pulse,* an existential meditation on loneliness, alienation, and suicidal depression wrapped in a terrifying and metaphor-friendly tale of ghosts in the city. The film is the very definition of *mood piece,* submerging the audience in a murky, miasmic zone of pale light and dark shadow, washed-out palette and unnerving sound design. Add stunningly elegant compositions courtesy of modern horror master Kiyoshi Kurosawa and you get a movie so atmospheric that the atmosphere itself (as in many of his films) is the main attraction. Stylistically, *Pulse* comes across as a cinematic hybrid, incorporating the methodical pacing of Kubrick, the psychological manipulation of Tourneur, and the emotional disaffection of Antonioni. With these elements in place, marshaled brilliantly by Kurosawa, it's no surprise the film is nothing short of a masterpiece.

Pulse is split into two parallel stories that eventually intersect. The A story focuses on Michi (Kumiko Aso), a woman working for a commercial florist; the B story concerns Kawashima (Haruhiko Kato), a college student. Here's the lowdown:

(A) Something's up with Taguchi (Kenji Mizuhashi). He hasn't been to work in a week and his co-workers Junko (Kurume Arisaka), Yabe (Masatoshi Matsuo), and Michi down at Sunny Plant Sales are getting worried. Eventually Michi finds the body, hanged, but only after talking with an evasive yet seemingly alive Taguchi. She also finds a diskette in his apartment containing an eerie image that intrigues Yabe. Before long, Yabe has found his way into a "forbidden room," where he encounters a terrifying ghost and is irrevocably damaged by the experience. Things go from bad to worse when Junko finds her way into the room. . . .

(B) Kawashima, an unassuming economics major, hooks his computer up to the internet and immediately connects to an enigmatic website that displays static, monochrome shots of gloomy rooms containing what could be ghosts (or just creepy, miserable Tokyoites). The images are sufficiently disturbing for him to seek out the help of Harue, an attractive computer science student whose morbid worldview and techno-savvy engender an instant fascination with the phenomenon. She's also sweet on Kawashima. Will she be destroyed by the darkness that obsesses her?

Kawashima meets Yoshizaki (Shinji Takeda), a computer science grad student who's figured out what's going on. It seems the netherworld has filled up, and ghosts are now spilling into the realm of the living, infecting its inhabitants with a virulent sense of isolation and loneliness that is gradually overtaking Tokyo like a plague. People are disappearing daily, some committing suicide, others simply fading away in the wake of this devastating, ghostly apocalypse. Michi and Kawashima each seek desperately to understand what's happening and help their friends cope with what could only be described as terminal despair.

The emotional landscape of *Pulse* is desolate, an unremittingly bleak take on humanity and modern life that deliberately blurs the line between the living and the dead. The "ghosts on the Internet" theme offers a wry comment on the idea of "online community" (i.e., a bunch of spectral goons looming in rooms). The film makes its fundamental thesis plain, that human beings are impossibly separate and doomed to a lifetime, and beyond that an eternity, completely and utterly alone. "We don't really connect, you know," Harue tells Kawashima. "We all live totally separately." (If the actress playing Harue looks familiar, you probably remember her as Tom Cruise's love interest in 2003's *The Last Samurai*.) Elsewhere, Michi's boss warns of the hazards of honesty in friendship: "Words said in friendship with the best of intentions always wind up hurting your friends deeply, and then you wind up getting hurt. Is friendship always that way? If that's so, what's left?" Nothing, it would appear, except a stain; when people die in *Pulse*, they tend to

Cure (Japan, 1997) Back in '97, this picture became Kiyoshi Kurosawa's international calling card, the film that broke him big after years of toil and battle in an unforgiving industry. It is a tale of hypnosis, and how a series of serial murders committed by random, unrelated, and perplexed perpetrators, is investigated by an intrepid police detective, Kenichi Takabe (longtime Kurosawa collaborator Koji Yakusho). Takabe eventually traces the killings to an enigmatic young man (who might be the devil), his every word and gesture a potent cue triggering a subconscious response in those around him. He seems the embodiment of hypnosis itself. Yet instead of "You are getting slee-py," his hypnotic suggestion is more, "You are getting homi-*ci*-dal." His MO involves chatting awhile, playing with his lighter, or getting a glass of water, and the next thing you know you've gone and carved a big red X in somebody's throat! Kurosawa plays the role of hypnotist as well, using long takes, slow pacing, and low lighting to lull the audience into a state somewhere just beyond or beneath waking consciousness. Folks with short attention spans will call this state "sleep," but the discerning filmgoer will recognize this slow-burn psychological cat-and-mouse piece for the masterpiece it is.

Kiyoshi Kurosawa (right)

© GOLDEN SCENE/DAIEI

Harue from *Pulse*

© GOLDEN SCENE/DAIEI

Michi from *Pulse*

Kawashima from *Pulse*

leave a splotchy black blot on the wall which itself eventually breaks into particles and blows away, a potent metaphor.

Pulse director Kiyoshi Kurosawa is an art house icon and darling of the international film festival circuit, but it wasn't always that way. The uncompromising filmmaker suffered professional exile and toiled in TV and V-cinema (the Japanese straight-to-video market) for the better part of the '80s and '90s, largely due to an unwavering (read: stubborn) dedication to his own artistic vision. He started at Nikkatsu in 1983, making the studio's trademark "roman porno" films (short for romantic pornography, basically softcore sex films) but made the commercial mistake of working artistic expression into the films, thus undermining the naughty bits. When Nikkatsu finally refused to release one of his films, he arranged to have it bought from the studio, and partially reshot, recut, retitled, and released it himself (as *The Excitement of the Do-Re-Mi-Fa Girl,* 1985), thus trumping his former employers. Humiliated, Nikkatsu retaliated by blackballing the director—he didn't work for the next four years. Kurosawa got a second chance with the Juzo Itami-produced *Sweet Home* (1989), a big-budget supernatural thriller. But when Itami later recut the film for TV and video release, a fuming Kurosawa sued his producer, further damaging his reputation in the industry. Fortunately, V-cinema, with its miniscule budgets and relative creative freedom, allowed Kurosawa to keep working and honing his skills for his eventual discovery by the world at large (not unlike fellow filmmaker Takashi Miike). This finally occurred in 1997 with his dark and hypnotic opus, *Cure.*

Watching *Pulse* reminded me at times of *Suicide Club* (see review) in that, although completely different in tone and approach, both films are emphatically stating that there is something very wrong with Japanese culture, that there is a deep disconnect within the society (as well as its individual members) that threatens to destroy the nation. Both films approach suicide as a symptom of a larger illness in the body politic. *Pulse* has its share of suicide scenes and, although relatively bloodless compared to *Suicide Club,* they have their own harrowing quality. Watch for the girl who leaps from the factory tower—it is one of the most stark and realistic suicides you're likely to see on screen.

Even if you don't go in for supernatural stuff, you'll still be moved by *Pulse,* a film that, like all of Kiyoshi Kurosawa's major works, pushes the boundaries of genre and defies expectations. And you'll have Kawashima as your representative, a character that has no use for or belief in ghosts. Even when confronted by one, he shouts, "I refuse to acknowledge death!" Way to go, Kawashima.

Three ... Extremes

2004

Japan/Hong Kong/
South Korea

118 min.

DIRECTORS: Takashi
Miike, Fruit Chan,
Park Chan-wook

CAST: Kyoko
Hasegawa, Atsuro
Watanabe, Miriam
Yeung Chin Wah, Bai
Ling, Lee Byeong-
heon, Im Won-hee,
Kang Hye-jeong, Mai
Suzuki, Yuu Suzuki

This pan-Asian, three-part anthology film is in fact the second install-ment in what will hopefully become a long and distinguished series. The first film, *Three* (*San Geng*, 2002), featured the directorial talents of Thai producer/director Nonzee Nimibutr (*Bang Rajan, Nang Nak*), Hong Kong producer/director Peter Chan (*He's a Woman, She's a Man, The Love Letter*), and South Korean director Kim Ji-woon (*The Quiet Family, A Tale of Two Sisters*). *Three ... Extremes* features another heavyweight tri-umvirate, this time composed of South Korea's auteur of revenge Park Chan-wook, edgy Hong Kong indy filmmaker Fruit Chan, and Japan's notorious Takashi Miike. Each director gets a one-word title giving us *Cut, Dumplings,* and *Box,* respectively. The first out of the box is . . .

BOX

This entry struck me as Miike doing his best Kiyoshi Kurosawa impres-sion. If you're familiar with Kurosawa's work, you'll know what I mean: striking compositions, jerky jump cuts when ghosts get near, slow and methodical pace, somber tone, and a generally pervasive melancholy. Miike sets his story of a woman (Kyoko Hasegawa) haunted by her past and the ghost of her dead sister in a wintery white landscape, achiev-ing breathtaking visual effects with dead trees and snow-bound set-tings, offset nicely by the warm red hues of a circus tent interior. Here we see flashbacks: Shoko and Kyoko (Mai and Yuu Suzuki), pre-teen twin girls, do delicate ballet routines and act as props for a mysterious, masked magician who might be their father (Atsuro Watanabe). If he is, what he appears to be getting up to with Shoko is incestuous as well as pedophilic, and Kyoko, in her perverse innocence, is jealous. The story flip-flops between past and present as Kyoko is plagued by painful memories and suffocating nightmares, culminating, regrettably, in an unrewarding, head-scratching denouement.

Miike fans will likely hate *Box,* offering as it does none of the di-rector's trademark verve, ultraviolence, and dark humor. It is instead a muted affair, dry and arty, offering little beyond visual aesthetics. In a way, it's a testament to Miike's reputation for extreme cinema: when he makes a dull film, it's *extremely* dull.

DUMPLINGS

Next up we have the centerpiece of the film, by far the best entry of the three. This is due in large part to a combination of understated presentation, airy musical cues, first-rate cinematography by Christopher Doyle, and horrific subject matter. Simply put, the juicy, pink dumplings of the title are made from human fetus meat.

Back in 1995, a report came out of the town of Shenzhen in mainland China concerning hospital staff eating aborted fetuses and offering them to others as a nutritional supplement. It's doubtful such practice is widespread, yet the story gained currency due in part to some unfortunate realities of Chinese culture, namely centuries-old beliefs about the nutritive powers of certain "foods" (particularly as they pertain to longevity and sexual potency). Rhino horns, tiger bones, toads, badgers, even the bile of bears are all considered legitimate components of traditional chinese medicine, and the demand created by these beliefs is resulting in the decimation of many endangered species. Such regrettable disregard for life has led many in the West to make the misguided leap of logic that Chinese people must not mind eating their own as well, whereas in reality, cannibalism is no doubt as abhorrent to Chinese people as any other group. Although the vast majority of human beings on this planet eat meat on a daily basis, the idea of eating the meat of another human is deeply repellant, a feeling seized upon brilliantly and exploited to the fullest in *Dumplings* by director Fruit Chan.

Mrs. Li (Miriam Yeung) is an aging TV actress with a peccant husband and a deep fear of aging. Enter Aunt Mei (Bai Ling), a sexy eccentric of indeterminate age—she looks as old as beautiful Bai Ling (here twenty-four), but claims her special dumplings keep her young (and indeed her dingy apartment is littered with photos and items that speak of a much older woman). Mrs. Li comes to said dingy apartment and soon she and Aunt Mei develop a fairly straightforward relationship in which Aunt Mei cooks the dumplings and Mrs. Li eats them. Aunt Mei's fetus connection is a nurse in a hospital in—wait for it—*Shenzhen.* Unfortunately, the press has gotten wind of the fetus scandal and the hospital is cracking down, which means no more dumpling supplies for awhile. Fortunately Aunt Mei is a resourceful woman of many talents and one of them is performing abortions. . . .

Dumplings is a truly shocking piece of work. What makes it so chilling is the casual, seemingly offhand way in which the subject matter is handled, centering on the nonchalance of Aunt Mei. Bai Ling gives a playfully perverse performance: wanton, amoral, an upbeat sociopath who truly couldn't care less. Given a different context, her blithe attitude toward life would be uplifting, motivational even. But under the circumstances she becomes a mordant ghoul, albeit a smiling, singing one. At one point she regales Mrs. Li on the merits of top-quality dumpling filling: "The best are those in the fifth or sixth month. You have to remove it only by breaking the water sac, then sliding it out. It's covered by a layer of creamy fat. The colors are defined; you can even see the cranium . . . The fifth month ones are perfect, kitten-like. So cute and nutritious!" Elsewhere we get dialog like this:

MRS. LI: What's this crunchiness about?

AUNT MEI: It's OK, they have hands and feet already you know. And ears, too.

MRS. LI: Those are bones?

AUNT MEI: Nah, their bones are hardly hard. I'll just chop finer next time.

MRS. LI: Simmer in broth next time, tastes less greasy.

Director Chan doesn't pull any punches visually. Food prep scenes are fairly disgusting, made more so by Christopher Doyle's beautiful cinematography, utilizing tight close-ups and creative camera angles (like up from the floor through a glass plate holding the main ingredient). Most of the film is suffused with a brightish white or creamy light, contrasting the dark themes and imposing an incongruous beauty on the proceedings. The music, too, imparts beauty, mainly via pretty piano pieces and the occasional traditional Northern song from Aunt Mei. These choices make sense when you consider the theme of cannibalism is interwoven with the quest for beauty and youth; Chan is obviously making a larger point about beautiful surfaces and the terrible reality that lies beneath. In fact, the thirty-seven-minute *Dumplings* is ripe for all sorts of metaphorical interpretation. It can certainly apply to drug addiction, with Aunt Mei the dealer and Mrs. Li the addict who requires stronger and stronger doses. There's a clear political parallel as well, in the way the rich Mrs. Li preys on the poor (like the Hong Kong schoolgirl whose fetus Aunt Mei aborts) to get what she wants. Mrs. Li is just as heinous as Aunt Mei, benefiting from her crimes, yet, like the political elite, never dirtying her own hands.

Just when you think *Dumplings* has gone as far as it can go, that it can't get any worse . . . it gets worse. Fruit Chan pushes the envelope of his singularly disturbing theme and, through sheer style and a refusal to flinch, manages to carry it off with aplomb and a lightness of touch. Chan initially shot enough for an entire film, edited down to a short for inclusion in *Three . . . Extremes*, and later released a full-length feature version. Whether it works at twice the length is debatable (Chan himself prefers the long version). But here, in its foreshortened form, *Dumplings* is the clear winner of the three films.

CUT

Finally, we come to an inventive, post-modern, yet ultimately static bit of violent nonsense from Park Chan-wook. Sadly, my favorite director of the three on offer has presented the weakest (and *longest*) entry. Like Miike's *Box*, Park's *Cut* has a contrived quality to it, a kind of forced artiness, as if the filmmaker felt compelled to come up with something that really wasn't in him. This is not to say Park isn't an artist, he is in fact a great one, but while *Sympathy for Mr. Vengeance* represents a cinematic achievement of high art, *Cut* just doesn't cut it.

In a nutshell, a film director (Lee Byeong-heon) comes home to find his wife (Kang Hye-jeong) held captive by a sociopathic extra (Im Won-hee) who's been in every one of his films. The director's house appears to be (actually is) the same set he was shooting a scene on earlier, perhaps making some point about the artificiality of home life. His wife, a pianist, is bound, gagged, and all rigged up at her piano in a massive web of wires extending to all points about the room like some doomed fly. Soon enough the director finds his hands bound and his midriff attached to the wall by a giant rubber band. Henceforth the extra proceeds to humiliate the director, chop off his wife's fingers, and attempt to force the director to strangle the life out of a little girl tied to the sofa. That's about it.

On the upside, *Cut* is shot with Park's trademark visual flair, creative camerawork, and crystal clarity. It's also nice to see Park film alumni Lee (*Joint Security Area*) and the exquisite Ms. Kang (*Oldboy*), although the latter isn't much to look at here, gagged and mascara-streaked as she is for the duration of the film. (Fortunately we have her performance in *Oldboy,* where she is impossibly gorgeous.) Too bad she's not given much to do here. On the other hand, Lee is put through all sorts of changes, but never really rises to the occasion. Altogether, *Cut* is a curiosity that overstays its welcome.

In the final analysis, I'd say *Three . . . Extremes* is worth a look, bookended as it is with subpar efforts from Miike and Park. *Dumplings* certainly makes the whole thing worthwhile and you really could do far worse (you could watch a *Guinea Pig* movie for instance). Perhaps I'm being too hard on Miike and Park; I'm only judging them according to their own past efforts, so maybe a newcomer would find their contributions here absolutely fabulous. Far be it for me to discourage any foray into the world of Asian film (unless it's a *Guinea Pig* movie).

We're Going to Eat You • Diyu wu men

1980

Hong Kong

90 min.

DIRECTOR: Tsui Hark

CAST: Norman Chu Siu Keung, Hon Kwok Choi, Margaret Lee Din Long, Eddie Ko Hung, Melvin Wong Gam San, Siu Gam, Fung Fung, Tam Tin Nam, Baan Yun Sang, David Wu Dai-Wai, Che Hung, Lung Tin Sang

If you don't eat people, they'll eat you.

Words to live by, and the folks in this film definitely do. If you haven't seen *We're Going to Eat You,* you're in for a rare film experience (or, if you prefer, well done). Only Hong Kong cinema could produce such a crazy kung fu cannibal comedy, stuffed to bursting with macabre merriment, gruesome guffaws, and hideously hilarious hijinks. Tsui Hark's masterful horror/action/black comedy swerves wildly between scenes of truly horrendous atrocity (people being sawn in half, disemboweled, chopped up, and cooked, often while they're still alive and kicking) and a mélange of broad, slapstick comedy and elaborately choreographed fight scenes (played mostly for laughs). Add a heroic operative from the Central Surveillance Agency, a wise guy thief, a bandit named Rolex, a demented chief of police, a young lady with a taste for human hearts, deformed freakazoid townies, and hordes of masked, cleaver-wielding mad butchers, all running from gag to gag-inducing gag at breakneck speed, and you start to get an idea of the insanity that is *We're Going to Eat You.*

Unfortunately, in the midst of all the chasing, capturing, escaping, punching, kicking, climbing, falling, thwacking, chopping, slicing, gutting, and, of course, eating, the film's script (or perhaps the person writing the English subtitles) tends to omit the names of many of the characters, leaving me to refer to them as "thief," "priest," "giant woman," etc. This won't harm your experience of the film—each character has a striking appearance and you're never in any doubt as to who's who—but it does make it a bit more cumbersome for the writer who's taken on the task of describing this indescribable film (that would be me).

The film opens with two "sample victims," luckless bird trappers (one has a weak bladder and stops to pee every minute) who have taken the ferry to a rustic island they soon learn is infested with the aforementioned cleaver-happy maniacs. One of the men (Baan Yun Sang) is killed in the woods. The other taken alive. Both are brought to an open-air abattoir where Mr. Weakbladder (David Wu) watches in horror as his friend is graphically eviscerated and his chickens cooked alive. Weakbladder's discomfort increases as a large, two-man crosscut saw is lowered to his midriff and employed to efficiently bisect him. This harrowing, no-holds barred sequence sets a dark tone at the outset that is alternately subverted and reestablished throughout the remainder of the film; just as the gleefully wacky fight sequences and sex farce scenes start to dull the sharp machete-edge of menace, some bit of violent grotesquery pops up, reminding us that we're still very much in the realm of dangerously demented, man-eating murderers.

In the village, many of the residents are afflicted with some deformity or physical handicap, and all of them are perpetually hungry. So they're ecstatic to hear the slaughterhouse is distributing fresh meat (plus some chickens). But their hopes are dashed as the despotic Chief of Police (Eddie Ko) steps in and takes thirty of the thirty-nine pieces of man-flesh for himself and his goon squad. When he tells the angry citizenry that they can have the chickens, one of them laments, "But how can they compare?" Standout freaks in the village include the local Taoist priest (played by character actor Fung Fung, whose lower face is remarkably warped), a giant (gland case Tam Tin Nam), and an enormous (and enormously amorous) "woman" I'll call Madame Large (giantism poster boy Siu Gam doing everybody's favorite "huge burly guy in drag" act, more recently perfected by burly Chatewut Watcharakhun in the Thai horror comedy *Body Jumper*). Other local characters of interest: a scholar (Che Hung) who keeps a slab of meat pressed between the pages of the book he carries (he claims it's a bookmark); Eileen (Margaret Lee), the Chief's girlfriend, whose favorite food is hearts (and I don't mean chicken hearts) and who somehow manages to become a sympathetic figure by film's end; and Eileen's timid brother (Lung Tin Sang) who proves an unlikely hero.

Before long a couple of strangers hit town, Agent 999 of the Central Surveillance Agency (Norman Chu) and a scrawny, wisecracking ne'er-do-well (Hon Kwok Choi) whom 999 soon learns is descended from a line of thieves (he finds out the hard way). Thief is full of worldly wisdom and says things like, "A cigarette without a match is like forgetting toilet paper after shitting." Soon he's accosted by Madame Large, eventually escaping down an alley yelling "Rape!" Agent 999 is on the trail of a notorious outlaw named Rolex (Melvin Wong), who he believes is hiding on the island. Obviously he's in for much more than he bargained for; he's got "fresh meat" written all over him!

Director Tsui Hark (who resembles a Chinese version of Pete Townshend), along with action directors Chin Yuet Sang and Corey Yuen Kwai, keeps the pace of *We're Going to Eat You* fast and furious, barely pausing long enough to let his actors or his audience take a breath. The score is properly weird and atmospherically disorienting, incorporating gongs, synth growls, odd orchestrations, bits of drumming, and demonic screaming lifted from the soundtrack of Dario Argento's *Sus-*

peria. This is frenetic '80s Hong Kong film frenzy at its finest, with great martial arts performances all around and a sense of fun that might be at odds with the more lurid realities of the story if this were made in a different region of the globe. But Hong Kong cinema's unique contribution to the horror genre is a willingness to play things for laughs no matter how shocking the subject matter. And the Hong Kong filmmakers of the '70s and '80s always manage to pull it off. Most likely it comes down to an ancient culture and an attendant seen-it-all attitude toward life. Perhaps no culture on Earth has suffered the slings and arrows of outrageous fortune as long and as enduringly as the Chinese. To make it through thousands of years of famine, poverty, and plague you have to develop a sense of humor, otherwise you'd never make it. Hence the frothy nature of Hong Kong horror.

Earlier I mentioned Fung Fung, the character actor with the bizarre, panel-beaten face and protruding ears. Don't be too quick to write off this bizarre-looking fellow; back in the '30s and '40s Fung regularly worked as a handsome leading man and eventually transitioned to writing and directing. It wasn't until 1950, after suffering a disfiguring mishap with an exercise machine, that Fung (for obvious reasons) switched to character acting. (That year also saw the release of *The Kid*, a film directed by and starring Fung and featuring a ten-year-old Bruce Lee). Over the next two decades Fung made dozens of features, contributing much to Cantonese cinema.

Those interested in writer, director, producer, actor, editor, and musician Tsui Hark will want to see *We're Going to Eat You,* Tsui's third film, for a peek into the origins of this talented Hong Kong veteran. Tsui went on to make the innovative *Zu: Warriors From The Magic Mountain* (1983), incorporating modern western special effects techniques like blue screen to breathe new life into the wuxia fantasy genre. He innovated again in 1984's *Shanghai Blues,* a hybrid of Hollywood screwball comedies and Chinese romantic comedies of the '30s and '40s. Memorable Tsui Hark features from more recent years include the Jet Li vehicle *Once Upon a Time in China* (1991), *Iron Monkey* and *Green Snake* (both 1993), and *Time and Tide* (2000). Of course, this is just a smattering of the forty-odd films Tsui has directed to date.

So if you like a bit of mirth in your mayhem and don't mind a little shtick in your bucket of blood, I'd highly recommend *We're Going to Eat You.* It's roaring good, gory fun and will leave you hungry for more Tsui Hark fare.

Modern communications and media technology are an undoubted boon, allowing us to reach out and interact with one another all around the globe. But what of those entities that lurk just beyond our sphere? An unfortunate side effect of technology is that it appears to have rent whopping great fissures in the fabric of our mundane plane, allowing unspeakable forces to enter from the nether regions. Seemingly innocent items such as personal computers, cell phones, even old VHS tapes can be the harbingers of some unspeakable fate. And while we're at it, what of modern medicine? What unexpected side effects might come with a set of transplanted eyes? We shall see. . . .

The Ring • Ringu

It's often said that the devil is in the details. While this tends be among the more negative of life's little epiphanies, in the case of Hideo Nakata's *The Ring,* it's the secret to success. Every nook and cranny of this film is jammed with details of delightful devilry, lending a touch of the sinister to the merest of mundane events. Everything from the sound of a telephone ringing to the swoosh of passing cars has been shifted slightly with subtle sound design; little bits of visual information are tucked into the corners of scenes for only your subconscious to see; performances are kept low-key so as not to upset the slow boil of the narrative. It's an

1998

Japan

96 min.

DIRECTOR: Hideo
Nakata

CAST: Nanako
Matsushima, Hiroyuki
Sanada, Yuko Takeuchi,
Yoichi Numata,
Rikiya Otaka, Masako,
Daisuke Ban, Rie Inou,
Chihiro Shirai

atmospheric tour de force, to J-horror what the Beatles were to the British Invasion. All the components of the paradigm are in place: you've got your extremely freaky female ghost with *long* black hair, your generation-spanning backstory, an emphasis on tone and ambience over cheap horror gags, as well as the optional bit of modern technology. This last component is the famed "cursed videotape," the watching of which causes death one week later, and it's to Nakata's credit that such a seemingly ludicrous concept (at least to the Western mind) is pulled off so convincingly. Perhaps, given the premise that ghosts exist, the electronic essence of a particularly pissed-off specter could so permeate the ethers as to imprint her malevolence onto magnetic tape. Who in this vast cosmos can really say?

One thing we know is that old-timey flashbacks (like the decades-old memories of a ghost) have to be shown in black and white, so of course the strange images on the deadly video are black and white, as well. Again, Nakata plays his hand with such surety that a detail like this just works without making a clank (like they don't have color in the spirit world!). This gimmick pays off later when our intrepid protagonists have their own psychic flashes that provide valuable plot points, also in black and white. But I'm getting ahead of myself. Let's run through the main characters:

- Tomoko Oishi (Yuko Takeuchi): The movie starts with teen Tomoko. She and a girlfriend and a couple of guys rented a cabin down the Izu peninsula south of Tokyo a week earlier and all watched a mysterious videotape together. You can guess the rest. Her aunt Reiko is a reporter, coincidentally pursuing the voodoo vid story. . . .
- Reiko Asakawa (Nanako Matsushima): TV journalist, careerist, mom, in that order. Reiko's heart seems in the right place—she loves her young son and fights desperately to protect him from the evil swirling around her—but she's never around. Is this a patriarchal wag of the finger embedded in the narrative, or just an unfortunate reality of the single mom? Anyway, at Tomoko's funeral Reiko talks to some classmates and starts putting things together. . . .
- Yoichi Asakawa (Rikiya Otaka): The aforementioned cherubic first-grader. Little Yoichi appears to have inherited certain psychic sensitivities from his parents. At Tomoko's funeral (held in the home) he follows a pair of ghostly legs running up the stairs to Tomoko's room. Later, after his mom and dad have both watched the tape (thus cursing themselves), he pops it on himself. Reiko is horrified to find him watching it; he explains that Tomoko told him to.

© GREG LOFRANO

The Ring: All's well that ends well

© GREG LOFRANO

Every day's a bad hair day for Sadako

© SEASONAL FILM CORP.

Hiroyuki Sanada back in his action days (from *Legend of the Ninja*, 1982)

- Ryuji Takayama (Hiroyuki Sanada): Reiko's ex-husband. Enigmatic and world-weary, Ryuji just oozes heaviosity. He's a college professor and seems to have some specialized knowledge regarding spirits and psychic phenomena (as well as certain powers of his own). Reiko calls him in to help with her investigation/mission. Together they've got to find a way to lift the curse and save themselves and their son.
- Shizuko Yamamura (Masako): Forty years back she threw herself into the volcano on Oshima island. Before that, she was a bit of a witchy woman, predicted stuff (volcano eruptions for one) and was eventually discovered and exploited by . . .
- Dr. Heihachiro Ikuma (Daisuke Ban): This guy was looking for a meal ticket and the superpsychic Shizuko was just the ticket. He tried to make a name for himself on her back (as well as enjoying himself on her front). In the end, all they produced was a child, but what a child!
- Sadako Yamamura (Rie Inou/Chihiro Shirai): Yes, little Sadako (played by Chihiro Shirai) was ten times more powerful than her mom and even killed a heckler at one of mother's psychic demonstrations just by willing it. Now, forty years later, grown-up ghost Sadako (Rie Inou) is terrorizing folks with the help of that cursed cassette. Can she be stopped? How did she die? And just how does a ghost grow up? Oh, never mind.
- Takashi Yamamura (Yoichi Numata): Shizuko's cousin. He's the only guy who knows the whole story, but the old-timer ain't talking. No worries. Ryuji, possessing as he does the power of psychometry, grabs old Yamamura's arm and we finally get that good, solid black-and-white flashback. Reiko wanders near the two men and gets sucked into the flashback as well; in it, Sadako grabs her forearm and, afterward, Reiko notices black, burn-like finger marks where the ghost had touched her.

I'll leave it to you to discover the secrets of Sadako. I've probably said too much already. But as I mentioned earlier, there's so much crammed into the corners of this film, you'll be digging out little gold nuggets for many screenings to come. The sound design alone is worthy of its own viewing (or hearing, as it were). Hideo Nakata definitely has a feel for . . . well, *feel*. Mood, pitch, pace, timbre, timing, framing, lighting, the guy knows how to create a vibe. Unfortunately, his storytelling skills occasionally fail him, as in such fun yet flawed films as *Don't Look Up* (1996), *Chaos* (1999), and *Dark Water* (2002). But to his credit, Nakata initiated major changes from *The Ring*'s original source novel by Koji Suzuki that make his film a more solid piece of cinema. For one thing, he did the old *His Girl Friday* switcheroo and changed the main character, the investigative reporter, from a man to a woman (and gave her a cute kid), changing the relationship with Ryuji from buddy to ex-husband (gets the family dynamic in there). Nakata also streamlined the Sadako character, originally an irresistibly beautiful hermaphroditic actress, to the more traditional vengeful Japanese ghost. And he jettisoned the original nature of the cursed videotape; in the novel, watching the tape actually gave the viewer a form of smallpox that killed him a week later, making it a virulent little bugger indeed. However, this mixture of biology and the supernatural might have made the film a tougher sell to moviegoers. Whatever the reason, the smallpox was removed and the curse retained, the cause of death changing to sheer fright on encountering Sadako. Nakata also had a personal motive for making these changes: there had already been a popular TV movie adaptation of *The Ring* on Fuji Television in 1995 (written by *Another Heaven*'s director Joji Iida and starring Yoshio Harada as Ryuji). Nakata wanted to put his own stamp on his film instead of just doing a retread of an old movie of the week.

Anyone who's seen Yoji Yamada's *The Twilight Samurai* (2002) or

The Ring (USA, 2002) OK, I finally sat through the Hollywood remake of *The Ring*. Competently made, it was less risible than I'd expected, but nevertheless replaced all the subtlety and style of Nakata's film with an embarrassingly condescending level of wordy exposition, clichéd tropes, and needless changes. Director Gore Verbinski and screenwriter Ehren Kruger obviously felt their American audience was not to be trusted with the slightest ambiguity or elliptical plot moments; thus, everything is S-P-E-L-L-E-D O-U-T, often for no particular reason, such as when, late in the film, Naomi Watts (playing the reporter/mom) has the unnecessary revelation that people die a week after seeing the cursed video because that's how long it took Samara (née Sadako) to die. There's some superfluous business about suicidal horses, bloody noses, picking flies out of video screens, and Naomi Watts coughing up a strand of long, black hair attached to an electrode. The deadly video is twice as long as the original, crammed full of weird images added for sensation, and of course the little boy is now the standard precocious, creepy mini-adult, his every line a portentous presentiment of doom. I beg you, don't spread the curse—see the original instead!

the Tom Cruise vehicle *The Last Samurai* (2003) will be familiar with Hiroyuki Sanada; he was the title character in the former film and the samurai that beat Cruise to a pulp with a *bokuto* (wooden sword) in the latter. In *The Ring*, he is Ryuji: sober, somber, and solid as a rock. In the 1970s, Sanada was an action star and member of superstar Sonny Chiba's Japan Action Club. As a leading member of the JAC, young Sanada was popular and in-demand, but in 1985, at the height of his kick-ass ninja powers, he turned his back on action films for a more serious acting career. He's since acquitted himself admirably with scores of films and live theater performances to his credit. Lesser known but no less worthy of praise is Yoichi Numata, here portraying old Takashi Yamamura, Sadako's uncle and first exploiter of her mother, Shizuko. Numata will forever be known and loved for his unforgettable, impossibly flamboyant performance as the demonic Tamura in Nobuo Nakagawa's horror masterpiece *Jigoku* (see review). Unfortunately, we don't get to see much of Rie Inou, the actress who plays Sadako; she has serious hair issues that keep her face mostly obscured. But what she does with contorted posture, creepy crawling and other assorted frightwiggery more than makes up for her lack of face time.

For those new to J-horror, my advice is start here. After all, *The Ring* got the ball rolling, so there's no better place to begin. Then you can move on to haunting teen ghost girl flicks *Shikoku* (1999, starring Chiaki Kuriyama from *Battle Royale* and *Kill Bill: Vol. 1*) and *Tomie* (1999, based on a disturbing manga by Junji Ito), Takashi Miike's horrendous "date movie" *Audition* (1999), body-jumping brain-muncher *Another Heaven* (2000), heady yakuza/zombie/samurai cocktail *Versus* (2000), and Kiyoshi Kurosawa's apocalyptic ghost epic *Pulse* (2001). This is just a short list; there are plenty more J-horror and J-horror-inspired films (such as the Korean entries, or K-horror). And if you can't get enough of the whole Ring mythos, there's always *Rasen* (1998, a simultaneously released sequel from *Another Heaven* director Joji Iida), *Ring 2* (1999, Nakata's sequel), *Ring 0* (2000, a prequel), *Ring Virus* (1999, the Korean version), and two Hollywood remakes. Collect 'em all!

Phone

The voice you heard on the phone was Jin-hee's. The voice of sad and vengeful Jin-hee.

Cultural anxieties about technology get expressed in film differently in

2002
South Korea
100 min.

DIRECTOR: Ahn Byeong-ki

CAST: Ha Ji-won, Kim Yoo-mi, Eun Seo-woo, Choi Woo-je, Jeong Seong-hwan, Choi Jeong-yoon

different countries. In the United States, it's all about artificial intelligence; the machines are going to develop consciousness and come after us (*The Terminator, The Matrix*). In Japan and Korea, however, where ancient, animistic beliefs still have influence, the approach is more a disturbing integration: *haunted technology.* We know there's something very wrong with the gadgets and inventions that augment our daily lives because they're lousy with ghosts! You've got your haunted videotape (*The Ring*), haunted Internet (*Pulse*), and here, in *Phone*—surprise, surprise—a *haunted cell phone.* Yet from these seemingly outlandish concepts come surprisingly cool films, owing much to elaborate backstories, impressive performances, and powerful production. Of course, there will be some who just can't get past the idea of a haunted phone, and will pass on this supernatural gem. That's a shame; there's more to this feisty Korean shocker than indicated by its modest title. Love, jealousy, revenge, issues of family and fertility, underage sex scandals, psychotic stalkers, possession, obsession, and Beethoven's Moonlight Sonata are all on hand, along with myriad plot twists and the most striking debut of a freaky little girl since Linda Blair.

Attractive, young, and single, Ji-won (Ha Ji-won) is on the hunt for men. No, not like that, she's a reporter, currently exposing a number of prominent Seoul professionals engaged in secret affairs with schoolgirls. This has made her unpopular with said men and at least one has made it his mission to harass her (or worse). The harassment begins through her cell phone, causing her to change her number. But the new number takes telephonic invasion to a whole new level, as there seems to be some malevolent force associated with it. The last three people who had the number have either died or disappeared. Ji-won doesn't know this, of course, and won't find out 'til later. Meanwhile, she needs a place to lay low for awhile, take a break from scandalous reportage, and work on her novel.

Ji-won's best friend Ho-jung (Kim Yoo-mi), formerly a painter, now lives only for her family, husband Lee Chang-hoon (Choi Woo-je) and five-year-old daughter Young-ju (the astounding Eun Seo-woo). Chang-hoon, wealthy CEO of Daehan Bonds, offers his house in Bangbae (the hip French section of Seoul) as a place for Ji-won to chill out and write. Ji-won takes him up on his offer but soon finds that her stalker problems aren't over, receiving strange, bloody images via email on her laptop. Things get weirder the next day when Ji-won goes to a museum with Ho-jung and little Young-ju. Young-ju answers Ji-won's ringing cell phone and hears something that sends her into paroxysms of shrieking fright, her eyes rolled back in her head, her face contorted into an evil grimace. The camera arcs round and round the screeching

© GREG LOFRANO

Young-ju acts out in *Phone*

child and two confounded adults, enhancing the sense of spiraling menace unleashed through the cell phone. It is the first of many memorable moments as the innocent Young-ju is pulled deeper and deeper into a vortex of possession and ghostly manipulation.

From here, otherworldly apparitions start ramping up. Ji-won dreams of a long-haired female ghost, Young-ju sees one peering at her from behind her dolls, Ji-won gives a lift to a rain-soaked ghost girl and later sees her in the bathroom mirror. All the while Young-ju is getting weirder and weirder, clearly overshadowed by a very angry spirit and acting out to beat the band. It's all becoming too much for Ji-won, who slaps her reporter cap on and starts digging into the mystery. Connections are made, secrets are revealed, and we eventually come to know "sad and vengeful Jin-hee," the phone-haunting ghost of the piece.

I'll leave it there, but the story is far from over. The third act is full of great plot twists and reveals, the taut storyline unraveling into dark, slithery strands that entwine and writhe like snakes in a pit. In fact, it's frustrating not to be able to discuss the third act, as it is here that the movie really takes off, but I don't blow endings, so you'll just have to take my word for it—it rocks. And like all movies with fantastic revelations at the end, *Phone* rewards repeat viewings.

Production-wise, *Phone* has a rather Hollywood feel, most noticeable in the bold score by Lee Sang-ho and slick cinematography by Mun Yong-sik. Costume and décor are exploited to great effect in presenting the Lees as the "perfect family" (think lots of *white*) and much is done with rain and snow to enhance the drama. Strong performances are given by Choi Jeong-yoon (who plays Jin-hee), and little Eun Seo-woo as Young-ju. Both young actresses give their adult counterparts a run for their money, and let's face it, the five year old steals the show. Eun Seo-woo's performance is sophisticated far beyond her years, yet she doesn't hold back, throwing herself (literally and figuratively) into her role with all the conviction of a New York method actor. Conversely, Ha Ji-won is a bit subdued in the central role, but perhaps it's just as well; her level-headed, if sedate, approach to the mounting horrors creates a stable through-line, allowing the other characters more latitude for their own out-freakage. (See the uproarious college sex comedy *Sex Is Zero* for a very different side of the lovely Ms. Ha.)

Phone is K-horror (as in very close to J-horror) and also a woman's picture. Sure, most J-horror revolves around a vengeful female ghost, but there's more "chick flick" material on offer here (which, in this case, is not a bad thing). The fundamental relationships that shape the story, both loving and hateful, are between women, and there's enough family, motherhood, jealousy, rivalry, and backstabbing, as well as murder, thrills, suspense, and scares, to keep both sexes glued to this movie until the final frame.

As of this writing, a U.S. remake of *Phone* is in the works, so by the time you read this you may have seen the reworked version. Hollywood is currently in a feeding frenzy over remake rights to Korean films, with *My Sassy Girl, Oldboy, A Tale of Two Sisters, My Wife is a Gangster* and *Hi, Dharma* (among others) all slated for the big-budget, big-name treatment. It's puzzling, as one thing that makes these films so great is the unique flavor of their cultural origin; it's like replacing kimchee with a Caesar salad. What was wrong with the kimchee? What if I *like* kimchee? But kimchee is spicy and therein lies the heart of the metaphor: the U.S. corporate entertainment complex wants to keep things nice and bland for plain ol' meat 'n' potatoes America (or rather, to keep America bland). I say accept no imitations, go for the real thing. And if you find kimchee's not to your taste, you're never far from a McDonald's.

A Snake of June • *Rokugatsu no hebi*

2002
Japan
77 min.
DIRECTOR: Shinya Tsukamoto
CAST: Asuka Kurosawa, Yuji Kotari, Shinya Tsukamoto, Susumu Terajima

There's a snake-like metal penis that comes out of Iguchi's corset.

But never mind that now. There are other things to get to before we encounter the eponymous snake, a yards-long, twisting, coiling, industrial phallus of black, oily metal. So put that image right out of your head. Instead, consider the dramatic potential of elements such as voyeurism, humiliation, blackmail, sexual awakening, terminal disease, fetishism, exhibitionism, and lots of lascivious photographs, plus a drowning chamber, snails, and a bunch of shackled *oyaji* (middle-aged men) with funnels strapped to their faces trying to get a peep at a live sex show. Welcome to Tokyo. Your tour guide for this evening, Mr. Shinya Tsukamoto.

A Snake of June is not as assaultive as earlier works like *Tetsuo: The*

© KAIJU THEATER

Rinko before

© KAIJU THEATER

Rinko after

Iron Man and *Tokyo Fist,* although, like all Tsukamoto films, there is a single-minded intensity in every frame. It is a stylistic hallmark of this two-fisted triple-threat that each of his movies is a total thesis, explored to its furthest reaches, leaving no conceptual stone unturned, no equivocal moments, no ellipses. One is often exhausted after a Tsukamoto film, wrung out, spent. *A Snake of June* reveals a subtler, simmering Tsukamoto. Like a child that's tired of fighting, here he is, content to spend the day picking up rocks and examining the squirmy things underneath. The film is a mood piece that is ultimately about love. Getting there, however, takes us on a twisted, adrenaline-fueled joyride of sordid, urban-noir encounters that, by the nature of their perversity, wrench something human out of the film's urban-dead characters.

A Snake of June is presented in black and white with a blue tint. The resultant blue/gray look highlights the two main motifs: concrete and water. The concrete is that of Tokyo, the real star of every Tsukamoto film. And the water—this is one of the wettest movies in film history. It rains throughout the picture, a constant, heavy downpour soaking the city to the bone. There are recurring images throughout the film of water gushing into storm drains, rain falling on flowers and snails, and the stormy cityscape itself looming like a massive, megalithic slab of wet oppression. Whatever the rain signifies in this picture, it is not our friend, although the camera loves it; as every filmmaker knows, water does interesting things to light. Tsukamoto takes full advantage of the myriad possibilities offered by falling rain and wet surfaces, particularly wet skin, more particularly the wet skin of a beautiful woman.

Tsukamoto plays the character Iguchi (the opening quote is his, from the making-of feature on the Tartan Asian Extreme DVD). Iguchi is kept deliberately mysterious in the first half of the film. He is a photographer, and early on we see him (from the back) submitting impressive pictures of dildos to the editor of a skin mag who asks him why he never takes any erotic photos, only pictures of products. As it turns out, he does take erotic photos, *lots* of them, but they're not for sale.

Rinko Tatsumi (Asuka Kurosawa) is a suicide hotline counselor at the County Mental Health Center. Although professional and self-assured on the phone, she is in reality extremely shy and repressed, afraid of confrontation, and stuck in a sexless marriage with an older man. When talking people out of topping themselves, her favorite line is, "Once you find what you really want to do, you'll be OK." This line will come back to haunt her, as one of her callers has taken a strong interest in her and has determined that she needs a dose of her own medicine. She's saved his life, and now he's going to save hers, in his own perverted way, whether she likes it or not. For, you see, Rinko is a hottie. What's more, she's a hottie who's never allowed herself to be hot. The caller, Iguchi, is going to change all that.

Shigehiko Tatsumi (Yuji Kotari) is Rinko's husband, an overweight *oyaji* with a chrome-dome and horn-rimmed glasses. He's a neat freak whose one great love appears to be cleaning the drain in the kitchen sink or the bathtub ("I love to do this"). He lives with Rinko in a nice, ultramodern stainless steel apartment, all severe right-angles and cubed edges.

Another motif that runs through *A Snake of June* is square versus round. Over and over we see the image of water rushing into a rectangular iron storm drain. However, whenever Rinko takes a bath, she gazes up at the rain hitting a circular skylight. The towering tombstone skyscrapers of the city contrast with the circular lens of the camera (itself an extension of the eye). The natural world is full of round things, whereas the man-made world is boxy and corner-ridden.

So Iguchi starts mailing things to Rinko: photos of her in compro-

Hiruko the Goblin (Yokai Hanta—Hiruko) (Japan, 1990) This is the story of a boy desperately searching for the head of the girl he loves. Sadly, he never got to express his feelings before the girl's noggin was appropriated by a spider-like goblin who wears it to cover his own ugly mug, creating a look akin to the head-with-spider-legs critter in John Carpenter's *The Thing*. This enjoyable horror romp, adapted from a novel by Daijiro Moroboshi, might seem like a departure for director Shinya Tsukamoto to folks who only know his experimental art house excursions like *Tetsuo: The Iron Man*. However, *Hiruko the Goblin*, a more commercial venture made for a major studio, is in fact closer to Tsukamoto's heart than his famed metal fetish freak out. It stars '60s rock 'n' roll singer Kenji Sawada (*Samurai Reincarnation, Happiness of the Katakuris*) as an entomophobic archeologist armed with an array of homemade *Ghostbusters*-type gadgets, as well as his trusty can of bug spray (which proves remarkably effective against goblins). Can he help young Masao (Masaki Kudo) realize his destiny as a three-horned queller of goblins? Will the bug spray run out at the crucial moment? Keep an eye out for old Toei exploitation film trouper Hideo Murota as Watanabe the gardener.

mising positions (taken from God knows where in private moments) and a cell phone. To get the negatives, she has to plug the cell phone into her ear and be his little puppet. He makes her do stuff like run around town in skimpy leather outfits with no underwear and ride up escalators. This is really hard on poor Rinko; she is so shy and consequently demoralized by the ordeal that she appears to be having a breakdown. Iguchi reminds her of the advice she gave him, about doing what she really wants to do. Then he orders her to buy a vibrator, insert it, leave the remote control where he can find it, and then purchase a cucumber, an eggplant, and a banana (ho ho). At the vegetable stand, he lets her have it. Not the negatives (she gets those eventually), but a few long blasts from the vibrator's remote. This brings Rinko literally to her knees, confusing the *yaoya* (green grocer). It is a devastating scene; her reactions, while spastic, are hardly erotic, and yet the knowledge of what's happening to her is titillating in a deviant sort of way. Whether it's sexy or merely pathetic will be determined by the tastes of the individual filmgoer, but it's clear that what we're witnessing is essentially a high-tech rape by remote control. Nevertheless, the experience seems to shake something loose within Rinko's psychosexual being. That night she showers, and later we find her kissing and caressing a leather chair.

Iguchi calls Rinko to inform her that she has breast cancer (he's such a good photographer, he can tell just by looking at nude pictures he's taken of her). He has cancer, too, and the knowledge of her affliction is tearing him up inside. Somehow, Iguchi has gotten it into his head that her husband Shigehiko is forcing her to get a mastectomy. Iguchi can't bear such a thought and goes after Shigehiko. Iguchi drugs him and spirits him off to a strange underground club where businessmen such as Rinko's husband are bound, fitted with large, face-hugging funnels (turning them into cameras, get it?), and shown live sex acts in which young couples are forced to copulate by tough-looking men in suits (probably yakuza). Afterward, the young couples are deposited in a chamber that rapidly fills with water as the audience (whose funnels have been opened to a wider aperture) watches them through a *round* window. Shigehiko is being liberated from his square world, into the realm of the round, albeit via voyeurism and murder.

Before it's all over, Iguchi will kick the shit out of Shigehiko with steel-toed boots, his long metal dick wrapped around Shigehiko's neck. He'd rather see Rinko dead than mutilated for the sake of something that's killing him as well. All the while, Rinko is transforming, getting hotter and hotter, and Shigehiko is becoming her biggest fan, following her surreptitiously about town. What will become of this obsessive little love triangle? And will it ever stop fucking raining?!

Shigehiko from *A Snake of June*

Rinko from *A Snake of June*

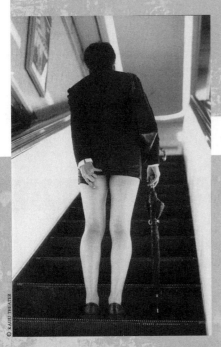

Rinko, controlled remotely by Iguchi

Iguchi from *A Snake of June*

Much praise must be given to the remarkable Asuka Kurosawa for her portrayal of Rinko. Here is an actress putting every ounce of herself into her role, making you suspect more than once that she was making a deep personal connection with the character. She says as much in interviews included on the DVD of the film: "I wanted to let myself go and explode. I wanted to be changed and become a new me, to have the rotten part of me driven out. 'Mr. Tsukamoto, help me!' was the cry in my heart." Normally this kind of talk is just promotional hype for a movie, but in this case, watching her gasping, weeping, screaming, passionate performance, you believe her. She claims that Rinko was the role she was waiting for all her life, and it's right up there on the screen. She's fantastic.

Yuji Kohtari, as Shigehiko, does a fine job, considering he's not a professional actor. A writer by trade, he is a good example of casting to type. His instincts are good and there's only one scene where he looks a little awkward. As for Shinya Tsukamoto, he "wanted to play a stalker for twenty years . . . there really wasn't much preparing for the role." If you've seen any of his other psychotic characters, you can imagine how much of a cakewalk a stalker would be for him. However, his Iguchi is more than your garden-variety, one-dimensional obsessed kook: while he is creepy and clearly has no right to put Rinko through the kinds of things he does, his actions are ameliorated by the positive effects they eventually bring about. In this way he can be likened dramatically to Puck in Shakespeare's *A Midsummer Night's Dream*, Zed in John Boorman's *Zardoz*, or even Q in Miike's *Visitor Q*. In fact, played a slightly different way, Iguchi could even have been a fantasy character, a manifestation of Rinko's subconscious à la Tyler Durden in *Fight Club*. In any case, Iguchi is rounded and realistic, played with subtle, tortured grace (and a big metal techno-weenie) by a talented actor, director, writer, and producer.

Organ

Organ. Just how does one describe a film like *Organ*? Oh, I could say the usual, "It's like nothing you've ever seen before," "You'll never get it's purulent images out of your head," "Like Kirk Douglas in *Detective Story*, you'll want to take your brain out of your head and hold it under a faucet to wash away the dirty pictures it put there," etc. But that just won't do. Perhaps I should start with the film's first impressions: A bloody face, a couple on the run, a rotting green, gooey multiple amputee in a hospital bed, a girl with an eyepatch vomiting blood—and we're not

1996

Japan

105 min.

DIRECTOR: Kei Fujiwara

CAST: Kenji Nasa,
Kimihiko Hasegawa,
Takaaki Furumoto, Kei
Fujiwara, Shun Sugata

even a minute into this unparalleled mélange of art house, film noir, psychodrama, splatgore, police procedural, yakuza, and psychedelic phantasmagoria. This directorial debut from Kei Fujiwara, the female lead in Shinya Tsukamoto's *Tetsuo* (aka *The Ironman*), has more ideas, impressions, impulses, convulsions, as well as buckets of blood, bile, pus, mucus, infections, distended abscesses, tumescent tumors, and, of course, organs (rolling around loose) than you're likely to see again in one 105-minute sitting.

Now some people might think a lead-in like that won't do much to sell the picture, and some people might be right. Too moody and dreamy for gore-hounds, too choppy and confusing for yakuza/crime fans, and too downright disgusting for just about anybody—who in their right mind would want to watch a movie like this? Maybe it's you and you just don't know it! I will admit it requires a couple of viewings before things start to gel (or coagulate, as it were) and for some this will simply be too tall an order. But you're a thrill-seeker, right? You came here looking for something different, something wholly other, the filmic equivalent of a gob-smack and a poke in the eye with a sharp stick, am I right? My friend, with *Organ* I gotcha covered.

> The odor of death in this city attracts the sellers of human organs. With newcomer Tosaka as my partner I was on stake-out behind the hospital where we had a lead.

Thus speaks Numata (Kenji Nasa), a tough cop who always seems to be losing partners à la Dirty Harry. His voice is heard over images of bikers kicking the shit out of an unfortunate individual dressed in like fashion. A rival gang member? A new recruit? Doesn't matter, he's about to become an organ donor. They deposit his limp frame by the back door of a hospital where he's discovered by an employee in a lab coat. Instead of bringing the biker in for medical attention, the guy brings his car around and does a Burke and Hare. Numata and Tosaka (Takaaki Furumoto) follow.

> The smell of death awakens a premonition that I am headed towards a maze with no exits.

The guy from the hospital leads the cops to a warehouse. Impersonating yakuza, Numata and Tosaka muscle in on his action and bluff their way into the building, but Yoko (Kei Fujiwara), the girl with the eyepatch at the door, is suspicious. A mysterious surgeon with a gimpy walk and a stylized, quasi-hockey-style surgical mask prepares to do a bit of vivisection on the biker. A yakuza with an antic disposition laughs maniacally and says, "This is great! He ain't dead, but he won't ever wake up. This means big bucks!" The doc turns the biker on his belly, grabs a scalpel and starts removing kidneys. Numata looks on in stunned silence, but it's too much for Tosaka—he loses it and blows their cover. All hell breaks loose. Numata struggles with the yakuza, burying a broken bottle in his butt; the biker flops around and makes sickening animal noises; Tosaka grabs a kidney and screams, "Put it back!" The doc jams a hypo full of green fluid into Numata's neck; in the melee, Numata escapes. The last thing he hears is Tosaka screaming. . . .

Tosaka disappeared after that scream. I was suspended and taken off the case.

Flash forward: Numata is now a disheveled, drunken down-and-out, reduced to the rubble of human wreckage by his horrific ordeal. He still haunts the warehouse where it all happened. Here he is confronted by two cops, one of whom is Tosaka's twin brother, Shinji (Takaaki Furumoto again). Needless to say, seeing the spitting image of his missing partner gives Numata a shock. However, it's clear that neither he nor Shinji have given up on the case, each cop dedicated to finding Tosaka.

Here the film shifts gears abruptly, turning its attention to the still, lifeless body of a blood-spattered schoolgirl. She lies discarded amidst foliage, her panties dangling from an ankle. Who is she? A gossipy girl's voice-over says, "This girl Saito's been absent for three months. But she's actually missing."

Koma (Hong Kong, 2004) Ching and Ling are young and pretty. One rich, one poor, one has kidney disease and the other might be a kidney thief. And they both love the same man. These two ladies have a lot in common! Love, friendship, betrayal, revenge, sharp scalpels, and involuntary organ donors waking up on ice make for one blood-spattered woman's picture in this slick, post-handover Hong Kong thriller. Outlandish? Yeah. Predictable? Pretty much. But there's something appealing about this film, namely the two female leads, Karena Lam and Angelica Lee. Both actresses give 110 percent, enlarging their sketchy characters with sheer presence and star power (and they're both easy on the eyes). *Koma* is big on entertainment value, but don't lean too heavily on the story or narrative structure; it's not some J-horror-style movie with elaborate backstory and moody, slow-burn atmosphere. We're firmly in the tradition of Hollywood blockbuster here, so enjoy it as you would its inevitable U.S. remake. Director Law Chi Leung has done all the work for his Hollywood counterpart, crafting the film with the familiar techniques of sound and vision that make Americans jump and scream (as he did with 2002's *Inner Senses*, also starring Lam). Recommended for Asian film newbies.

We are now drawn into the world of the mysterious surgeon, Junichi Soeki (Kimihiko Hasegawa). He's a high school biology teacher, his office walls covered with framed butterflies. Adjoining his office is his private lab, which contains myriad plants, live butterflies, a small fridge full of drugs, and Officer Tosaka all rigged up in a cabinet with an IV drip and plants. His legs and hands have been amputated, his limbs terminating in bloody stumps whose redness contrasts the bright green of the leafy plant life surrounding him in his little case. Lolling in semi-consciousness, he has become a gruesome science experiment, a hapless human lab rat.

Soeki is pinning butterflies to a board when he's visited by a female student. She complains about her low marks in biology and appears to come on to him in her nerdy, awkward way. This stimulates a response in Soeki: orange, viscous slime starts to ooze through his shirt in the region of his abdomen, apparently from some concealed wound. As he rolls the ropey, mucilaginous muck around on his fingers, images of the dead schoolgirl flash across the screen, creating an *aha!* moment: When Soeki gets turned on, (1) he oozes, (2) he rapes, and (3) he kills. Orange slime oozes from the student's mouth as well, perhaps indicating a metaphor for sordid sexuality. In any case, he takes her into his private lab, assuring her that she won't have to worry about her grades anymore. . . .

In the afterglow of his sexual/surgical moment with the student (now quite dead), Soeki stares at a butterfly cocoon and begins to hallucinate, seeing a woman emerge from the viscid folds of its fissure. "There are caterpillars in my belly," she moans, pulling out a long, gluey, blue-green sample and fondling it suggestively. Later, Soeki visits Yoko (the girl with the eyepatch) and we learn that they are brother and sister. She chides him for murdering a second student.

Meanwhile, Numata is drinking sake with some old guy in a flophouse. The conversation soon turns to a very cop-like line of questioning, indicating that Numata's new persona as bum isn't so much a lifestyle choice as cover for his continuing, albeit independent, investigation. He shows the oyaji, Nakanishi (Shun Sugata), a photo and the latter mumbles something about "my kids." It's soon revealed that Nakanishi is a former, much respected yakuza and his kids are none other than Soeki and Yoko.

The key scene of the film, the moment that transforms Soeki and Yoko into three-dimensional, almost sympathetic characters, comes as Soeki is rolling around on his futon, apparently in great physical distress. He cries out to his henchman Shige, "Call Yoko for the drugs!" He opens his shirt to reveal an abscessed, open wound. In the throes of his agony, his fevered brain flashes back to his childhood, to POV images of his psychotic mother ranting about her unfaithful husband and vowing never to let young Junichi follow in his footsteps. To ensure this, she takes a knife to his genitals and in the fracas, mom also pokes out little Yoko's eye. Later, at the hospital, the doctor announces that he managed to save Jun's penis (although the injury explains why he walks with a limp). Soon, mom has run in, murdered the doctor, taken the children to the woods, and made them cut her open, screaming, "Tear my belly and kill this baby! He's coming into hell! This world is hell!" You don't have to be Sigmund Freud to understand why Jun and Yoko grew up to become *bakemono* (monsters, a recurring term in the film).

From here, the film descends into ever-widening spirals of depravity, cruelty, and revenge, served up with copious amounts of chartreuse goo and crimson gore. The use of bright greens (and, to a lesser degree, oranges and browns) creates a visual cue conveying disease and decay, major themes in the film. Wounds are another theme, and in some cases exist wholly as metaphors. For example, after several miraculous recoveries, it becomes clear that Soeki's wound isn't an actual one, but in fact his *inner* wound, and that the drugs he's taking to ameliorate the pain are further warping his demented brain. The wound grows larger and larger throughout the film, covering his chest, shooting green pus, and, at one point, projecting into a fetus-sized protuberance. These metamorphoses depict the real Soeki, the man inside. How revealing (and revolting) it would be to witness this side of the people around us in our everyday lives.

According to Brian Thomas' Psychotronic Film Society website (http://www.psychotronic.info), *Organ* was originally a stage play, a production of Kei Fujiwara's Organ Vital group. It was apparently quite a hit, but there must have been more than a few theatergoers leaving performances covered in glutinous secretions. I imagine the front row of the audience swathed in plastic, like fans of some watermelon-smashing prop comic.

As mentioned earlier, *Organ* requires a second viewing to really grasp everything that's going on. Fujiwara was juggling a lot of balls thematically and plot-wise, and was apparently still coming to grips with the subtleties of film editing. There are jumpy bits where a few extra seconds, an additional scene, or line of dialog would have cleared up the confusion. The film is not for the squeamish or the faint of heart, but definitely worth a look. For my money, *Organ* makes a worthy addition to any horror film library. Just be careful who you show it to; you might be taken for hentai or bakemono!

The Eye • *Jian gui*

2002

Hong Kong/Thailand

98 min.

DIRECTOR: Pang
Brothers

CAST: Angelica Lee
Sum Kit, Edmund
Chen Chi Choi,
Wilson Yip Wai Shun,
Lawrence Chou Jun
Wai, Yut Lai So

Millions of moviegoers enjoyed hearing the words "I see dead people" spoken by creepily cherubic Haley Joel Osment in *The Sixth Sense* (1999). Me, I'd prefer to hear it in Cantonese from a pretty girl who's just had a cornea transplant in a haunted Hong Kong hospital. Actually, it's not just the hospital—the whole city is haunted, there are ghosts everywhere! In the elevators, in the restaurants, walking down the middle of the highway. The lucky ones are escorted away to the afterlife by urban-cool, Grim Reaper types, tenebrous, whisper-thin fellows in black turtlenecks with blurry, white faces. These "shadowy men," as Mun (Angelica Lee), the central character, calls them, will figure largely in the grand finale of the film.

The protagonist of *The Eye* is a lithe yet strong-willed young blind woman, the aforementioned Mun, who's just had a cornea transplant. Mun is befriended by a chemo-bald eleven-year-old girl (yeah, they had to put a kid in there) named Ying Ying (Yut Lai So). Ying Ying is undergoing a series of operations to remove a brain tumor and is a spunky little thing, but after awhile you get the feeling that it's only a matter of time before a shadowy man comes around for her. Ying Ying has a little pink camera that will come into play later in the film, when one of her photos reveals something shocking to Mun.

Mun's operation is a success, but the joy of regaining her sense of sight (she lost it at the age of two) is soon marred by the realization that with it comes a second sight, an acute awareness of the wandering dead all around her. The reality of this newfound perception isn't immediately apparent to Mun who, at first, can only see blurry outlines of people, thus making it difficult to distinguish who's alive and who isn't. Things eventually clear up, though, and poor Mun becomes so traumatized by the daily hauntings that soon she's holed up in her room, curtains drawn, light bulbs out, dark glasses on, simultaneously returning to the womb, as well as the comfort of her former phantom-free blindness.

Mun's love interest is her psychotherapist, whom we'll call young Dr. Lo (singer Lawrence Chou) in contradistinction to his uncle, who performed Mun's eye surgery, whom we'll call old Dr. Lo (Edmund Chen). Young Dr. Lo, who looks fourteen, is incredulous on first hearing Mun's ghost stories, and as for old Dr. Lo, he just thinks she's nuts. Both men eventually come around, though, and decide, against the code of medical ethics, to help her find out more about the donor of her cursed

© APPLAUSE/FORTISSIMO

Mun and Dr. Lo in *The Eye*

corneas. Mun's quest leads her and young Dr. Lo to Thailand and many revelations.

Also present, more as a chorus than a character, is a Taoist priest who pontificates on all manner of ghostly issues, such as: "Those who die a sudden death have no recollection of the instance of death. Their souls remain in this world as if they're still alive. But there are others who intentionally refuse to leave, mostly due to unresolved problems during their lifetime. These souls can't be consoled while their problems remain. There is only one way to help them, and that is to resolve what they left unsettled." This is, in a nutshell, the whole narrative thrust of the film.

In discussing *The Eye*, references to *The Sixth Sense* are inevitable; everyone saw the latter film back in 1999 and was affected by its calculated creepiness, its clammy, claustrophobic atmosphere, and moving (if lugubrious) storyline. While *The Eye* lacks the heavy bummer vibe (nobody is slow-poisoned with Drano in their food), it has its own compelling qualities and is, pound for pound, a scarier picture. The ghosts here are not merely lifeless losers wandering the lower strata of the astral plane—they're the sneak-up-behind-you-and-go-"Boo!" variety. One move they use frequently is to appear before Mun a little ways in the distance, disappear, then reappear right behind her and croak or scream something suitably terrifying. Elsewhere, they're swooping down on or even running through her. The Pang Brothers are throwing down the cinematic gauntlet. "You want ghosts?" they seem to be saying, "Sit the fuck down, pal, we'll give you ghosts!"

One image that's worth pointing out (because it's entirely possible to miss) is that of a ghoulish face in a window. Look for it in the scene where Mun and young Dr. Lo are on a train and Mun has her revelation with Ying Ying's photo. The scene is gripping, featuring a crucial plot point, but watch the window to the right of the two main characters: every time the train goes into a tunnel, you can see a faint yet menacing visage hovering just outside the glass. Nobody notices it, no musical cues draw our attention to it, it's just *there*. A nice, eerie touch from the brothers Pang.

What's perhaps most shocking about *The Eye* is not so much what we see as what we hear. Orchestration and high-tech sound design are employed to a frightening and assaultive extent reminiscent of *The Exorcist*. Several ghosts' appearances are accompanied by cacophonous or-

Angelica Lee

chestral crescendos right out of The Beatles' *Day in the Life*. Listen for these moments of soundtrack intensity when Mun goes for her calligraphy lesson, has lunch in a restaurant, or gets on her building's elevator; the ghosts she encounters in these scenes are unnerving enough on their own, but with the added aural dimension your heart will quickly reach palpitation point. Note also the pounding, percussive music that accompanies Mun's recurring nightmare.

The Eye directors Danny and Oxide Pang head up a multinational cast and crew in this truly pan-Asian production. Twin brothers Oxide (formerly a colorist) and Danny (an editor) are Hong Kong natives who started out in advertising, a background shared by Thai filmmakers Wisit Sasanatieng (*Tears of the Black Tiger*) and Pen-ek Ratanaruang (*Last Life in the Universe*). The brothers moved to Thailand, joining the vanguard of that country's new and exciting cinema at the turn of the millennium. The two stars of the film are also imports: Angelica Lee is Malaysian, Lawrence Chou Chinese-Canadian. This multitude of Asian nationalities is even worked into the film itself. In one scene, Mun's grandma suggests that she move to Toronto with her father. And, of course, the filmmakers make a point of setting the action partly in Hong Kong and partly in Thailand. This is not entirely uncalculated: making movies that appeal to a wider swath of Asia means a lot more box offices, which means a lot more money. The production company responsible for *The Eye*, Hong Kong-based Applause Pictures, specializes in pan-Asian films, making foreign distribution central to their business strategy. For this film they brought in Singapore-based Raintree Pictures. Raintree put up

Danny & Oxide Pang

30 percent of the financing, helped with distribution in Singapore and Malaysia, and supplied Edmund Chen and Pierre Png (who portrayed Dr. Eak, the Thai doctor with all the answers). Raintree's CEO, Daniel Yun, sees things this way: "The next lap of the regional film industry is not led by Hong Kong, but by countries such as Thailand and Korea . . . we have to stay in the loop by working with these countries" (Karl Ho, "An Eye on Asian Film Market," *Straits Times*, June 22, 2002.)

The Pang Brothers' first collaboration was *Bangkok Dangerous* (1999), a gritty urban crime story about a deaf-mute hit man and the people who pass into and (often violently) out of his life. By then Oxide had already made his solo directorial debut with *Who Is Running?* (1997), a film concerning a man who gets hold of tomorrow's newspaper and sets about trying to avert the deaths described in it. The film was a flop, panned in Hong Kong, but proved a big hit on the international festival circuit, garnering specific praise at the Asia Pacific Film Festival and the Vancouver Film Festival, thus putting Oxide on the map as one to watch. Following the international success of *The Eye,* the Pang Brothers directed the inevitable sequel, *The Eye 2,* featuring the fetching Taiwanese-born Shu Qi (*The Storm Riders, So Close*).

I'd recommend *The Eye* to anyone who liked *The Sixth Sense* as a spicy Hong Kong/Thai alternative. It's also a good pick for those worn out by the Sadako-style ghost of oh-so-many J-horror and Korean shockers. The Pang Brothers offer up just as plausible and pitiable a selection of lost souls as M. Night Shyamalan, but up the ante when it comes to the fright factor.

5 CONFINEMENT

What a fate to be locked away. And how much the worse for the man or woman imprisoned unjustly. Ah, horrible! One might well cling to dreams of vengeance for solace through the dark nights. What savagery would years of such obsession finally unleash! But before sweet revenge can be wrought, other dangers await. One's time confined, be it in a prison, a convent, or on a tropical isle, is a bloody battle, a never-ending struggle against the oppressors as well as the oppressed. Sooner or later one has to kill to survive. Occasionally, weapons are provided. . . .

Oldboy

2003
South Korea
120 min.
DIRECTOR: Park Chan-wook

CAST: Choi Min-sik, Yoo Ji-tae, Kang Hye-jeong, Ji Dae-han, Oh Kwang-rok

If you were mad at someone, you might whack him with a hammer. If you were *really* mad, you'd use the claw end. And if you were burning with white hot rage at having been kidnapped and imprisoned for untold years, you might just duct-tape the guy to a chair and use the claw end for a little impromptu dental surgery. . . .

Meet Oh Dae-su (Choi Min-sik), drunken Korean salaryman. He's sitting in a police station, charged with harassing women, fighting, and who knows what other drunken shenanigans. Far from sitting quietly in the presence of the law, he's a wild man: he's trying to urinate in the corner, he's taking his clothes off, he's ranting and raving, he's modeling his three-year-old daughter's angel wings (her birthday pres-

Oldboy's Oh Dae-su: "15 years of this wallpaper would choke you too!"

ent) and singing a little song, he's attacking the cops with a coat stand, he's weeping. His name means "getting along with people"—so why can't he get along? His friend Joo-hwan (Ji Dae-han) bails him out, only to lose him in the dark, rainy night. Where did he go? Did he wander off to pass out in some public park? Has he gone home? No, Oh Dae-su has disappeared.

What becomes of Oh Dae-su is beyond comprehension: He is imprisoned in an illegal private jail for fifteen years. In a cell made up like a shabby hotel room, our protagonist lives out the lonely years with nothing but a television and a pile of green notebooks into which he pours the confessions and bitter reflections of a lifetime. Deeper and deeper he sinks into despair, hallucinating wildly, and masturbating to idol singers on the TV. He learns that his wife has been murdered and he's been framed—by the same party that's holding him prisoner. He slashes his wrists repeatedly. But he doesn't give up. Gradually he regains his sense of himself, the spunky, fighting Oh Dae-su. He draws an outline of a man on the wall, a sparring partner upon which to beat out his frustrations. He begins to dig his way out through the wall, brick by brick. Soon he will be free. . . .

And then one day, much to his surprise, Oh Dae-su finds himself on the grassy roof of an apartment building, free as a bird. From this point forward, we follow him on a single-minded and ferocious quest for vengeance unlike anything seen before in the whole long history of revenge tragedy. We're talking Senecan here, we're talking Shakespearean. And, in common with his fellow revengers, Oh Dae-su will get more than he bargained for; his vengeance will get the better of him, and he will end up paying a far greater price than just fifteen years of his life for his transgressions (whatever those are—that's one part of his mission, to learn what he's done to warrant such cruel and unusual punishment).

But what makes *Oldboy* such a uniquely brilliant and devastating film? Beyond the complex storylines, eye-popping cinematography, breathtaking pace, and masterful direction by Park Chan-wook, there is the performance of Choi Min-sik. At the end of the day, Choi Min-sik *is* the movie. From beginning to end, it's his film, and he gives what is probably the performance of his life. Very few actors can convey a range and degree of human emotions with such seamless verisimilitude. He is by turns tender, brutal, numb, intellectual, psychotic, vulnerable, invincible, goofy, sadistic, garrulous, pathetic, paternal, amorous, confused, introspective, and nauseous. His physicality is nonpareil as well; whether he's taking on twenty guys with a knife stuck in his back or chowing down on a live octopus, it's clear that Choi Min-sik is up for anything when it comes to using his "instrument."

Like fellow screen greats such as Japan's Tatsuya Nakadai, England's Lawrence Olivier, and Italy's Gian Maria Volonte, Choi Min-sik began in live theater and divides his time between screen and stage acting. He first worked with Park Chan-wook in the film *Our Twisted Hero* (1992) and appeared in stage plays, television dramas, and films throughout the '90s. He was a bright spot in the otherwise tepid mob flick *No. 3* (1997), countering Han Suk-kyu's embattled syndicate boss as a ballsy, tough-as-nails DA who hates gangsters and literally slaps them around in public. (Choi had previously appeared with Han in the popular South Korean TV show *Moon Over Seoul* in 1994.) In 1998, Choi showed off his comedy chops in Kim Ji-woon's riotous black comedy *The Quiet Family* as slobby Uncle Chang-ku, whose chief household duties include burying corpses and keeping an eye on his peeping tom nephew Yeong-Min (played brilliantly by versatile screen star Song Kang-ho).

But it was his explosive portrayal of a North Korean special forces commander in *Shiri* (1999) that catapulted Choi Min-sik to superstardom. Once again he played opposite handsome leading man Han Suk-kyu, the latter a good-guy special agent bent on stopping Choi and his elite team from detonating a devastating high-tech explosive planted in a sports arena during a soccer game. (Song Kang-ho is also on board as Han's funny-yet-astute partner.) Choi's performance won him the Korean Grand Bell Award for Best Actor in 1999, a year that also saw him

Sympathy for Lady Vengeance (Chinjeolhan geumjassi) **(South Korea, 2005)**

Oh boy, there goes the franchise. The third time is *not* a charm in Park Chan-wook's famed Revenge Trilogy. While *Lady Vengeance* has its moments, it's ultimately muddled, uneven, and ill conceived. It doesn't hold a candle to its predecessors *Sympathy for Mr. Vengeance* and *Oldboy*. Frankly, it's not hard to understand; like Welles after *Citizen Kane* or Radiohead after *OK Computer*, sometimes your toughest competition is yourself. How do you follow an act like *Oldboy*? A savvy artist would try something different, to be sure, yet not abandon those strengths that made him what he is. *Lady* starts off promising, with a decidedly lighter tone, setting up plenty of interesting characters and plot possibilities. But in an effort to move away from *Oldboy* territory, the new directions the film takes make for a frustrating and tedious third act. The big revenge, when it *finally* comes, is accompanied by rabbit-out-of-a-hat plot revelations and lots of superfluous scenes and dialog that sap it of any impact. Bad guy Choi Min-sik is given little to do and other Trilogy alumni are barely glimpsed, while miscast Lee Young-ae is forced to carry the film. Here's hoping for a return to form for Park next time out.

© SHOW EAST/EGG FILM

Oh Dae-su plots a trajectory in *Oldboy*

play *Hamlet* on stage and star in *Happy End*, a dark tale of betrayal and murder, which caused a stir at home for its graphic violence and near-porno sex scenes. 2001's *Failan* found Choi playing a loser thug who falls in love with the dead wife he never knew; it's one of the saddest pictures ever made. In 2002, Choi garnered accolades for his portrayal of renowned Korean painter Jang Seung-eop in *Chihwaseon*.

Which brings us back to *Oldboy*. The villain of the piece is the enigmatic and super-rich Lee Wu-jin (Yoo Ji-tae). He is the one who has imprisoned, as well as released, Oh Dae-su for reasons known only to him. Immediately after Oh's liberation, Lee sees to it that he is supplied with money and a cell phone. Oh finds a sushi restaurant and, after chatting pleasantly with female sushi chef Mi-do (the stunning Kang Hye-jeong), receives a call from Lee, who informs him that his mission is to discover (1) who imprisoned him and (2) why. Lee says cryptic things like, "Be it a grain of sand or a rock, in water they sink as the same." Oh becomes enraged and afterward orders something alive. Mi-do serves him an octopus and Oh proceeds to eat the wriggling thing, causing U.S. critics to scream like schoolgirls and blow the scene out of all proportion in their reviews. If you've been around the block, you know that, however unfortunate, cruelty to animals comes with the territory in many Korean films. Consider the live-fish sashimi scene in Kim Ki-duk's *The Isle* (2000), his lesser torture of frogs and fish in *Spring, Summer, Autumn, Winter . . . and Spring* (2003), or the massive frog annihilation scene at the beginning of Kang Hyeon-il's art house freak out *Mago* (2002).

Choi Min-sik   Kang Hye-jeong   Yoo Ji-tae

Oh Dae-su's nemesis, Lee Wu-jin, is played with smirking arrogance by actor, model, and graduate student Yoo Ji-tae. Yu first came to the attention of audiences in 1999's uproarious social satire *Attack the Gas Station* as a punk painter with white-dyed hair and a criminal attitude. In *Oldboy*, he is suave and confident, a slick sociopath with all the time in the world to send the wretched Oh scuttling down the narrow passages of the dark Skinner box he has created; rewarding here, punishing there, Oh's every move is plotted out and planned for by this self-appointed master of his destiny. We eventually learn that Lee is an old classmate of Oh's, that they are Sangnok High School "Evergreen Oldboys" (hence the film's title). This does constitute a flaw in the film, as actor Yoo Ji-tae is fourteen years Choi Min-sik's junior. Perhaps we are to assume that Lee's privileged existence has allowed him to keep fit and young-looking, whereas Oh's dissipated salaryman lifestyle plus fifteen years in stir has led to his considerably more bedraggled appearance. In any case, Lee Wu-jin has created a monster in Oh Dae-su, even jokingly calling him "Mr. Monster"—this long after Oh himself has the thought, "I've become a monster."

Oldboy is based on a Japanese manga by Garon Tsuchiya and Nobuaki Minegishi and, like all manga adaptations, is filled with extreme storytelling that makes for unforgettable scenes, such as Oh Dae-su taking on twenty assailants in a dank hallway with nothing but his trusty hammer. It is a set-piece at once brutal and balletic,

Yoo Ji-tae, Park Chan-wook, Kang Hye-jeong, and Choi Min-sik

the entire sequence captured in one continuous take. The camera tracks gradually left and right as it follows the tidal movement of the brawl, our hero attacking, connecting, flailing, falling, rallying and attacking again, at one point acquiring a knife in his back which remains there for the remainder of the fracas. There are hallucinatory sequences involving ants that, according to the internal logic of the film, appear in the minds of the very lonely. Oh Dae-su sees them coming out of his skin in enveloping waves; Mi-do encounters an eight-foot-tall variety on a subway train.

Oldboy makes good use of recurring catch phrases that seem trite at first, but take on meaning and significance as the events of the story unfold. "Laugh and the world laughs with you, weep and you weep alone" is a good example, or the aforementioned "Be it a grain of sand or a rock, in water they sink as the same." A suicidal man at one point says to Oh Dae-su, "Even though I'm no better than a beast, don't I have the right to live?" This one sticks in Oh's head and resurfaces again and again. Other memorable utterances include

> The television is both a clock and calendar. It's your school, home, church, friend, and lover . . . but my lover's song is too short.

> Each [tooth] I yank out will make you age one year.

> I'm going to kill every woman you love until you die.

There are moments in *Oldboy* when Choi Min-sik reminds me of Gary Oldman. As of this writing, plans for a Hollywood remake are going forward, yet I can't imagine they'll hire Oldman, the only possible choice for this role. He'll be passed over for some less-talented but more-bankable star, one of the usual, square-jawed suspects. Luckily for us, we live in an age in which we can acquire the original product; masterpieces of cinema like *Oldboy* not only stand up to their imitators, they invariably outshine them by comparison.

In terms of popularity, *Oldboy* has been an international phenomenon. It's truly gratifying for fans of extreme Asian cinema to see how this film has been embraced and awarded around the world. In addition to box-office success, it took the Grand Prix at the Fifty-seventh Cannes Film Festival and Best Asian Film Award at the Twenty-fourth Hong Kong Film Awards. At home in South Korea it was given Best Picture at the 2004 Korea Film Awards, Kang Hye-jeong won the prestigious Blue Dragon Award for Best Supporting Actress, it even won the Bo-Gwan Order of Cultural Merit from the government's Minister of Culture and Tourism (even though the film is hardly a picturesque travelogue—it might, on the other hand, inspire tourists interested in a little kidnapping, murder, forced confinement, and ultraviolence).

Female Prisoner #701: Scorpion • Joshuu 701-go: Sasori

1972
Japan
87 min.
DIRECTOR: Shunya Ito
CAST: Meiko Kaji, Rie Yokoyama, Isao Natsuyagi, Fumio Watanabe, Yoichi Numata, Saburo Date, Yayoi Watanabe, Yoko Mihara

You're a beautiful flower
His words flatter you today
But once you're in full bloom
He'll just toss you away
Foolish, foolish, foolish woman's song of vengeance

So sings Meiko Kaji, star of *Female Prisoner #701: Scorpion,* the lyrics nicely setting up the larger plot arc of the film (wickedly betrayed by her lover, she will have her revenge). Kaji's smoky alto and a haunting arrangement make for a catchy, torchy little number; the song, "Urami Bushi" ("Song of Vengeance," literally "Grudge Song") was a hit in Japan, helped by the popularity of the Female Prisoner #701 franchise (four films with Kaji in 1972 and 1973 and a couple of lesser installments later in the '70s without her). Here, the song plays over an opening credits sequence featuring nude lady convicts exercising on an apparatus seemingly designed for the benefit of the pervo guards leering below. Earlier, Kaji's character, Nami Matsushima (aka 701 aka Matsu aka Sasori), made a break for it with her mute friend Yuki (lovely Yayoi Watanabe). But as the two women were running, Yuki got her period. Consequently, her pace was hampered by crippling cramps; the trail of menstrual blood also made it easier for the dogs to follow. Recaptured, the two women lie hog-tied, Japanese rope bondage-style, in a drippy cell, receiving daily tortures from a sadistic trustee.

Cue expressionistic flashback: Nami doesn't know it, but her boyfriend and first love, Sugimi (Isao Natsuyagi), is actually a villainous cad and

女優 梶 芽衣子

強烈な個性の代表作一挙上映!

701号怨み節
猛る! 黒い殺意!
復讐の呪経が闇中にひびき
さそりの刑事狩りが始まる

日程	作品
9/23～26	女囚701号・さそり
9/27～29	女囚さそり第41雑居房
9/30～10/3	女囚さそり・けもの部屋
10/4～6	女囚さそり・701号怨み節
10/7～10	女番長・野良猫ロック
10/11～13	野良猫ロック・セックスハンター
10/14～17	野良猫ロック・マシンアニマル
10/18～20	反逆のメロディー
10/21～24	修羅雪姫
10/25～27	修羅雪姫・怨み恋歌

Meiko Kaji in her Scorpion persona

corrupt narc (one so detestable that every time he appears on screen a sinister fanfare blares out, seemingly encouraging you to hiss). He convinces Nami to assist him in a sting operation on Kaizu Enterprises, a marijuana-trafficking yakuza outfit. In a series of colorful, non-realistic scenes played out on a soundstage, we witness it all go horribly wrong as Nami is gang-raped by the Kaizu thugs ("If you're not going to talk, we'll ask your body!"), and a laughing Sugimi receives a payoff from their boss (Saburo Date). Sugimi drops a few bills on Nami's ravaged form and saunters out. Clearly this guy never heard that old chestnut about "a woman scorned," a proverb that goes double for Nami. Sadly, she chooses to attack him with a knife right in front of the police station, where a group of uniformed officers thwart her efforts and haul her away.

We later learn that Nami never testified against Sugimi or any of her yakuza assailants in court. In fact, our heroine doesn't say much of anything, a departure from the foul-mouthed Nami of the original manga by Toru Shinohara. As Kaji herself recalls,

I saw that [the screenplay] had kept most of the obscenities the character spoke in the comics. I told [director Shunya Ito] that was unacceptable, that it would end up making the film seem cheap and sleazy. . . . He agreed with me and came to believe it would be more interesting if my character hardly spoke any dialog. (Chris Desjardins, *Outlaw Masters of Japanese Film*, p. 68)

Christopher Lee made a similar decision in *Dracula: Prince of Darkness*

(1966), choosing to forego his lines and consequently improving that picture as Kaji does here. Kaji communicates her state of mind largely with her eyes; once someone pushes her too far and she gives them *the stare*, you know it's all over. Trust me, that stare will stay with you long after the initial shock of the ultraviolence has faded.

What ultraviolence, you ask? Let's see, people are beaten with truncheons and burned with hot soup, the warden receives a long shard of glass in his eye, Nami endures hot light bulb abuse where no woman should ever have a hot light bulb (and this from another woman, evoking the electrified dildo scene in *Ilsa, She Wolf of the SS*), and in one riot sequence, the great Yoichi Numata (*Jigoku, The Ring*), here playing a lascivious guard, gets brained by one of the inmates with a shovel, geysers of blood shooting from his head. But if this were the only thing going for *Female Prisoner #701: Scorpion*, it would be very thin soil indeed (like the brutal, yet deadly dull fourth installment, *Female Prisoner Scorpion: #701's Grudge Song*).

No, what really elevates this movie is the stylistic flourishes im-

In Praise of Manga Movies If you're looking for a shortcut to extreme Asian cinema, you can't go far wrong with a film adapted from Japanese manga (comic book). While Hollywood cranks out one tepid popcorn film after another based on American comic books (usually concerning someone with superpowers and a form-fitting costume), manga movies are far different, owing to the fact that manga itself is very different from what we consider a "comic book" in the States. First off, the range of topic and target audience is far broader for manga; you've got manga for kids, young adults, and adults offering cuddly creatures, supernatural tales, crime drama, samurai action, shojo (girl stuff), sports, yakuza wars, corporate intrigue, hentai (porno)—anything you like! And yes, extreme violence is definitely on the table, such as the prison saga *Riki-oh*, on which the Hong Kong splatterfest *The Story of Ricky* is based, as well as *Seiju gakuen*, an S/M-in-a-nunnery *gekiga* (like manga but far more dark) penned by Norifumi Suzuki, who later adapted it as Toei Studios' nunsploitation classic *Convent of the Sacred Beast*.

If you liked *The Story of Ricky* and *Convent of the Sacred Beast* and crave a hybrid, you might go in for the women's prison manga movie series Female Prisoner Scorpion starring Meiko Kaji (four films, 1973–74). The series is packed with more mutilation, humiliation, and torture than you can shake a truncheon at, all delivered with style and verve, a masterpiece of mid-'70s "pinky violence" from Toei. The hypnotic Ms. Kaji starred simultaneously in the title role of both *Lady Snowblood* pictures for Daiei Studios, portraying a woman living only for vengeance in Meiji-era Japan. Lady Snowblood was the creation of stellar manga scribe Kazuo Koike, also responsible for manga movie series Lone Wolf and Cub (six films, 1972–74) and The Razor (three films, 1972–74), both classics of samurai exploitation cinema.

More recently we've seen the release of manga movies *Shark Skin Man and Peach Hip Girl* (1998) and *Ichi the Killer* (2001), both starring Tadanobu Asano, both filled with bizarre and unforgettable characters, and both wildly perverted and violent (*Ichi* far more so). The Korean revenge odyssey *Oldboy* (2003) is manga-based, with a performance by Choi Min-sik to rival anything by De Niro, Brando, or Oldman.

The key to manga movies is manga, a creative environment of complete freedom, allowing for bold, willfully provocative explorations of the farthest reaches and the darkest depths. To bring such stories into the realm of film is to blow the doors of perception open with a fistful of C4. See you in the burn ward.

Meiko Kaji sporting her '70s look

Meiko Kaji in tradional Japanese attire

parted by director Shunya Ito. Having served as assistant director to the deliriously depraved and brazenly talented Teruo Ishii, Ito knew a few things about visual style and how to make an exploitation film with just the right blend of prurience and panache. Therefore, in Nami's flashback sequence we see her wrapped in a long, white cloth against a solid blue background and gradually, sensually unrolled by her lover. Later, as she is raped, we see the scene from below through a transparent glass floor. A rotating platform flips a wall around to reveal Saburo Date sitting at a desk. After Sugimi drops the money on Nami, a green spotlight falls on her face, deep crimson pours up through the glass floor and, in a series of jump cuts, her long black hair rearranges into a splayed-out mane. The combination of these last effects and Kaji's expression transforms Nami into the familiar vengeful ghost of Japanese folklore. A similar yet stylistically different transformation scene comes when Nami confronts corrupt, redheaded trustee Masaki (exploitation veteran Yoko Mihara), sending her face through a window. When the enraged Masaki looks up, in addition to a gash on her forehead, she's now made up in *kumadori*, the stylized Kabuki "shadow painting" traditionally used to accentuate a fierce or grimacing face. She chases Nami, brandishing a shard of glass, a howling theremin freak out playing throughout. Nami deftly maneuvers her toward the warden, stepping out of the way just in time for an impromptu eyeball-ectomy (the shock of which magically wipes the kumadori from Masaki's face).

The warden is played by Fumio Watanabe, a Toei Studios pink film favorite who also portrayed wonderfully loathsome characters in Teruo Ishii's *Shogun's Joy of Torture* and Norifumi Suzuki's *Convent of the Sacred Beast*. I already mentioned Yoichi Numata, here in a criminally small guard role (although he dies magnificently). If you're a fan of Japanese megastar Shintaro Katsu, you'll no doubt recognize Saburo Date as the yakuza boss; he was in practically every Zatoichi film ever made and was always popping up in Katsu projects. Props must be given to Yayoi Watanabe, one of the prettiest actresses in exploitationdom, for her role as the sweet and innocent Yuki. She plays a similar character, and is similarly punished for her good deeds, in *Convent of the Sacred Beast*, even getting defiled by surname-mate Fumio Watanabe (no relation). She also returns to the Sasori series in the third film, *Female Prisoner Scorpion: Beast Stable* (1973). And we mustn't overlook the enjoyably sleazy, *kumadori*-enhanced performance of Yoko Mihara. If you're into Japanese exploitation cinema, you've seen her around. She was tits up in a bathtub full of blood in *Zero Woman: Red Handcuffs* (1974, another heinous Toei flick based on another twisted manga from Sasori author Toru Shinohara); she was the cruel yet horny nun who got what was coming to her in *Convent of the Sacred Beast* (damn, *everybody* was in that!); she was in *Tokugawa Sex Ban: Lustful Lord, Hot Springs Kiss Geisha, Sukeban Guerilla*, as well as *Female Prisoner #701: Scorpion*—and that was just in 1972! However, her career covered much more than just '70s exploitation; starting out in the '50s, Mihara acted in many a fine film by prestige directors such as *Sword of the Beast* (1965, Hideo Gosha), *Blackmail Is My Life* (1968, Kinji Fukasaku), and a bunch of Abashiri Prison pictures (mid-'60s, Teruo Ishii). Hats off to Yoko Mihara.

But the real jewel in the crown is Meiko Kaji. A stunning natural beauty, her performance in *Female Prisoner #701: Scorpion* is understated yet smoldering, the essence of bottled rage. Born Masako Ota, Kaji had previously been at Nikkatsu studios, playing tough chick roles like the girl gang leader in the popular Stray Cat Rock series, but left in 1972 for Toei, having no interest in participating in Nikkatsu's switch to all "roman porno" (romantic pornography) all the time. The years 1972 and 1973 were a professional peak for Kaji. She appeared in four Female Prisoner Scorpion films, as well as two legendary period exploitation pictures for Toho, *Lady Snowblood: Blizzard from the Netherworld* and *Lady Snowblood 2: Love Song of Vengeance* (both based on a manga by Kazuo Koike). Kaji went on to work with acclaimed directors Kinji Fukasaku and Yasuzo Masumura.

It's been asserted that the second film in the Sasori series, *Female Prisoner Scorpion: Jailhouse 41* (1972) is the best of the series, but I'm not so sure. It's definitely more surreal, and the girls get to break out, rampage across the countryside, and hold a busload of amoral businessmen hostage, but for my money *Female Prisoner #701: Scorpion* is more true to the classic W.I.P. formula, while simultaneously taking it a dozen steps further. Granted, the whole "Devil's Punishment" sequence, basically involving an extended forced dig, does go on a bit (although if you've ever had to dig a large hole, you're sure to relate to the torturous aspects of this *Cool Hand Luke*-inspired segment). What I found impressive about this first film is how compelling it was. Many a first film in a series is mired in tedious exposition and pace-destroying flashbacks. But Junya Ito's inspired, surreal approach bridges chasms that lesser filmmakers would surely have tumbled down, establishing a dreamy strangeness that keeps things from going stale. An impressive first outing.

I never did get around to the lesbian love scene or Katagiri (Rie Yokoyama), the inmate hired by Sugimi to off Nami, or the gloriously over-the-top revenge sequences. Nor should I. It's more important if I've whetted your appetite for some surprisingly rewarding pinky violence. They just don't make them like this anymore. But be sure to see these films while you can; you never know when they'll go out of print.

Convent of the Sacred Beast • Seiju gakuen

1974
Japan
91 min.
DIRECTOR: Norifumi Suzuki
CAST: Yumi Takigawa, Emiko Yamauchi, Yayoi Watanabe, Fumio Watanabe, Hayato Tani, Ryouko Ima, Marie Antoinette, Kyouko Negishi

Occasionally, one finds an exploitation film that is so artfully made, so beautifully rendered that it bridges the chasm separating it from art, demanding a whole new classification: anyone for *artsploitation*? The notorious *Convent of the Sacred Beast* (aka *School of the Holy Beast*) certainly qualifies, presenting as it does all the more lurid aspects of forbidden sex and violence with grand flourishes of color, style, and composition to seduce the eye and intoxicate the mind of the viewer. Gloriously blasphemous, gleefully wicked, and jam-packed with exquisite young Japanese women in (and frequently out of) habit and wimple, *Convent of the Sacred Beast* is a rapturous epic of torture, depravity, and revenge that's sure to make a Toei pink film convert out of you (if you aren't one already).

Convent of the Sacred Beast (adapted from an adult manga, or *gekiga*, originally written by director Norifumi Suzuki and published in *Comic & Comic* magazine) contains multiple characters and plotlines, so let's begin with an overview of the dramatis personae:

• Maya Takigawa (Yumi Takigawa): Maya is the central character, a young woman of eighteen who, at film's beginning, spends a breezy, free 'n' easy day of fun, food, and casual sex in Tokyo, only to join the Convent of Saint Kuroashi the following day. Her motivation for doing so is not made immediately clear; only gradually do we find out it has something to do with her mother. What we do learn at the outset is that she's a strong-willed, independent "mo-gal" (modern gal) with a taste for hockey, men on motorcycles, and purple martinis.

- Matsuko Ishida (Emiko Yamauchi): Ishida is one tough customer, a cynical, no-nonsense nun who's only in the convent because her dad couldn't handle her problem-child ways. She calls it like she sees it, hates spies and hypocrisy, and you just know she's not going to let herself be "punished" by the twisted sisters of St. Kuroashi. At first she's suspicious of Maya, but they eventually become friends, Matsuko even rescuing Maya at one point and castigating her torturers: "You bitches don't play fair, do you? You're no better than criminals." She whips out a knife. "Don't make a fuss. You hysteric sisters, I accept this fight." She's fond of whiskey and pot and gets all the best lines in the film.

- Hisako Kitano (Yayoi Watanabe): She's the sweet one, the only true nun in the place, it would seem. She's genuinely committed to serving God and obeying the tenets of purity and penance set forth by the order. Of course this means that she'll suffer horribly at the hands of her cruel and faithless elders. It's also worth mentioning that, along with Maya, Matsuko and other fellow nuns, she's quite a looker, a gorgeous young woman whose tragic torment is heartbreaking to watch.

- Janet (Marie Antoinette): Here we have the hot import in the cloister, a fiery redhead who enjoys lusty lesbian liaisons with her Japanese girlfriend among the hothouse flowers. The scene in the hothouse is made memorable by its inventive representation of cunnilingus: a close-up of Janet's face, swooning in sexual ecstasy, is intercut with scenes of her lover licking her between her . . . fingers. The digits make a surprisingly effective stand-in for Janet's legs and the scene is surprisingly erotic.

Zero Woman: Red Handcuffs (Zero no onna: Akai wappa) (Japan, 1974) A vicious gang of deranged sociopaths goes on a rampage and it's up to ex-cop Zero Woman (exploitation siren Miki Sugimoto) to stop them. Good lord, what a brutal flick. There's enough rape, kidnapping, murder, psychotic laughter, and bad singing to keep you wincing for weeks. Seriously, a scene where the cops hold a blowtorch to a guy's belly—you know that stuff is fake. But enduring Miki Sugimoto's off-key interpretation of the theme song not once but *twice*—that's real torture! She's nice to look at, though, an alluring lady in red with matching accessories: red purse, red gun, and those handcuffs. They have an extra long chain, a lethal weapon of bloody strangulation in Miki's hands. Too bad she spends most of the film standing by while the murderous crazies rape and assault everyone in sight (including her). Her mission, to rescue the daughter of a bigwig politico (played by the inevitable Tetsuro Tamba) and dispose of the gang, gets a little lost in the melee, but then so do we. Toei released this feral film the same year as *Convent of the Sacred Beast*; watch them back-to-back to see just how different (yet effective) two exploitation films can be.

Yumi Takigawa

Fumio Watanabe

- Priest Kakinuma (Fumio Watanabe): Rasputin look-alike Kakinuma is a church big-wig from Rome who swings by the convent now and then for a little "private mass" with some unfortunate sister who doesn't have the wits or the will to escape his insidious designs. When Hisako confesses to him that she's stolen money from the convent for her father's operation, he kindly gives her the sum she needs to replace it, but soon turns nasty and rapes her, rationalizing that it's God's will (of course). He's a gloomy character, his faith poisoned by lust, obsession, and bitterness over Nagasaki and Auschwitz. Kakinuma's God is cruel and perverse, and he makes every effort to embody such qualities in his private life, all the while preaching the gospel of peace and love.
- Kenta Aoki (Hayato Tani): An easygoing playboy type, Aoki spends an enjoyable day and night with Maya at the beginning of the film. We don't hear from him again until later in the film, when Maya recruits him (and a comedic sidekick) to help her take revenge against a cruel and particularly repressed senior nun, resulting in a "Don't! Stop! . . . Don't stop!!" seduction scene.
- Natalie Green (Ryouko Ima): The convent's very own Witchfinder General, this egregious individual is flown in by Priest Kakinuma to crack down on the convent after one of his sinister schemes fails. She's clearly a Japanese woman, so why her name is Natalie Green is anybody's guess. Perhaps the foreign name makes her seem more evil. Ms. Green sets her sights on Hisako and Maya, employing old-school tortures originally used to extract confessions of heresy and witchcraft back in the Tokugawa era. Hisako doesn't stand a chance, but can the wicked Ms. Green break Maya?
- Michiko Shinohara (Kyouko Negishi): Maya's mother. Long dead, she too was a sister at St. Kuroashi. Now Maya seeks to learn the truth about what happened to her. We will eventually meet her in flashbacks and learn the whole awful truth. . . .

Yumi Takigawa receives The 13th Punishment

In addition, there's a host of foul, despotic senior nuns, including the headmistress and assistant headmistress, who deal out most of the punishments. Director Suzuki makes clear how much lascivious enjoyment they derive from the young nuns' suffering with close-ups of their aroused expressions during torture sequences. Punishments include (but are not limited to) a forced topless whip duel between two offending nuns ("I want you to whip each other until all your skin is flowing with blood!"—this for stealing ham, no less); being bound (topless) and jerked around by long, thorny rose bush vines (artistic images of blood running down thorns and across breasts); and The Thirteenth Punishment: the thorn-bound victim, Maya, is repeatedly whipped with long-stemmed roses by one senior nun after another, writhing in slow motion as petals float about her head, her skin left scored and bloody. In purely aesthetic terms, the scene possesses its own perverse beauty, despite the torture aspect (or, for some, because of it). Soon enough, however, Maya is rescued by Miss Ishida and cut loose from her bloody bonds.

Early in *Convent of the Sacred Beast*, we are told that the white of a nun's habit represents purity; the black, penance. Combine this with the red of blood and roses, and you wind up with a powerful triumvirate of color. Any graphic designer will tell you that black, white, and red make for the most potent color combination going; Hitler was certainly hip to it. So too is Norifumi Suzuki, exploiting it expertly, along with all the possibilities of candlelight, stained glass, and the saturated neon colors of the city (for his contrasting Tokyo scenes). Complimenting the meticulously crafted lighting and color is the score by Masao Yagi, revolving as it does around a catchy harpsichord motif punctuated by chorus-of-angels-type vocal swells that highlight and amplify the brutal irony of vile debasements carried out in sacred halls of worship.

Convent of the Sacred Beast saw the screen debut of the alluring Yumi

Movie posters outside theater in Asakusa, Tokyo (*Zero Woman: Red Handcuffs* poster far right)

Miki Sugimoto confronts a kinky creep (movie still outside theater, Asakusa, Tokyo)

Takigawa and, sadly, the camera never saw as much of her again (skin-wise), although she did go on to a successful film career. In interviews over the years, she's distanced herself from the film, considering it a somewhat embarrassing stepping-stone to better things. The following year she starred opposite Tetsuya Watari in Kinji Fukasaku's first-rate yakuza flick *Graveyard of Honor* and never looked back. Fumio Watanabe, here playing unsavory Priest Kakinuma, is no stranger to exploitation cinema, having appeared as the wicked warden in the first two installments of the Female Prisoner Scorpion (1972–73) series and as sadistic Lord Nambara in Teruo Ishii's infamous *Shogun's Joy of Torture* (1968). This is not to take away from a long and illustrious career during which he worked with such distinguished directors as Nagisa Oshima, Yasujiro Ozu, and Masahiro Shinoda.

Director Norifumi Suzuki, one of the more gifted house directors at Toei, was among the leading lights of the studio's early-'70s "pinky violence" film line, helming classics like *The Insatiable* (1971), *Tokugawa Sex Prohibition—Lustful Lord* (1972), *Girl Gang—Guerilla* (1973), and the late-entry *Star of David: Beauty Hunting* (1979, also adapted from a gekiga). Prior to his pinky period, Suzuki worked on yakuza pictures, contributing to the Big Boss in a Silk Hat series (starring Tomisaburo Wakayama) and the lady gambler Red Peony series. Following the fall of pinky violence, Suzuki spent the remainder of the '70s focusing primarily on his Truck Guys action/comedy series starring Bunta Sugawara and Kinya Aikawa. In the '80s, Suzuki kept the riotous action films coming with Hiroyuki Sanada vehicles like *Shogun's Ninja* (1980) and *Roaring Iron Fist* (1981), as well as *Kabamaru the Ninja* (1983, starring Sonny Chiba), and *The Samurai* (1987).

I should mention that in describing the characters and events of *Convent of the Sacred Beast,* I've left out a lot. There's more breathtaking debauchery and jaw-dropping plot twists crammed into its ninety-one-minute running time than I could or would want to reveal. Such discoveries, as well as the mystery of Maya's mother, our protagonist's whole *raison d'être,* I leave to you. Call it nunsploitation, call it artsploitation, call it a sick 'n' twisted fetish film, there's no denying the cinematic filmcraft and sheer artistic brio of *Convent of the Sacred Beast.* If only all exploitation movies were this good.

Riki-Oh—The Story of Ricky • *Lai wong*

Hong Kong

1991

90 min.

DIRECTOR: Nam Nai Choi

CAST: Louis Fan Siu Wong, Fan Mui Sang, William Ho Ka Kui, Yukari Oshima, Tetsuro Tamba, Gloria Yip Wan Yi, Philip Kwok Chung Fung, Frankie Chin Chi Leung, Chen Jing

Imagine, if you will, the supreme fighter: a person of immense physical strength far beyond that of any human being, able to hit and kick with unstoppable force. Practically speaking, it would stand to reason that if you went up against such a person and received, say, a blow to the midriff, his fist would go right through your body like a punch press. Likewise, if hit in the head, your brain, skull, eyeballs, and other assorted components (en masse or, more likely, in pieces) would go flying to the four winds. It is this fundamental assumption, that someone could be so powerful as to literally kick the shit out of you, that makes *The Story of Ricky* such a unique film experience. That, and a Macanese prison full of colorful characters, including a buffed pretty-boy hero, a villainous assistant warden with a hook, a needle-throwing malignant dwarf, a suspiciously feminine kung fu killer, a head-crushing giant, assorted bullies, snitches and other stock prison picture types, and a lot of cheap yet effective special effects.

The Story of Ricky is a film based on a Japanese manga by Masahiko Takajo (story) and Tetsuya Saruwatari (art) and directed by Nam Nai Choi. As such, it is nothing less than a completely insane movie. Manga movies are always nuts, but add Nam to the mix, a director known for frenetic brain-fryers like *The Seventh Curse, Erotic Ghost Story*, and *The Cat,* and you've just cubed the equation. The only thing stopping Nam from realizing his grand vision of extreme manga mayhem is his special effects budget, obviously woefully inadequate to the task. Let's face it, some of the cut-to-the-dummy shots are just plain laughable. In most cases, however, the simple fact of what he's attempting to depict is shocking enough to carry the audience over the edge—our imaginations wind up doing half the work for him.

In *The Story of Ricky*, like most prison pictures, the protagonist is incarcerated at the beginning and endures a series of conflicts with various cons and screws, ultimately facing off with the warden. Here, however, said conflicts tend to end in someone being pulped, perforated, crushed, lacerated, gutted, ground into chop meat, strangled with intestines—one guy even gets lathed. In other words, the story doesn't follow a plot so much as a series of mutilations. So, rather than going through some kind of sickening synopsis, let's take a look at the dramatis personae:

- Ricky (Louis Fan): He's a mixture of raw, muscular he-man and sensitive soul. His cut physique and martial arts prowess are offset by big eyes, pooched-out lips, and delicate bone structure, striking just the right balance for a character who alternately punches people's heads off and plays lilting melodies on his flute.
- Assistant Warden (Fan Mui Sang): Yikes, could they make this guy any more repellent? He's ugly, brutal, and big as a house. He likes to gorge himself on buffet lunches in his office, then pop a few breath mints he keeps concealed in his glass eyeball. His bookshelves are filled with porno tapes, but thankfully we never have to see him enjoying them. He doesn't like Ricky one bit; on their first meeting, he drives his jumbo-sized metal hook prosthesis through the back of our hero's hand to make a point.
- Hai (Frankie Chin): One of the Gang of Four, badass convicts that run the four wings of the prison (the subtitles refer to them as "cells," which is confusing). The formidably muscled and tattooed Hai is the head of North Cell and is the first to be tasked with getting rid of Ricky.
- Huang Chuan (Yukari Oshima): Don't be fooled by his girlish looks, slight build, and earrings; West Cell chief Huang Chuan is the toughest of the lot, a master of esoteric kung fu killing techniques. Personal hobbies include skinning people. Played by real-life female action star Oshima (aka Cynthia Luster), veteran of some sixty-plus (mostly Chinese) films.
- Uncle Shan Kuei (Tetsuro Tamba): Not satisfied appearing in every Japanese film ever made, Tetsuro "Never Turns Down a Role" Tamba is here, too, providing his late-period Avuncular Wise Man services to a young Ricky (actually the same Ricky in school uniform) during the fight-training flashback sequences.
- Kuang (Philip Kwok): Action director Kwok does double duty here

in a brief and unrewarding role, taking a serrated axe to the face and then being hung on a cross.

- Centipede (Chen Jing): He's a dirty snitch, causing the innocent to suffer. Ricky will deal with him later. In the meantime, enjoy his little post-potty dance as he sings, "A playboy keeps going to the toilet—not knowing if he needs to or not."
- Warden (William Ko): The warden dresses like a pimp, has a fat, bratty kid, and a big secret. You'll learn the secret at the end of the movie and it's a doozy, as is the way Ricky deals with it. For now, just know that this warden isn't a very nice person.

Louis Fan does an admirable job as Ricky, playing the role straight and managing to infuse his character with pathos and real angst. He began his acting career at the age of five and by fourteen was training in martial arts. Having appeared in a number of films, Fan achieved greater success on television in hit shows like *Fist of Power* and *New Story of Shaolin*. His father, veteran character actor Fan Mui Sang, plays the corpulent, despicable assistant warden—don't look for a family resemblance, there isn't one (Ricky's mother must have been some beauty). The elder Fan's career stretches back to the mid-'60s with appearances in Shaw Brothers films like *One-Armed Swordsman* and *Trail of the Broken Blade* (both 1967). He went on to appear in some fifty-odd films in the '70s and '80s, including Yuen Woo Ping's kung fu classic *The Magnificent Butcher* with Sammo Hung. Look for Fan Miu San in *Death Duel* (1977), *Jade Tiger* (1977), *The Buddhist Fist* (1980), *The Postman Strikes Back* (1982), and Michael Cimino's Mickey Rourke vehicle *Year of the Dragon* (1985).

Men Behind the Sun (Hei tai yang 731) **(China, 1988)** Alright folks, this is it: the most disturbing prison film I've ever witnessed (maybe you've seen worse). *Men Behind the Sun* is ostensibly an exposé of the heinous medical experiments and mind-bending atrocities carried out by the Japanese Army's infamous Unit 731 in Harbin, Manchuria, during the waning days of World War II. Well executed as the film is, however, director T.F. Mous pushes it past historical docudrama into the realm of shameless exploitation. Characters including women, children, and the handicapped are sentimentalized and subsequently mutilated, vivisected, and casually murdered; ultra-gore sequences linger long and luridly; and scenes of unnecessarily sadistic (and real) animal cruelty make one question the motives of the filmmaker. Some critics defend the film as a true depiction of the horrors perpetrated by Unit 731, and they have a point—many characters and events in the film are a matter of record, and the fictitious elements are likely composites, as well. My misgivings are in the manner of the telling, not the tale itself. I realize there's no way to truly explore this material without inflicting trauma. But there is an undertone of *wrongness* in this picture that goes beyond the hideous historical events it depicts.

Critically speaking, *The Story of Ricky* is a train wreck, or, more to the point, a freeway pile-up; as gruesome as it is, there's something about it—you can't turn away. You have to keep looking, and just as you'd crane your neck as you passed the wreckage on the road, savoring the ghastly view until it's well out of sight, so you'll watch this movie to the very end. At times the special effects can be so bad that the scene becomes even more grotesque than it would have been otherwise. For example, early in the film Ricky is attacked in the showers by a gigantic, bald, morbidly obese inmate named Silly Lung. Ricky punches a hole in Silly Lung's enormous belly, and the camera cuts to a close-up of an unrealistic belly pouring out gallons of some viscous red fluid through a ragged hole. Half the shock of the scene is in the disorientation we feel transitioning from real actors to such an obviously artificial (but nevertheless disgusting) effect. Moments like these are what put *The Story of Ricky* in a class by itself: the ultimate gross-out prison picture.

Battle Royale

2000
Japan
109 min.

DIRECTOR: Kinji Fukasaku

CAST: Takeshi Kitano, Tatsuya Fujiwara, Aki Maeda, Taro Yamamoto, Masanobu Ando, Chiaki Kuriyama, Kou Shibasaki, Yukihiro Kotani, Hirohito Honda

Ah, high school days. A time of discovery and wonder mixed with sadness and confusion. We all have high school memories that will last a lifetime. Making friends, cheering for the team, cramming for tests, falling in love, getting picked on by cliques, your first gunshot wound, taking an arrow in the neck or an axe in the head, blowing students away five at a time with an uzi, committing suicide, making bombs, being stabbed repeatedly in the groin—and who can forget that talkative girl in the back of class that teacher had to discipline by throwing a knife at her forehead? These are the memories of Class B in Kinji Fukasaku's *Battle Royale*, a teenage bloodbath epic with a heart. Like high school, you'll never forget this millennial meditation on intergenerational conflict; there are multiple metaphors bubbling under the surface here, as well as beautiful tropical vistas, a stirring score, great cinematography, and lots of attractive young actors giving 110 percent performances. It really doesn't get any better, or darker, than this.

It seems that Japan has gone all fascist (again). The opening exposition cards read, "At the dawn of the millennium, the nation collapsed. At 15 percent unemployment, 10,000,000 were out of work. 800,000 students boycotted school. The adults lost confidence and, fearing the youth, eventually passed the Millennium Educational Reform Act aka the BR Act." Class B, forty ninth-graders on an end-of-term class trip, are drugged and spirited away to the tiny island of Okishima, where they

Takeshi from *Battle Royale*

awaken in a dark classroom. They are greeted by their old seventh-grade teacher Mr. Kitano (played by comedian/actor/director/TV host/household word Takeshi Kitano), who tells them, "Today's lesson is . . . you kill each other off until there's only one left. Nothing's against the rules." It seems the Millennium Educational Reform Act is all about scaring the shit out of the youth of Japan; by annually picking classes by impartial lottery and plunking them down on an island for three days of mind-bending violence, the government effectively reinforces the fascist logic of "rule by fear."

Mr. Kitano shows the class a video that explains what will be happening during the next three days. The video features a cute and perky, scantily uniformed female presenter (anime voice-over veteran Yuko Miyamura) who describes the island and explains the high-tech, metallic collars the class is now wearing: they monitor heart rate, send out tracking signals, and serve as self-destruct mechanisms for the unfortunate teenager that wanders into one of the "danger zones" (which change hourly, of course). Mr. Kitano demonstrates the efficacy of the "necklace" on Nobu (Yukihiro Kotani), a punk who slashed Kitano's posterior with a butterfly knife in an earlier scene. Nobu's throat is blown out in a geyser of blood, whistling over his windpipe in a moment of chilling sound design. The video girl goes on to tell the class that everyone will receive a kit with food, water, a compass, a map, and a mystery weapon (each different and wide-ranging in their lethality in order to eliminate natural advantages). As the final kicker, if there isn't a clear winner by the end of the third day, all the necklaces will explode! "Why are you doing this?" a student asks Kitano. "It's your own damned fault," he replies. "You guys mock grown-ups. Go ahead and mock us, but don't you forget: Life is a game. So fight for survival and find out if you're worth it."

Everyone gets their kit and heads out into the dark, uncertain

© TOEI

Shuya from *Battle Royale*

night. From here on in, it's a free-for-all. Shuya (Tatsuya Fujiwara) and Noriko (Aki Maeda), the protagonists of the piece, are dismayed to find that their "weapons" consist of binoculars for her and a pot lid for him. Never mind, they'll get through this somehow. Before long, several deadly front-runners emerge from the pack: There are the two "transfer students," Kiriyama (Masanobu Ando) and Kawada (Taro Yamamoto), the former a silent, red-haired demon, the latter a Rambo-esque action man of mysterious motivations. Then there's the stunning Mitsuko (Kou Shibasaki), as lovely as she is lethal, who discovers early on the dark delight she takes in killing. "What's wrong with killing?" she muses after shooting the leader of her clique. "Everyone's got their reasons."

I won't catalog the numerous murders, suicides, and deaths by misadventure depicted in *Battle Royale*—where's the fun in that? Director Kinji Fukasaku has already done a masterful job, the gory goings-on buoyed by an ironic wit born out of the existential ethos permeating the piece. If you want meticulous details on who killed whom and in what order, the Internet is a great resource, with numerous fan sites offering up such statistics. Talking of weapons, implements of destruction (or protection) include the aforementioned pot lid and binoculars, a hand axe, a stun gun, grenades, various knives, a megaphone, a vial of KCN (potassium cyanide), a sickle, a crossbow, a bulletproof vest, a cane sword, a paper fan, a GPS tracker, nunchucks, and guns, lots of guns.

As more and more kids bite the dust, we are provided with periodic on-screen score cards, such as "Boys #16 Niida dead—22 to go." (The #16 is his class number, not the number of boys killed.) Niida is played by Hirohito Honda, who also starred in the innovative, low-budget shocker *Living Hell*. He makes the mistake of trying to force a sexual encounter with Chigusa (Chiaki Kuriyama) at crossbow-point. With a ferocious, jungle-cat look in her feline eyes, Chigusa flicks her

Noriko from *Battle Royale*

jack knife and growls, "Come at me. Every inch of me will resist you." Niida winds up taking the knife right in the naughty bits, then Mitsuko appears out of nowhere and shoots the fleeing Chigusa, mortally wounding her. Many will recognize the striking Chiaki Kuriyama as the spiked-ball-on-a-chain-wielding Go Go Yubari from Quentin Tarantino's *Kill Bill: Vol. 1* (2003), but she's been in plenty of other pictures, including J-horror films like *Shikoku* (1999) and the original *Ju-on* (2000). More recently, she's starred in Takashi Miike's remake of the spooks 'n' samurai classic *The Big Spook War* (*Yokai Daisenso*, 2005). Asked her thoughts on *Battle Royale,* she said, "There is something weird going on with the youth in our society. To be honest, whenever I go shopping in Shibuya, I find that I'm actually scared of girls my age. When I hear news about some violent crime being caused by a person in my age, I am petrified. . . . Ironically, in *Battle Royale* I found myself playing the kind of girl that scares me" (*Asian Cult Cinema* #42, 2004, p. 33).

Standing at the center of the violent maelstrom that is *Battle Royale* we find "Beat" Takeshi Kitano, a man universally famous in Japan. Kitano first came to prominence in the '70s as "Beat Takeshi," one half of the manic *manzai* comic duo The Two Beats (along with Beat Kiyoshi). During the '80s, Beat Takeshi came to dominate the airwaves, doing his own brand of edgy comedy on radio (*All Night Nippon,* a Howard Stern-style broadcast), and on popular TV shows like *It's Time to Laugh!* (*Waratteru Baai Desu Yo!*) and *We're Wild and Crazy Guys* (*Oretachi Hyokinzoku*). During the late '80s, he hosted the deliriously deranged and highly dangerous game show *Takeshi-jo* (*Takeshi's Castle*), which has since gained worldwide cult status; humorously dubbed versions of the show have aired in Italy, India, Germany, Great Britain, Australia, Spain, and in the United States as MXC (Most Extreme Elimination Challenge). During the '90s, Kitano started making movies and proved a formidable talent

Battle Royale: The Girls of Class B
(and their weapons)

Battle Royale: The Boys of Class B (and their weapons)

with *Boiling Point (3–4x jugatsu,* 1990*), Sonatine* (1993*), Fireworks (Hanabi,* 1997*),* and *Kikujiro* (1999). In the summer of 1994, Kitano suffered a serious motor scooter crash that left his face scarred, partially paralyzed, and afflicted with tics. During his recovery he began to paint, launching yet another artistic career! The painting his character displays at the end of *Battle Royale* is a Takeshi Kitano original.

Heaps of praise are due the young cast of *Battle Royale* without whose talent and verve the film could easily have fallen into a forgettable, trashy exercise. Tatsuya Fujiwara, the hero of the piece who never kills a classmate (well, maybe), gives a tour-de-force performance, his manga-like facial features forever contorted in grimaces of rage and anguish as he witnesses death after brutal death of his friends and fellow classmates. The fact that a seventeen-year-old actor was capable of conveying such levels of grief and angst is remarkable, attributable in part to the directing talents of the seventy-year-old Kinji Fukasaku, himself a World War II survivor. Like European contemporary Paul Verhoeven, Fukasaku knew a few things about war and was always capable of channeling such personal horrors into his film work. Also good in the picture is Masanobu Ando as the malevolent Kiriyama, the "transfer student" who signed up for fun; with his shock of orange hair and black school uniform, he strikes just the right balance between slouching juvenile delinquent and psychotic killing machine. He may have gotten the gig through Beat Takeshi: Ando starred in Kitano's 1996 boxing picture, *Kid's Return.* In addition, *Battle Royale* was the launch pad to a successful and award-winning film, TV, and singing career for Kou Shibasaki, the merciless murderess Mitsuko. Quentin Tarantino was so taken with her, he wrote a whole revenge subplot for her in the original script for *Kill Bill* as Go Go Yubari's sister Yuki; unfortunately for her (and us) Miss Shibasaki turned down the part and the character was deleted. It's worth noting that in the classic go-for-it tradition of Japanese film, no stunt doubles were used for any of the teen cast members; they did all their own stunts and the film is that much more vital and visceral for it.

Some may be surprised to learn that the fictional island of Okishima, where the bloody conflicts of *Battle Royale* are played out, is in fact an amalgam of various locations not far from Tokyo. Only a couple of scenes actually feature an island, in this case Hachijo-Kojima, some 300 miles south of Tokyo in the Izu island chain. Other locations include a house (the clinic) and an old school in Kanagawa Prefecture (just southwest of Tokyo), rocks, caves, and Tsurugizaki lighthouse along the Miura Peninsula in Tokyo Bay, as well as botanical gardens, various ramshackle Shinto shrines, and a ruined amusement park, all not far

© TOEI

Chigusa Kiriyama Mitsuko Kawada

from The Megalopolis. This is an eye-opener for folks who don't realize just how lush and verdant a country Japan really is.

Enhancing the grandeur of the natural settings, as well as amplifying and refining the violent drama of the story, *Battle Royale* boasts a bombastic score by Masamichi Amano, all orchestral crescendos and operatic voices. The score is punctuated by classical pieces by Verdi, Strauss, Schubert, and Bach, chosen (at times perversely) to compliment specific moments in the teenage rampage. For example, as Kiriyama shoots Mitsuko repeatedly in a rickety, rain-soaked warehouse, she glides gracefully backward in slow motion (à la Peckinpah) to the beautiful strains of Bach's Air in G; the combination of music and image conjures a feeling of wistful redemption, as if Mitsuko's soul is being released and all her sins forgiven. Elsewhere, Strauss' Blue Danube underscores images of the fascist Japanese army forces, throwing up the irony of stately elegance (the music) joined with the mundane, thug-like presence of the troops.

The irony is thick in *Battle Royale*, pointing to larger metaphors. Like Kitano says at the outset, "Life is a game. So fight for survival and see if you're worth it." But if to survive is to kill your friends, where's the worth in that? The film is making a larger point about life itself, particularly life in Japan (be it academic competition or the post-academic rat race of modern urban existence). Early in the film we see a boy and girl on a cliff. They clearly have no intention of playing, choosing suicide instead.

YAMAMOTO: What will happen to us?
OGAWA: I know one thing: I'll never play this game.

Another couple also take their own lives, choosing to hang together (literally). How many people in Japan (and elsewhere) routinely choose death over a shitty life in this hard old world? Others, like Mimura (Takashi Tsukamoto) and his gang decide to rebel, use technology, make bombs, hack computers, and take down the system. Then there are those who thrive on the game, revel in the viciousness, life's predators (who usually prevail) like Kiriyama and Mitsuko. After shooting cute little Kotohiki, Mitsuko remarks coldly, "Nobody will rescue you. That's just life." *Battle Royale* is littered with dual-use lines like this, providing salient allegories throughout the story. We all know some callous jerk like Kitano who says things like, "It's tough when friends die on you, but hang in there." In the end, it's probably best to follow the example of strong, noble Shuya, who says simply, "I'll keep fighting, even though I don't know how."

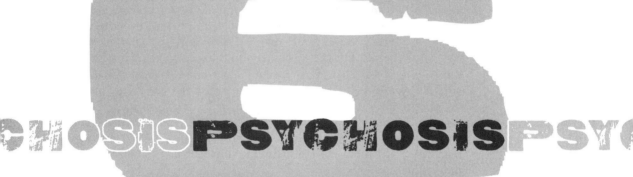

CHOSISPSYCHOSISPSYC

A mind is a terrible thing to waste. However, it's a worse thing to lose, for you often take others with you. At least that's what happens in the films discussed here. The dangerously unstable are all around us in these movies: hitchhikers, psychiatrists, cabbies, monks, restaurateurs, you name it. There's just no escaping the fact that there's just no escaping them. Sooner or later you're going to come up against a bloodspattered fiend with a diseased brain, a knife, and no compunction at all about slicing you up as a treat. There's nothing for it, you might as well start screaming now.

Tell Me Something

1999
South Korea
118 min.
DIRECTOR: Chang Yoon-hyun
CAST: Han Suk-kyu, Shim Eun-ha, Jang Hang-seon, Yeom Jeong-ah, Yu Jun-sang

Most critics compare the ultranoir crime thriller *Tell Me Something* to David Fincher's *Se7en*, but how much better would the denouement of *Se7en* have been if we had actually gotten to see Gwyneth Paltrow's severed head in that box? Hollywood films tend to pull their punches at such cinematic moments; Korean filmmakers are much more hardcore, as *Tell Me Something* illustrates in spades. Two minutes into the film we've already witnessed a graphic arm amputation, announcing a dominant theme and signaling to those in the audience with weak stomachs that perhaps now might be a good time to take their popcorn and leave.

Tell Me Something was the second-largest grossing film in South Korea in 1999 (after *Shiri*) and it's easy to see why: it's what's popularly known as an "instant classic," a film noir tour-de-force. Strip away the gore and stylized '90s production values and what you've got is a good old-fashioned Chandleresque detective story; director Chang Yoon-hyun sticks to the genre rulebook and shows us just how effective those well-worn tropes can still be. You've got your mysterious femme fatale, your bewildered everyman trying to make sense of it all, lots of rain, wet streets at night (whether raining or not), venetian blinds making stripey patterns on walls, lots of reflective surfaces (table tops, computer monitors, car windows, gelled hair) creating interesting effects, the old looking-down-the-long-stairwell effect, poking around in the dark with a flashlight (at one point you can see the smoke employed to pick up the beam), and just plain old darkness itself. There are only two or three scenes in the film where we see sunlight. Otherwise it's raining, it's night, it's inside a dark space, or some combination. Then, of course, there are the crime thriller/police procedural elements: the scandalized, loose-cannon cop; his loveable, ultimately doomed partner; the cranky commissioner who says things like, "You're off the case!"; and that other asshole cop who goads our hero until he gets a punch in the chops for his insolence. You've even got the scene where the cop is speeding to the scene of the crime and sticks the magnetic police light on the car roof.

And then there's the dismemberment. There are so many body parts flying around in this picture that even the wily and cantankerous coroner, Professor Yu, is having trouble keeping things straight. Big black bin bags are showing up around Seoul, you see, containing dismembered "corpses," but the various pieces are all mixed 'n' matched from a variety of different bodies. One bag has a guy with another guy's legs. Another has the guy who matches the legs, but his heart is missing, etc. It's up to Lieutenant Cho (Han Suk-kyu) to get things sorted, as it were. One thing Prof. Yu does know for sure is that the victims were sedated but alive when they were cut apart, dying from the resultant massive blood loss. So we're essentially talking death *by* dismemberment. Damned efficient, that.

Discovery of the black bags makes for some of the more jaw-dropping moments in the film, such as the bag left lying on the highway that is hit by a careless trucker: body parts go skittering across the pavement and blood rains down on windshields, causing a spectacular pileup. But by far the most shocking unveiling—and for my money the most memorable moment in the picture—comes just twelve minutes in, when a kid on a crowded shopping center elevator notices a bulging bag in the corner and decides to ram it with a shopping cart. Sploosh! Flesh and blood everywhere—instant pandemonium, total freak out: people panicking, pressing buttons, screaming, one girl slipping in the gore and landing face-to-face with the severed head, screeching, getting blood all over her long hair. It's a mess. What makes the scene so ghastly is the suddenness of it. There's no buildup, it just happens, much like it would in real life.

Three bags are found initially, and Prof. Yu and Lt. Cho eventually identify all three victims. What's more, when Lt. Cho questions a pretty yet aloof young lady named Chae Su-yeon (Shim Eun-ha), she reveals that she knew all three of the guys. It turns out she was in fact romantically involved with the three men (an artist, a violinist, and a philosophy professor, respectively), but she's not terribly forthcoming with details and seems to have something to hide. This apparently doesn't faze Lt. Cho, who never questions her innocence and even takes her into his home when it appears that an intruder has broken into her place.

However, we haven't seen the last of those black plastic bags. A fourth one appears (the one the trucker hits) containing the segmented corpse of Cho's prime suspect (er, most of him) causing Cho and his partner Lt. Oh to direct their investigations elsewhere. Severed heads continue to pop up (one in Cho's car), along with new suspects like Chae Su-yeon's father, a famous artist who we learn in a series of flashbacks enjoyed alternately painting and molesting his daughter while she was growing up. He will figure in the horrific finale of the film.

Art and artists play a crucial role in *Tell Me Something,* and a little knowledge of art history can help us get to the bottom of the somewhat confounding third act of the film. For example, under the opening credits we see details, and finally a full shot, of a painting depicting a

Memories of Murder (Salinui chueok) (South Korea, 2003) This film portrayal of Korea's first serial killer case, set in rural Gyeonggi province, was the big hit of 2003. It features a pair of brutal country-bumpkin cops, a smart detective from the big city (Seoul), and a whole lot of wrong suspects. You see, the string of murders, occurring between 1986 and 1991, was never solved. This puts the kibosh on a satisfying denouement, but the story is nevertheless compelling, due in no small part to Song Kang-ho as Detective Park, a rural cop who routinely tortures and frames his suspects with the help of his less intelligent but far more vicious partner, Cho (Kim Roi-ha). Song gives a complex performance, tempering his character's casual cruelty with just the right touch of humanity to make him sympathetic. Detective Park thinks he can see criminality in the eyes of his suspects, but this new case, with its string of raped and murdered local girls, finds him completely out of his depth. Enter Detective Suh (Kim Sang-kyeong), the sophisticated city cop who shows Park how it's done, learning a few things about his own threshold for violence into the bargain. Tension turns to teamwork as the two cops struggle to unravel the baffling case.

number of men dissecting a human corpse. Some of the faces are Asian although the costumes are seventeenth-century European. The painting is in fact a reinterpretation of Rembrandt's *The Anatomy Lesson of Dr. Nicolaes Tulp* (1632), an iconic work celebrating then-modern medicine and the dispassionate will of the scientific mind. We are never told the name of the re-worked painting in the film, nor its artist; it shows up in Su-yeon's father's house as well as his workshop (the latter also containing the surgery where all the dismemberments took place). Su-yeon tells Lt. Cho that it was her father's favorite painting and that it gave her nightmares as a child. From this we can deduce that either the father is the killer or that the painting influenced Su-yeon's incest-traumatized psyche, storing something there for later. . . .

Another fine art reference/clue comes fairly early in the story when Lt. Cho and Lt. Oh pay their first visit to Su-yeon's home and, while Oh is questioning Su-yeon, Cho casually snoops around her place. He finds a postcard-sized print of John Everett Millais' Pre-Raphaelite masterpiece, *Ophelia* (1851–52). Later we see a painting in Su-yeon's country house (presumably painted by her father) of Su-yeon herself *as Ophelia*. If you know your Shakespeare, you'll recall that Ophelia was Hamlet's doomed girlfriend, destined to go mad and drown herself in a river. Sure enough, we learn from Su-yeon's friend, Seung-min (Yeom Jeong-ah), that Su-yeon had attempted suicide several times in the past. These narrative parallels between Ophelia and Su-yeon lead inevitably to the supposition that if Su-yeon shares Ophelia's suicidal tendencies, shouldn't she share her madness as well?

As mentioned earlier, things get a little frayed at the end of *Tell Me Something*. Perhaps it was done deliberately to preserve the perverse sense of senselessness conveyed by the heinous murders themselves. Or perhaps director Chang Yoon-hyun pulled an Orson Welles and lost interest in post-production, leaving things in the hands of lesser talents. Maybe he and fellow scripter In Eun-ah simply wrote themselves into a corner. In any case, the dangling strands of plot don't significantly damage the film experience, and many confusions clear up on second and third viewings—there are tricky little shots that slip through the net of attention the first time around. So, if you watch the film and feel a little lost, don't worry, you're not as lost as you think. Go back and watch it again. This is the kind of picture that rewards repeat screenings. Upon its release, so many Korean fans were perplexed that a number of Internet chat rooms sprung up to help crack the mystery posed by the remaining fragments of the case left unsolved by the filmmakers. But again, they're really very minor details, A-to-B issues that could have been easily fixed. And as Joel Hodgson sang in the *Mystery Science*

Theater 3000 theme song, "Repeat to yourself it's just a show, I should really just relax."

Dr. Lamb • Gao yang yi sheng

1992

Hong Kong

90 min.

DIRECTOR: Danny Lee Sau Yin, Billy Tang Hin Sing

CAST: Simon Yam Tat Wah, Danny Lee Sau Yin, Kent Cheng Jak Si, Eric Kee Ka Fat, Emily Kwan Bo Wai, Lam King Kong, Parkman Wong Pak Man

For the record, there's no "Dr. Lamb" in *Dr. Lamb*. There's a guy named Lin, and, depending on the literature you might read elsewhere, he's based on an actual serial killer named Lam—the fact of the matter is that this film was released on the heels of *The Silence of the Lambs* and there's a certain cash-in factor to the title. One thing's for sure, *Dr. Lamb* shines on a whole other level from the Jonathan Demme picture; it may not have the production values of its namesake, but, my God, does it deliver on sheer psychosis. It stands among the great psychokiller films, right up there with *Psycho, Henry: Portrait of a Serial Killer,* and *Peeping Tom.*

Dr. Lamb is a police procedural and, as such, has it's own internal logic and investigative attraction. What ups the ante here is that the story is set in Hong Kong in 1982 and the cops have no compunction about what methodologies they employ to get a confession out of their suspect—they beat the living shit out of him. While this is, of course, morally reprehensible and legally intolerable, it nevertheless makes for compelling viewing. American cinema cops might wring their hands and punch the wall at the prospect of a less-than-forthcoming suspect; these Hong Kong guys just pull out the trusty, fat old Kowloon phone book (that's right, many Chins) and use it in all the ways you do when interrogating a prisoner. Of course their efforts fail, providing a neat "torture doesn't work" message to defuse your concerns that there might be some right-wing message lurking in the narrative. No, it's the culprit's *family* that gets him to confess.

You see, Lin (Simon Yam), a taxi driver, was living in a tiny flat with a dad, brother, sister, and niece at the time of the murders. Working nights, he somehow managed to coordinate his schedule so that other household members were away while he indulged in his peculiar pastime, namely photographing and dismembering wayward women he'd previously picked up in his hack and strangled. Cutting them up was only part of the fun, however, as we later discover . . . Lin's self-absorbed family members remained oblivious, even as Lin was hauling out boxes of body parts right in front of them; dad was always talking to his two pet birds, sister was preoccupied with her daughter, and brother had hairdo issues to deal with.

Since Lin is captured early on, the film is by necessity made up of interrogation sequences and flashbacks. Inspector Li (Danny Lee) is in charge of the investigation, assisted by the aptly named Fat Bing (Kent Cheng), volatile Bully Hung (Parkman Wong), preening pretty boy Eric (Eric Kee), and cute 'n' plucky Bo (Emily Kwan). With the exception of Kent Cheng, this is the same team that cracked the human pork bun case the same year in *The Untold Story,* although here they're far more professional. There's still the odd bit of comic business, such as when Fat Bing discovers a severed breast and it winds up stuck on Bo's back (ho, ho).

At first Lin refuses to answer questions, despite the considerable physical abuse dealt out by Bully Hung. This extends to beating the soles of his feet and getting whacked repeatedly in the chest with a hammer (the aforementioned phonebook used as a buffer). His family members are also dragged down to the station and roughed up a bit, but are in total denial until some pedophilic photos of Lin's young niece are found among the suspect's belongings. This convinces the family that Lin is a sicko, and they are in turn set loose on him. He might have been tough with the cops, but everyone knows what being alone in a room with your family can do to a man, and soon he succumbs to their blows and excoriations and confesses to murder.

Ever wonder how much of a mess you'd make with a human corpse and a Makita circular saw? Lin finds out with his first victim, as do we. Yikes! Cleanup is *not* a breeze. By the second murder, he's bought surgical tools and is consulting an anatomy book. From buzz saw to scalpel in just two murders—not bad for a beginner. Simon Yam's performance as Lin is riveting; he really pulls some dark stuff out of his soul for this role and, despite an occasional tendency to howl like a wolf, his psycho portrayal is balanced and effective. Much time and attention is devoted to observing Yam when he's alone with his victims, both before and after their deaths; the camera lingers on him, as if trying to penetrate his psychotic mind, striving to understand what he's going through, what drives him, and what he's getting out of his dark deeds.

By the third woman, Lin is taking souvenirs (remember that breast?). Since the first three were all somewhere between floozy and prostitute, he is contemptuous of them and plays out the by-now standard psycho line of, "I'm doing the world a favor by ridding it of these dirty whores," etc. But the fourth woman is different. A sweet young thing of seventeen, "pure and innocent" as Lin never tires of saying to her (both alive and dead), she was never an intended target. They just got to talking as he drove her in his cab and one thing led to another. You know how it goes, one minute you're chatting agreeably and then all of a sudden she gets freaked out for some reason and you have to handcuff her. Before long you're chasing her through the rain. What's a fella to do? *Not* choke the life out of her? Just let her go? I think not. (Jeez, you think I've seen too many of these flicks?) Later, Lin decides that this is really the girl for him. Back at the pad he tells her lifeless form, "You and I are virgins. Our marriage is perfect." You can see where this is going. . . .

Dr. Lamb is one of the great Category III films. Category III is Hong Kong's most severe rating, essentially the same as NC-17 in the United States (you gotta be over eighteen to see a Category III film). But whereas NC-17 is just a rating, Category III has become something of its own genre, namely extreme violence with or without softcore sex. Amazon.com has a Category III sub-section under its Hong Kong movie selection. Category III is your shortcut to dark, shocking Hong Kong cinema; most of the Hong Kong films reviewed in this book are Category III. If these films interest you, I'd recommend buying a region-free DVD player. Why? Because while you can buy some titles on Amazon, you'll have a wider selection and get them much cheaper in other regions. You can often pick up Hong Kong films in Region 2 or Region 3 for less than ten dollars. However you may have to contend with wonky subtitles. My *Dr. Lamb* disk had some pretty hilarious translations (which, I find, often enhances the viewing experience). Particularly funny are the subtitles for words already spoken in English. Hong Kong was a British Colony for some 150 years and many English words and phrases are sprinkled in among the Cantonese. So you get a situation where someone onscreen says, "Take it easy" and the subtitle reads, "leave him alone," or you hear, "Asshole!" and the translation reads, "Bastard!" There's also a tendency to swear in English, no doubt to get around the censors.

Dr. Lamb was the first of many gruesome, true-crime films to come out of the '90s before Hong Kong became the Hong Kong Special Administrative Region of the People's Republic of China in 1997. It makes an excellent double feature with *The Untold Story* (if you can take that much psychosis in one sitting); you've got the same investigative team in place, and two very different perps. Danny Lee co-directed *Dr. Lamb* with Billy Tang (*Run and Kill, Brother of Darkness*) and *The Untold Story* with Herman Yau (*Ebola Syndrome, Taxi Hunter*); Lee handled the police procedural stuff and let his respective collaborators handle the psycho sequences. Both partners acquitted themselves admirably in this writer's opinion. Hong Kong action fans will know Danny Lee from his star turn opposite Chow Yun Fat in John Woo's *The Killer* (1989), a film inspired by the French classic *Le Samourai* (1967, directed by Jean-Pierre Melville and starring Alain Delon).

So there it is, I've suggested the most horrendous double feature imaginable. I think I should stop now.

Ichi the Killer • Koroshiya 1

2001

Japan

124 min.

DIRECTOR: Takashi Miike

CAST: Tadanobu Asano, Nao Omori, Shinya Tsukamoto, Sabu, Alien Sun, Shun Sugata, Kee, Satoshi Niizuma, Susumu Terajima, Yoshiki Arizono, Nao Maori, Suzuki Matsuo, Hiroshi Kobayashi, Mai Goto

There's something inhuman to this carnage. Most people have a touch of both sadism and masochism inside them, but this Ichi is 100 percent pure sadist.

But you'd never know it to look at him. Our Ichi is an unassuming, pleasant-looking young fellow—shy, keeps to himself, big on video games. He is usually smiling a sweetly retarded kind of smile or sobbing uncontrollably, his face stung with hot tears of fear and rage. You don't want to see the crying face. . . .

The year 2001's *Ichi the Killer* has the distinction of being the most shocking in director Takashi Miike's not inconsiderable stable of jaw-dropping films. Beyond the garroting of *Audition*, the necrophilia of *Visitor Q*, the vaginal blow-darts of *Fudoh*, Ichi stands atop a mountain of mutilated body parts and internal organs, a veritable endurance test for the squeamish and faint of heart. Invite your friends over for a screening—watching other people freak out is half the fun of this film. Because at the end of the day, as perverse as it might sound, *Ichi the Killer* is about fun. It is a fantasy, based on a popular manga by Hideo Yamamoto, and so beyond the pale that there's really no way for a reasonable person to take it seriously. Those who try tend to find it unbearable. During its initial festival run, walkouts were so common that those close to the film would monitor which scenes got to people most. Those who made it through the tongue-slicing scene would often bail at the nipplectomy, and so on. No doubt about it, *Ichi the Killer* is in the running for the most gratuitously violent film ever made.

At the heart of *Ichi the Killer* stands Jijii (Shinya Tsukamoto), the gray-haired puppet master of the piece. For reasons of his own, this enigmatic little man has vowed to destroy the Anjo-gumi, a Shinjuku-based yakuza group whose titular head is eviscerated at film's opening by Jijii's secret weapon, Ichi (Nao Omori). Decked out in a black body suit resembling heavily fortified riding leather (with a big yellow #1 on his back), our boy Ichi's preferred method of attack is a wicked butterfly kick made lethal by concealed blades in the heels of his shoes. Before you can say, "Not my jugular!" you're doing an impression of a lawn sprinkler. Most folks who go up against Ichi wind up doing the sprin-

© PRENOM/OMEGA

Kakihara from *Ichi the Killer*

kler thing, but others lose limbs, and one, a particularly brutal pimp, gets halved, top to bottom, the fact only dawning on him as he slowly begins to come apart. But where Ichi really shines is in his group work: once he gets going there's no stopping him—he's like a human Cuisinart. (To depict the aftermath of one such scene, a room was covered with the blood and organs of two whole pigs; copious amounts of vanilla extract were used on-set to cover the stench while filming.)

Jijii controls Ichi with a combination of hypnosis, avuncular caring, and good old-fashioned mind-fuck. For example, Ichi hates bullies (himself the embodiment of bully-related trauma), so Jijii never fails to point out the similarity between whoever is next on his hit list and the boys who bullied Ichi so mercilessly in the past. But this is not the only factor that motivates Ichi; he has his own warped sexuality to deal with, and it invariably revolves around, that's right, violence. As this review's opening quote states, he's a sadist. Shy boy that he is, however, his release is always auto-erotic; the things that arouse his ardor exist in the darkness that surrounds heinous murders he grows ever more horrified at committing. Poor Ichi, he's a mess.

And who's going around saying Ichi's 100 percent sadist? None other than Boss Anjo's successor, the brilliantly twisted Kakihara (played with foppish flair by Tadanobu Asano), who so steals the show that he tends to overshadow the title character as the focal point of the film. Maybe it's his devilish good looks, his bright blond hair, his tastefully arranged facial scars, or his magnificent wardrobe. Or perhaps it's the fact that his cheeks are sliced from corner of mouth to top of jaw, held together with two small ringlets, and when he likes he can open his mouth like an alligator and chomp you. Kakihara initially sets out to find his boss. Unbeknownst to him, Boss Anjo's remains were so neatly removed and cleaned up after by Jijii and his assistants Longie (Kee) and Inoue (Satoshi Niizuma) following Ichi's fancy footwork that you'd never know he'd been strewn about his apartment like wrapping paper on Christmas morning. Kakihara eventually learns the truth, though, and before long he's on a collision course with Ichi. Along the way he tortures quite a lot of people with his weapon of choice: long, thin metal skewers. Good lord, the things he gets up to with those wicked spike-needles. Ironically, deep inside he's a masochist, heartbroken at the loss of Boss Anjo, the only one who truly knew how to make it hurt so good. He tries unsuccessfully to train his girlfriend Karen (Alien Sun) in the fine art of pain: "Listen, when you're hurting someone, don't think of the pain that he feels. Only concentrate on the pleasure of causing him pain. That's the only way to show true compassion for your partner." But it's no good. As freaky as she is, she just doesn't have the goods. No one does. Later, in a fight with Longie, Kakihara comments, "There's no love in your punches." Poor Kakihara. That's why he's so jacked about meeting Ichi: the ultimate S/M experience!

Also in the mix is Kaneko (Sabu), Boss Anjo's bodyguard, who's understandably mortified and out to catch his boss's killer; his son Takeshi (Hiroshi Kobayashi), who Ichi inadvertently helps out of a jam with some bullies; Jiro and Saburo (Suzuki Matsuo), twin detectives so psychotic that Kakihara seeks *their* help in tracking down Ichi; Sarah (Mai Goto), a hapless prostitute whose disfiguring beatings at the hands of her pimp turn Ichi on like nothing else; and Suzuki (Susumu Terajima), a bandage-bedecked rival yakuza out for revenge after being

Miike on Miike

TROUBLE Trouble puts us into a position where we have to be creative. So the more problems we encounter, the more interesting the film can be. . . . If there's no trouble, it doesn't matter who directs it. I'm sure it has some kind of personality, but when someone is in trouble, that's when you see his true power.

ACTORS Omori and I didn't discuss about what Ichi was like, but we just started filming to understand Ichi. I didn't really talk to actors, because I didn't know what I wanted either. If I directed actors to act in certain ways, it would be boring.

CONTINUITY We didn't have a person recording how scenes connect and make sense. As long as the actors act the way they feel I don't care if the scenes don't connect to each other. It doesn't matter if the actors didn't know what they were supposed to do. I'm not worried about details like that . . . I should enjoy myself instead of trying to make a film that makes sense. So I don't think I can become a good director, and I don't wish to be one.

CHARACTERS Everyone knows their true self, but they pretend they don't know it. But your true self comes out once in a while. If you accept your true self and watch this film, you'll understand the characters' feelings in the film. They are very honest about what they believe. They don't lie to themselves. Everyone in this film is very pure. So I felt really good shooting these characters.

MIIKE Being born into this world is an accident to me. I don't question why I'm here, but I try to think what I can do.

(From the DVD commentary, *Ichi the Killer* [Uncut Special Edition], Tokyo Shock TSDVD0317)

hung up on hooks, lanced with skewers, and doused with boiling tempura oil by Kakihara.

Ichi the Killer is a wild ride, made all the more intoxicating by the score by composer Seiichi Yamamoto. Unlike most films, where the music is composed after shooting, the striking themes and psychedelic strains heard here were actually created as a reaction to the original manga on which the film is based. The music was delivered en masse to Miike, who then chose which parts he felt best fit the various scenes and sequences of the film. Miike admits that the music also influenced the editing of the film, becoming a more integral part of the narrative than it would have been with standard post-sync methods. Also, the fact that the music was inspired by the manga rather than the film creates a thematic bridge between the original work and the film interpretation. The origin and integration of the score is one of many facets that make *Ichi the Killer* a truly unique work of art rather than merely some sick film (although it is that, too!).

In addition to its unique score, the cast of *Ichi the Killer* is something of a remarkable assemblage. For one thing, there are other Japanese cult film directors in it! Shinya Tsukamoto, playing Jijii, hardly needs an introduction; with films like *Tetsuo: The Ironman* (1988), *Hiruko the Goblin* (1990), *Tokyo Fist* (1995), *Gemini (1999)*, and *A Snake of June* (2002) to his credit, he's a modern auteur who shares Miike's fascination with Tokyo and taste for extreme storytelling. Playing the disgraced ex-cop and bodyguard Kaneko, Sabu (née Hiroyuki Tanaka) is no slouch either, having made kinetic, absorbing films like *Postman Blues* (1997), *Unlucky Monkey* (1998), *Monday* (2000), and *Drive* (2002). Before becoming a film director, Sabu had worked as an actor, appearing in a number of Miike films and here, returning after an acting hiatus of some years, he acquits himself nicely.

Gorgeous Alien Sun (née Pauline Suen Kai-Kwan) was Miss Singapore in 1994; not the greatest actress, she compensated with creative innovation on the set, such as her character Karen's polyglot speech pattern (randomly drifting into English, Japanese, and Cantonese), lending an eerie eccentricity to the role. Nao Omori is the son of acclaimed actor Akaji Maro who, in addition to playing bald cop Murata in *Suicide Club* and Boss Ozawa in *Kill Bill: Vol. 1*, has also appeared in films directed by Miike, Tsukamoto, and Sabu, making him a triple alumnus. Talking of *Kill Bill*, Tarantino was completely floored by *Ichi the Killer*, appropriating a portion of its swagger and unflinching gore for his own opus (as well as Shun Sugata, Kakihara's hulking lieutenant, to play the part of Boss Benta).

Tadanobu Asano had previously begged off appearing in Miike

A rogue's gallery from *Ichi the Killer:* Jijii, Ichi, Kakihara, Karen, and Kaneko

films prior to *Ichi*. The reason? Miike's films were too violent. This might make his taking the role of Kakihara seem incomprehensible but for the fact that Asano got it: *Ichi the Killer* is an imaginative work, adapted from a manga fantasy and as such is not subject to the same moral scrutiny of, say, a serious dramatic work. Japanese culture has always been more indulgent toward extreme forms of entertainment, and Asano was reflecting this enlightened aesthetic sensibility. Satoshi Niizuma, however, had no such issues with violence or violent roles. Before trying his hand at acting (here playing Jijii's junkie underling Kano Inoue), Niizuma had been a professional kick boxer, and subsequently left acting for work as a high-level bodyguard for showbiz and yakuza figures. Niizuma also turns in a wonderfully menacing performance as a kimchee-munching Korean assassin in Miike's *Fudoh: The New Generation*. And who could miss Susumu Terajima as the unluckiest yakuza in the world, Suzuki, hung naked from the ceiling on a dozen small meat hooks. A prolific character actor in Japanese film since the early '90s, he is another Miike/Tsukamoto/Sabu alumnus and a frequent face in the films of Beat Takeshi.

And then there's Takashi Miike. My take: In a nutshell, Miike is all about process. He thrives on filmmaking as a creative act in itself, not something done in service to some larger vision. What happens on the set is the most important thing to Miike, and that includes the inevitable problems that arise; he views these as unique opportunities

© PRENOM/OMEGA

Ichi from *Ichi the Killer*

for innovation and invention (see sidebar). This is the key to understanding both Miike's filmic fecundity (he loves to shoot—half a dozen films a year, on average) and his dodgy quality control (an occupational hazard for anyone who makes so many films). With *Ichi the Killer*, he's created a film that truly bears scrutiny, all the more amazing for the fact that he used no script supervisor for continuity. There is one big gaffe, however, involving a sizeable forehead gash Kakihara receives late in the film, only to disappear in a subsequent close-up. Oh well.

There are a few scenes where it's hard to miss the use of computer-generated effects—fakey-looking gushing blood, for example (there isn't that much fake blood in all of Japan!). However, you might be surprised to know how much CG is going on right in front of you that you don't notice. Boss Anjo's blood-spattered apartment, for example; all that blood on the walls came not from the abattoir but from a computer. Or in the scene where poor Suzuki is hung on all those hooks: you might have marveled at the makeup job, the way it really looks like a yakuza hanging by his tattooed skin on two lines of sharp hooks. However, CG was employed later to cover the seams between the latex and Susumu Terajima's real skin, a brilliant example of technology extending verisimilitude. This didn't lessen Terajima's discomfort, though; he still had to spend twelve hours in makeup and another twelve on the set all rigged up like some hideous human hammock.

In the end, I know that no matter how I sing the praises of *Ichi the Killer*, there will be many who just won't like it, and I understand. How can anybody's idea of a good time be to watch two people play tug-of-war with a man's face? Or see walls spattered simultaneously with blood and semen? Hey, I'm happy if you're still *reading* this. But thrill-seekers and aficionados of extreme film recognize *Ichi the Killer* as something special, a cut above the lurid trash cinema with which it's often lumped. Remember, the best way to approach it is as the live-action manga it is; watch it like you'd watch *The Matrix*. Nobody's up in arms about all the cops that got blown away in that film, right? It's OK because it's fantasy/sci-fi, right? Maybe *Ichi the Killer* should be cut the same slack.

Say Yes

2001
South Korea
104 min.
DIRECTOR: Kim Sung-hong

CAST: Park Joong-hoon, Chu Sang-mi, Kim Ju-hyuk, Ki Joo-bong

If there's one thing we've learned from the movies, it's never pick up hitchhikers. Whether we're talking regular guy Tom Neal in *Detour*, menacing Lawrence Tierney in *The Devil Thumbs a Ride*, or demonic Rutger Hauer in *The Hitcher*, it's inevitable: if you give this man a ride, sweet memory will die. But no unstable stranger-cum-traveling companion can hold a candle to Park Joong-hoon in *Say Yes*, a film that is the very definition of harrowing journey. Park is positively diabolical as the dark stranger who attaches himself to a young couple, bent on their destruction but clearly in no hurry. With all the sadistic playfulness of a cat with some luckless, living prey, he toys with them, relentlessly ratcheting up his assault, both physical and psychological, with each new encounter. There's no chance of their escaping unscathed. The question is, will they escape at all?

Pretty Kim Yoon-hee (Chu Sang-mi) is a newlywed working part-time translating French texts into Korean. Her husband, bespectacled aspiring novelist Jung-hyun (Kim Ju-hyuk), decides to celebrate their one-year anniversary, as well as his first book deal, with a little vacation up the eastern coast. All in all, they're a fairly average young couple, their interactions shifting from whimsy to lighthearted bickering to sentimental moments. Considerable time and care is devoted to developing their characters (vacuous as they might be), groundwork that will pay off later. What comes across is that basically they are *happy*. Unfortunately, this quality also comes across to a man sitting alone at a roadside rest stop looking very *unhappy*. Getting back on the road, Jung-hyun backs into the stranger with his car and, naturally mortified, grants the man's request for a ride to their destination, the seaside resort town of Sokcho. En route, the stranger says, "You two . . . how much longer do you want to live? I haven't decided whether to kill you two or not." This comment doesn't sit well with Jung-hyun, who demands

© CINEMA SERVIC/MVP/HWANG KI SUNG FILMS

Say Yes

the stranger get out of his car. The man very unconvincingly claims it was a joke, and the uneasy ride continues. Later, as he exits the car at Sokcho, his parting words are, "I never joke around."

The Kims try to forget their unpleasant rider with some frolicking on the beach, a romantic dinner, and some hot sex, but a large rock through the window interrupts their lovemaking. Next day, on the road again, a mysterious black SUV swoops down on their little white car, inflicting all manner of vehicular assault. By the time Jung-hyun finally catches up to the SUV, parked in the next town, he's in such a lather that he beats the driver (yes, it's the stranger, mumbling dirty things about Yoon-hee) to a bloody pulp. Jung-hyun thinks he's taught the guy a lesson and the whole thing is over. But it's only just begun. . . .

So much more is in store for the Kims (and you) in *Say Yes*. It's the type of film that just keeps going, getting more and more intense, never letting up, reaching crescendos of violence and suspense that almost dare you to keep watching. Playing the stranger, Park Joong-hoon is of course unstoppable, surviving numerous movie-ending deaths only to continue his rampage on the unfortunate couple. Various other folks get murdered *en passant*, including a cop, which gets the attention of an intrepid police detective played by diminutive yet ubiquitous character actor Ki Joo-bong. He's one step behind his perp, appearing at each new crime scene with a look of grim determination, offering a hope that someone will get to Park before he can commit yet another heinous act. Cliché? Sure, the whole premise of the film is a cliché. But the interest lies in where director Kim Sung-hong takes it, and the uniquely visceral touches one finds in Korean film, like a character grinding broken glass into his own hand, lighting someone's face on fire, or brutally beating a hospital patient.

Another element that makes *Say Yes* so agonizing is how personally involved Park gets with his victims. Any cop will tell you that in most cases, a murder is committed by an assailant known to the victim, often a spouse, friend, or relative. Far from some removed tormentor, striking at his victims from afar, Park wants intimacy with the Kims, to talk, have dinner, travel with them, all sorts of up close and personal stuff (while intermittently torturing them, or course). This close proximity with a lonely, deranged person makes for an oppressive, claustrophobic film experience. Fact is, most of us live our lives safe in the knowledge that we won't be attacked by vampires or aliens, but becoming the victim of an unbalanced person who seeks to harm us for some irrational reason of his own, that's very possible. Statistically, there are millions of such people in this world, and it's really only a matter of luck, timing, karma, or some combination that keeps us from crossing paths with them. Let's face it, there's nothing like the true horror of another human being. This is the premise played out so effectively in *Say Yes*.

And hats off to Park Joong-hoon for his frightening, ferocious performance. Park is an unusual-looking man; with trapezoidal head (wider at the top), boxer's nose, and thick lips, it's no wonder he made his name in comedies like the 1993 hit *Two Cops*. More recently, the journeyman actor has branched out, playing thuggish Detective Woo in *Nowhere to Hide* (1999) and creepy crook Lee in Jonathan Demme's 2002 *Charade* remake, *The Truth About Charlie*. Here in *Say Yes*, he's been fitted with blue contact lenses that add an eerie quality to his singular, yet not-unattractive, countenance. He wears a blue track suit, sneakers, and an overcoat for most of the movie, a look that might diminish the intimidation factor of a lesser actor, but Park is all maniac, offering up a particularly virulent strain of malicious intent. Kudos as well to Chu Sang-mi and Kim Ju-hyuk for their believable interpretations of two people caught in a never-ending nightmare of mounting mayhem.

I won't kid you, *Say Yes* is a rough ride, and there will be some that won't be able to make it to the blood-soaked end, but I'd encourage you to stick it out. Coming out the other side you'll experience feelings of exhaustion and exhilaration, leaving no doubt in your mind that you've *been through something*. Truly harrowing.

The Untold Story • Ba Xian fan dian zhi ren rou cha shao bao

1993
Hong Kong
95 min.
DIRECTOR: Herman Yau
Lai To

CAST: Anthony Wong
Chau Sang, Danny
Lee Sau Yin, Emily
Kwan Bo Wai, Eric
Kee Ka Fat, Parkman
Wong Pak Man, Lam
King Kong, Shing Fui
On, Julie Lee Wah Yet,
James Ha

The Untold Story (actual title: *Eight Immortals Restaurant: Human Meat Roast Pork Buns*) is the kind of film that will make you wonder about yourself, chiefly whether you're a sick and demented person for liking such a sick and demented movie. "What's up with me?" you may ask yourself as you consider what you have just witnessed, a bizarre mélange of the goofy and the grotesque, a harrowing journey into the warped mind of a brutal serial killer intercut with kooky cop antics. After awhile and a few more viewings, however, you'll feel better about yourself and realize that the film is much more well-made than you'd first realized, overwhelmed as you were by the extreme subject matter. That, and the fact that what makes this film so absorbing, what manages to sell the proposition that one can be entertained by a tale of cannibalism, rape, torture, child murder, and the restaurant business, is the amazing performance of legendary Hong Kong actor Anthony Wong. Wong's "Bunman" is a grimacing, cleaver-wielding maelstrom of violent rage so unhinged and over the top that all other cinematic psychokillers pale in comparison.

As is the case with many Hong Kong horror/crime films, *The Untold Story* is based on a true story. According to director Herman Yau, "It occurred in 1978 in Hong Kong. Newspapers and magazines treated it as big news and said the flesh of the victims was made into buns that were sold in the restaurant. The 'human pork buns' might be just a rumor but for people who had eaten the buns sold by the restaurant, it was enough to feel sick even if the possibility of the reporting being true was only one percent" (Lisa Stokes and Michael Hoover, "An Exclusive Interview with Herman Yau," *Asian Cult Cinema* #35, p. 35).

The events in the movie are shifted to Macau in the mid-'80s, where Wong Chi Hang (Anthony Wong) is running the Eight Immortals restaurant (after emigrating from Hong Kong where he torched a guy in a gambling dispute, presumably his first murder). The eponymous "untold story" concerns just how Wong came to be the boss of the Eight Immortals and what happened to the previous owner, Cheng Lam (Lau Siu Ming), as well as his wife and their five young children. They've mysteriously vanished and Cheng Lam's brother keeps writing to the local cops to find out what happened.

The cops, meanwhile, are investigating some severed limbs that have washed up on the beach. Aside from their boss, they're a rather thick and shiftless lot and include:

- Officer Lee (Danny Lee): He's the lead detective, smooth and savvy, always has a sexy hooker on his arm, and is the only one who knows what's going on. He has his staff follow leads, but he's the one who's actually solving the case.
- Bull (Parkman Wong): Second in command to Officer Lee and head boob among the staff.
- King Kong (Lam King Kong): The young one, a guy with a bowl haircut and not much brains underneath.
- Ah Bo (Emily Kwan): The girl. The guys make her do all the dirty work and make fun of her small breasts. She's funny and gutsy and has a crush on Officer Lee. What do those whores have that she doesn't?
- Robert (Eric Kee): The womanizer. He's all muscle-tees and chat-up lines, always on the make with Officer Lee's girls, and even hits on Ah Bo, but supercop he ain't.

This same bunch features in the true crime shocker *Dr. Lamb* (1992), although they are considerably more competent in that film (perhaps because they're Hong Kong cops, whereas in *The Untold Story* they're Macau cops?). Various combinations of these actors appeared in many another Hong Kong crime film during the '90s.

The only thing Officer Lee's staff seems good at is beating the shit out of Wong once he's finally apprehended. By this point, in addition to the Cheng family, he's murdered and served up both his waitress (Julie Lee) and cook (James Ha), leaving the audience to wonder how he managed to run a restaurant all by himself. However, there's no doubt that though Wong may be as crazy as a loon, he's an assertive, can-do kind of guy. Minutes after jamming a receipt spike in his cook's eye and bludgeoning him to death with a big ladle, he's got the corpse up on the block and is slicing away. All of the chopping goes on below the frame, but Anthony Wong conveys the whole lurid business with his body and facial expressions; his performance is so intense, it's easy to believe he's really carving someone up. And of course he picks up his handiwork for the camera once he finishes a task, showing us a large pile of entrails (which go into the "pig's organ soup" pot) and a sizeable slab of red meat that looks to be the gluteus maximus. The waitress's fate is worse, as she is sadistically terrorized, tortured, and raped before finally expiring on the business end of a fistful of chopsticks.

Such gruesome scenes alternate with bits of comic business with the cops. One priceless scene features Ah Bo and King Kong trying to fingerprint a bloated severed arm and accidentally yanking the finger off. Another comes when the cops all enjoy the delicious pork buns

Wong has given them on their initial visit to the Eight Immortals restaurant (!). Scenes like these are inserted ostensibly to lighten things up a little, but the shifts in tone can be bewildering. Here in the U.S. we take our horror seriously, especially when the subject matter verges into the serial killer genre. Films like *Henry: Portrait of a Serial Killer, The Silence of the Lambs, Se7en,* and the like are all business, solemn affairs not to be taken lightly. But why not? Who's to say? I'll admit that the first time I saw *The Untold Story,* I found the tonal variations jarring, but this was only because of my cultural conditioning. For me, instead of breaking up the tension, it actually had the opposite effect: the gruesome scenes were that much more gruesome *because* things had been light and silly just a moment before. That's what makes Asian film (and foreign film in general) so unique and compelling: you take away a measure of cultural insight you didn't have before, not only into the foreign culture, but your own as well. There's a lot of pussyfooting that happens in Hollywood movies, a lot of filters, even in supposedly hard-hitting movies, that just aren't there in Asian film. Is there a scene of a young child being beheaded in this film? Yes, there is. Did Anthony Wong win the Hong Kong Film Award (the Hong Kong version of the Oscar) for best actor for his performance in *The Untold Story?* Yes, he did. Will you ever see an Oscar-winning Hollywood film with this level of graphic violence? No way.

Anthony Wong is an institution in contemporary Hong Kong cinema, having already appeared in over 150 films since 1985 (twenty-two in 2000 alone). His range is considerable, from the suave chief detective Wong in *Infernal Affairs* (2002) to the formidable villain Johnny in *Hard Boiled* (1992) to the sage, bearded Sword Saint in *Storm Riders* (1998) to horny demon Wu Tung in *Erotic Ghost Story II* (1991). But his Bunman in *The Untold Story* is probably his most intense performance. Every movement, expression, every gesture is nuanced, conveying menace. When he isn't killing people, his manner is hasty, blunt, almost as if he were an animal, a vicious dog, say, inhabiting the body of a man and still getting the hang of it. He displays the low cunning of an animal as well, and when he attacks, that's when the beast is truly unleashed. Also, his look is perfectly matched to his performance: His head is shorn almost bald and he wears oversized glasses with thick, dark frames. The glasses serve a threefold purpose: (1) They enhance the maniacal look in his eyes, (2) they give him a nerdy appearance at odds with his imposing physique and brusque mannerisms, and (3) they make for a handy windshield against the blood that routinely splashes his face while he's "at work."

The third act of *The Untold Story* is concerned with the efforts of the cops to get a confession out of the Bunman. They try the obvious first, lots of beatings down at the station, but he's a tough customer and takes everything they can dish out. One cop even complains that it's like he's made out of rubber. Wong, as cagey as he is stubborn, seizes an opportunity to run out into the hallway and show the reporters his bruises to get the cops in trouble. Fortunately, Cheng Poon (Shing Fui On), the brother of the murdered owner of the Eight Immortals restaurant, is serving time on his own murder rap. Why not let him do the beating? The cops arrange things so Cheng Poon can pay little visits to Wong, during which the Bunman is repeatedly beaten to a pulp and subjected to all manner of abuse including the ol' soap-in-the-sock routine (like poor Vincent D'Onofrio in *Full Metal Jacket*). Wong attempts suicide and is hospitalized, giving Officer Lee an idea, and soon the cops and hospital staff are working together, using modern medical technology to torture a confession out of Wong. Will their efforts pay off?

There is a frankness, a stark quality to *The Untold Story,* playing more as a docudrama than a moody, atmospheric piece. Rather than being lured into a dark lair and bitten by a snake, the effect is more like being attacked on the street in broad daylight. "I had a long time in the industry as a cinematographer and I care about camerawork very much," says Herman Yau. "For the killing of the waitress and family, I didn't want low-key lighting because I thought it would be more horrible and different from the usual treatment of other directors." We all know how terrible we look under fluorescent lights, imagine how much worse you'd look in pieces and you get an idea of what Yau was going for. But it works. There's something about this film that transcends its equivocal tone and ghastly events, a combination of Anthony Wong's dedication to the role of Bunman and Herman Yau's directorial and cinematographic sensibilities. Highly recommended.

Under the Blossoming Cherry Trees • *Sakura no mori no mankai no shita*

"Kill that woman for me!"
"She doesn't have to be killed . . . think of her as a maid."
"You killed my husband but you hesitate to kill your wife? How can I be your wife then?"

This charming *tête-à-tête* comes early in the relationship between an unnamed man and woman (samurai film veterans Tomisaburo

1975

Japan

95 min.

DIRECTOR: Masahiro Shinoda

CAST: Tomisaburo Wakayama, Shima Iwashita, Ko Nishimura

Wakayama and Shima Iwashita, respectively) and illustrates how much the woman has already gotten the upper hand. In fact, the two have only just met; earlier in the day, the woman, her husband, and a servant had found themselves at the mercy of burly, mustachioed mountain bandit Wakayama along a lonely country road. Wakayama, instantly smitten with the alluring Iwashita, never before having seen such beauty, draws his sword and makes quick work of the two men, but reassures Iwashita, "You're too beautiful to kill." On the spot, he decides to make her his wife. Far from being appalled or terrified at her situation, Iwashita immediately accepts the situation and starts right in on her new hubby, making him carry her on his back up the side of a mountain, berating him and questioning his manhood every step of the way.

The setting is twelfth-century Japan, and the blossoming cherry trees, nowadays so beloved, were during this time regarded as something to be feared, nature's preeminent symbol of death, emanating a monstrous, malefic force. As the opening narration declares, "People thought they'd lose their minds by walking under the blossoms. Travelers made detours, going out of their way to avoid the flowering trees." Wakayama does the same as he carries his new bride home to his mountain retreat. Once there, Iwashita is revolted by the sight of seven grubby, homely women already living in Wakayama's house ("Seven Brides for Katsu's Brother," as one wag put it), and immediately makes the demand quoted at the beginning of this review. However, once Wakayama draws his sword and does her bidding, she becomes intoxicated by the killing and demands the death of another wife and another, until only one, a girl with a malformed leg, remains. This one will be her maid. Wakayama is, by this time, caught up in his own bloodlust, but Iwashita forbids him from skewering the crippled girl. "You silly thing," she chides him, "she lives because I say so."

Despite Wakayama's total devotion and effective cunnilingual technique, Iwashita soon tires of life in the mountains. Even though her new husband brings her the nice things she desires like combs, makeup, musical instruments, and lovely kimonos (by casually slaughtering travelers along the road), she longs to return to The Capital, her true home. She eventually talks him into going and, once there, things take a gruesome turn.

You see, our lady has a thing about heads. Severed heads. She loves them, can't get enough of them, they're all she lives for. Wakayama becomes her hatchet man, so to speak (really he uses his trusty sword), supplying Iwashita with the noggins she needs. At first she plays with them like dolls, acting out conversations between them. For example, when Wakayama surprises the vile Lord Daiganon as he is attempting

A rare shot of a young, smiling Tomisaburo Wakayama

to rape lovely young Lady Rokujo, soon enough Iwashita is reenacting the drama with their freshly severed heads. She ad-libs both roles and encourages Daiganon to bite the princess's cheek, neck, and eyeball. The camera pans down to the floor and a dozen more heads—this has been going on awhile! As her insanity deepens, Iwashita starts interacting with the heads, kissing them, even suckling an old, perverted monk Wakayama has recently dispatched, along with his young male paramour: "Suck on it. The taste of a woman's nipple is quite exquisite, too. Have you ever had anybody besides young boys? How do you find the taste? Suck harder, harder. Good . . . I'll take you to Nirvana (gasp, moan)." Heady stuff.

While Iwashita is perfectly content to sit in a dingy house, playing endless games with her menagerie of heads (soon in varying stages of decay), Wakayama suffers from a growing ennui. He takes no pleasure in his wife's head trips, and he's definitely not enjoying life in The Capital; he is mocked by the city folk for his bumpkinish ways, such as staring at turnips in the marketplace, drinking sake like an animal, and not even knowing how to use money. Even the head chopping, which might have provided an opportunity to vent some frustration, now only depresses him. One day he inadvertently steals some oranges and is pursued and caught by The Pardoned Ones, former thieves and murderers who have been recruited by a city official (Ko Nishimura) and formed into a local constabulary. These corrupt and loathsome characters wear red and white uniforms, brandish long red spears, and laugh maniacally when in pursuit of their prey. Wakayama is beaten and tortured for awhile, Nishimura questioning him about the mysterious Head Chopper who's been terrorizing The Capital of late. Our man doesn't talk, but soon enough he's wearing one of those red and white uniforms. However, he's not the uniform-wearing type, and in a triumphant moment of release and revenge, he lops off Nishimura's head in a gloriously gory freeze-frame.

Eventually husband and wife decide to return to the mountains. When Wakayama wonders if Iwashita can be happy without her beloved, bodiless friends, she reassures him:

Shima Iwashita in the early days

Shima Iwashita circa *Under the Blossoming Cherry Trees*

"If I have to choose between you and the heads, I'll choose you."

"Are you sure?"

"I can easily give up the heads for you. I just want you."

However, on the way back, Wakayama, emboldened by his woman's love and overjoyed to be returning to the mountains, decides to take the path through the cherry trees. Something happens there, something very strange. . . .

Under the Blossoming Cherry Trees, based on a novel and play by Ango Sakaguchi (1906–55), is an overlooked masterpiece of Japanese cinema, as unique as it is macabre and, as of this writing, only recently released on DVD (in Japan). It was directed by acclaimed auteur Masahiro Shinoda who, along with fellow filmmakers Shohei Imamura, Yasuzo Masumura, Nagisa Oshima, and others, set out to redefine Japanese cinema in the early '60s, kicking off what's come to be known as the Japanese New Wave. As a youth, Shinoda had pursued physics and higher mathematics. Then came World War II and, shattered by his experiences, young Masahiro lost faith in the purity of science, coming to regard war as its most immediate product. At Waseda University, he embraced the traditional Japanese theatrical art forms of Kabuki, Bunraku, and Noh, and eventually found his way to Shochiku Studios, where he began directing features in 1960. The central theme in Shinoda's work is that of self-sacrifice and self-destruction, elements of human nature that confounded him. Other great Shinoda films include *Pale Flower* (1964), *Assassination* (1964), *Samurai Spy* (1965), *Double Suicide* (1969), *Buraikan* (1970), *Ballad of Orin* (1977), *Gonza the Spearman* (1986), *Owl's Castle* (1999), and *Spy Sorge* (2003).

Samurai film fans will derive special gratification from *Under the Blossoming Cherry Trees*, featuring as it does the acting talents, fighting abilities, and sheer presence of the legendary Tomisaburo Wakayama. Although a striking and formidable force in samurai films dating back to the '50s, the actor is best known in the West as Ogami Itto, rogue assassin of the Lone Wolf and Cub series (six films, 1972–74), wherein his character had formerly occupied the post of Kogikaishakunin, official head chopper for the shogun. Perhaps his popularity in Japan as Ogami Itto influenced his casting here, as he does quite a lot of decapitating, albeit for the sake of his wife, not the shogun. When we first encounter Wakayama, he is a hulking, formidable bear of a man, wearing a vest of animal furs and sporting big, barbarian/pompadour-style hair, graying at the temples, and a long straight-edged sword. He robs and kills travelers with abandon and loves his life as freelance mountain bandit. Shortly after abducting his new wife, while carrying her up the hill to his A-frame hideaway, he boasts, "All the mountains you can see belong to me . . . every single tree in the mountains, and every ravine, even the fog and clouds in the mountains are mine!" Later, while hunting deer, he exclaims, "I must be the strongest man on earth!" Clearly his identity and self-image are all wrapped up in this mountain marauder lifestyle, a feeling not shared by his wife, who is bored out of her mind with country living and longs only to get back to the city.

Strangely, once the wife gets to The Capital (that would be ancient Kyoto, but I call it "The Capital" to be consistent with the film), she shows no interest in seeing her old friends unless they come to her sans body. Only their heads interest her. Monks, officials, lords and ladies, whole families, are brought to her by her faithful husband, and she holds court. This scenario suggests some interesting metaphors: Are we saying here that city folk are as useless and dull as a roomful of moldering heads? Perhaps Iwashita's manipulation of the heads, the way she plays with and fusses over them, represents the kind of vicious social games played out by women of her class in The Capital. We don't really have a backstory on her, so this could just be simple revenge, taken out on all those who formerly manipulated and abused her. One thing's for sure, while she was climbing the walls in Wakayama's mountain retreat, she is completely sustained and entertained in a similarly dreary city dwelling, never going out, endlessly captivated by the scintillating company of her vacant, staring companions.

At the end of the day, it is this country-life-versus-city-life dichotomy that lies at the heart of *Under the Blossoming Cherry Trees*, despite all the head-chopping, insanity, and spooky pink trees. Communion with nature lies at the heart of Japanese art and culture, and although both main characters are sociopathic to say the least, it is Wakayama (country) who maintains his sanity and sense of self, while Iwashita (city) allows herself to drift in and out of fantasy and dementia, and is ultimately completely dependent on Wakayama.

Shima Iwashita, Shinoda's wife and personal muse, appeared in all the director's major works, as well as an impressive roster of fine films for other directors, including *Harakiri* (Masaki Kobayashi, 1962), *Sword of the Beast* (Hideo Gosha, 1965), *Festival of Gion* (Daisuke Ito, 1968), and *Red Lion* (Kihachi Okamoto, 1969). Her performance in *Under the Blossoming Cherry Trees* is chilling and wonderful, keeping the audience forever uncertain as to just how much of her behavior is calculated, and how much is just plain psychosis. It is the triumvirate of Shinoda, Iwashita, and Wakayama that elevates this sordid tale of banditry, obsession, and murder into a compelling, engrossing piece of film art to be savored and treasured.

Angulimala

2003

Thailand

101 min.

DIRECTOR: Sutape Tunnirut

CAST: Jayanama Nopachai, Stella Malucchi, Alisa Kajornchaiyakul, John Rattanaveroj, Kamron Gunatilaka

His original rosary was not enough to count the evildoers he delivered from suffering. He then made a rosary beaded with their fingers. That was why he was named Angulimala.

Anguli = finger, *mala* = rosary. Talk about accessorizing for maximum impact! Angulimala was a religious fanatic and mass murderer in ancient India who, as legend has it, believed the path to enlightenment was strewn with 1,000 corpses, and once he'd relieved that number of people from their burdensome existence (taking the pinky of their right hand as a souvenir) he would reach Nirvana or, as they call it in the movie, the *dharma core*. In a way, it's hard to argue with the logic of his basic assumption: when you cut someone's head off, you do relieve them of their suffering. The logic unravels, though, when you take into consideration the added suffering felt by the victim's loved ones. Angulimala, while not the clearest of thinkers, nevertheless makes for a riveting title character in this lush, atmospheric spectacle of butchery and Buddhism.

It seems that the madman with the finger garland moniker was originally born Ahimsaka (*ahimsa* is the Sanskrit word for non-violence) into a prominent Brahmin family around 500 B.C. His birth was marred by bad omens (like all the weapons in the vicinity glowing and emitting eerie flames, a clear indication that an evil bandit has been born). His father was all for killing him in his crib, but cooler heads prevailed and young Ahimsaka was instead sent to Taxila, a city in the far north of India (now in northern Pakistan near Islamabad), renowned as a seat of learning and religious study. There he would live and perfect himself in the pursuit of dharma, the law of the universe as described by the Vedas and Upanishads.

Unfortunately, shortly after Ahimsaka's mother Mantani (Alisa Kajornchaiyakul) drops him off at his new home in Taxila (leaving him her own mala as a keepsake), the monastery's guru, Brahmin Sati (Kamron Gunatilaka), has a vision of the lad's bloody future: "He is destined to be a murderous bandit, robbing of life those he owes a debt of gratitude," says the venerable master. Wishing to isolate him from the rest of the students, the guru puts Ahimsaka in charge of the goats. The kid makes the best of the situation, spending his time meditating and watching the goats, but he's clearly an outsider.

As time goes on, we observe young Ahimsaka having formative experiences that will play a vital part in shaping his future identity as Angulimala. Early on, he is taken hostage by a muddy bandit and then rescued by Vidhura (John Rattanaveroj), a noble Brahmin warrior, who, untroubled by the knife at Ahimsaka's throat, shoots the bandit through the eye with his bow and arrow. When the boy asks why Vidhura killed the bandit, he's told the man was "a follower of the Niratta cult practicing physical invulnerability and committing crimes without conscience." Later, Ahimsaka is shocked to find the people of Taxila participating in a ceremonial mass goat slaughter. Brahmin Sati explains that whoever kills 1,000 goats will be reborn in heaven, but that evildoers will be reborn as untouchables. This guru, while possessing certain psychic abilities, gradually reveals himself to be a rather unsavory individual. For one thing, he's a horny old bugger with a hot young fiancée on the way to Taxila. Also, he's not very cordial to Mantani when she comes to visit her son. Still distraught over Ahimsaka's predetermined fate as a serial killer, Mantani mentions a chat she recently had with a certain enlightened individual:

> "I once heard from an ascetic that everything is impermanent. I asked him if impermanence also included destiny, and he confirmed it to be so."

> "To which doctrine does that dharma belong?"

Mantani tries to duck the question, but the increasingly perturbed guru repeats it. Finally, she admits,

> "It's the dharma of an ascetic from the Shakya clan."

That ascetic would be one Siddhartha Gautama, more commonly

© FILM BANGKOK/CHALERMTHAI

Angulimala

known as the Buddha. On hearing this, Sati goes ballistic, pouring milk all over the floor (to purify it) and exclaiming hotly, "What a misfortune it is! Saying the words of that unconventional doctrine in this sacred place!" Looks like somebody feels a little threatened.

Nandha (Stella Malucchi), the young bride-to-be, arrives, but Sati's geezer lust is soon thwarted by the news that (1) although her father is a Brahmin, her mother is in fact an untouchable, making *her* an untouchable, and (2) the king has canceled the Great Brahma Worship Ceremony and converted to the teaching of that ascetic from the Shakya clan. Sensing no future in Taxila, Nandha jumps into the river. She is rescued by Ahimsaka, who's immediately accused of abducting her and attacked by Sati's followers. Ahimsaka and Nandha run away and hole up in a cave. Here, Ahimsaka encounters an amorphous, luminous being with a deep, echoey voice. It's the Holy Mountain's God, and it tells him that he needs to start sacrificing evildoers. "Stop them before they commit more evils. Evildoers are everywhere on earth. Once you sacrifice a thousand evildoers, you will attain dharma." The God also mentions that Ahimsaka is imbued with certain gifts and once he's got sword in hand, he'll gain supernatural powers, making him a lean, mean killing machine.

And so Angulimala is born. At first he only goes after bandits, dispatching them with ruthless efficiency (and a lot of gory special effects). When he meets an old teacher from Taxila who's recently switched over to following the Buddha, he kills him too, adding people who don't worship the Great Brahma to his list of evildoers. Before long it occurs to him that *every* man suffers and deserves to be delivered and that's when the carnage shifts into high gear. The guy's unstoppable, wiping out whole villages (and any armed detachment that comes after him), yet back at the cave with Nandha, he's a solemn and respectful companion (they're just friends). Who can stop him? And will he reach his goal of a thousand kills?

Three years in the making, *Angulimala* is a movie of epic sweep and grandeur (like *Suriyothai* or *Bang Rajan*, only more ancient), treating as it does a big name in the history of Buddhism (Angulimala has his own sutra in the Buddhist canon). Thai film is often infused with Buddhist thought, and *Angulimala* has it in spades. Those untroubled by all the gruesome murders will find the film doubles as a crash course in the fundamentals of Buddhist philosophy (one imagines young guys running to the theater for the mayhem and emerging wearing saffron robes). Those interested in historical epics will enjoy *Angulimala*, too, with its striking landscapes, haunting atmospheric theme of chanting voices by Chatchai Pongprapaphan (who also scored *Bang Rajan*), and elegantly tattered costume design by Natthorn Rakchana. Sure, the acting could be a little better, but isn't that always the way with epics? Pitched battles, broadly drawn characters, and straightforward plotlines are the order of the day, the genre all but precluding a meaningful dramatic performance. But what the film might lack in thespian quality it makes up for in psychedelic meditation sequences, gore-enhancing sound design, tasteful use of digital effects (such as following arrows from bow to target), sumptuous cinematography courtesy of Nattawut Kittikhun, and, of course, an ongoing discussion of karma, dharma, and the impermanence of all things.

Needless to say, *Angulimala* can be seen as a cautionary tale of the dangers of fanaticism, but there's also some ambiguity regarding the eponymous character's mental state. What's really up with him? He's hearing the Mountain God and seeing the spirits of his victims give him a gentle *wai* (bow with palms together) following their brutal demise. Could it be that he's really just fucking nuts? The script sets up plot elements that pay off later to support this analysis; Vidhura's rationalization for killing the "evildoer," the ideal of sacrificing a thousand goats (and him the goat boy), even his attachment to his mother's mala (he makes his own, remember?), all these elements could get scrambled up in the mind of a psychotic, leading to his eventual killing spree. Or you could choose to take things literally and just roll with all the supernatural stuff. It works either way, thus rewarding repeat viewings.

This is not the first film adaptation of the Angulimala legend; an Indian version was filmed by director Vijay Bhatt in 1960. It is, however, the bloodiest. As of this writing, *Angulimala* is not that easy to come by. Hopefully things will change in the future, but if not, you'll have to hit up a foreign distributor like ethaicd.com. But it's certainly worth it; films like this don't come along every day. If you think a fusion of bestial violence and sublime spiritual teachings is your cup of chai, you can't go far wrong with this remarkable film.

Inner Senses • Yee do hung gaan

2002
Hong Kong
100 min.
DIRECTOR: Law Chi Leung
CAST: Leslie Cheung Kwok Wing, Karena Lam Kar Yan, Waise Lee Chi Hung, Valerie Chow Kar Ling, Norman Chu Siu Keung

I normally refrain from blowing the endings of movies, but in the case of *Inner Senses,* there's simply no avoiding it. The subject matter of the film and the death of star Leslie Cheung soon after its release are so inextricably entwined, it's impossible to have a meaningful discussion without spoiling the film's ending. For those of you who, like me, *hate* having movies spoiled, my deepest apologies. Stop reading now, go watch *Inner Senses* (it's excellent), then come back. For those who've seen it or don't mind spoilers, read on.

A shortsighted reviewer might dismiss *Inner Senses* as a cross between M. Night Shyamalan's *The Sixth Sense* and Hideo Nakata's *Dark Water.* It's true, similarities to both films do exist. However, *Inner Senses* is very much its own film, with its own creative and cultural identity, and shouldn't be written off due to superficial resemblance or confluence of themes. Yes, there's the inevitable "I see dead people" line, but it's spoken by a grown woman to her psychiatrist, without the precious, childlike phrasing made so memorable by Haley Joel Osment; she simply says, "I see ghosts" (in Cantonese). The *Dark Water* similarities extend to a woman taking a creepy, most-likely haunted apartment with a leaky tap (as well as some J-horror references toward the end). There is admittedly a strong Hollywood influence in terms of score, sound design, pace, and production values like many a post-handover Hong Kong offering. But in the end, *Inner Senses* succeeds as a decidedly Chinese take on the modern ghost film.

Early in the film, we attend a lecture by Dr. Jim P.L. Law (Leslie Cheung), a leading psychiatrist, and hear his views on ghosts and culture. "We Chinese are a strange lot," he muses. "Our parents like to use ghosts to teach their children. If you're naughty? Ghosts will come to get you." Law uses cultural analysis to explain why, even though ghosts don't exist, everyone believes in them anyway—it's all just so much conditioning. His thesis: "Ghosts only exist in your brain." This creates a conflict later with a colleague who questions whether, since he doesn't buy in to the ghost thing, Law even believes in God. Nope, he doesn't go in for that either. Dr. Law is a *man of science.*

So when he gets a referral from his friend and colleague Dr. Wilson Chan (Waise Lee), a troubled young woman named Cheung Yan (Karena Lam) who sees ghosts, you just know he's not about to buy into the booga-booga bit. He keeps things purely clinical, although he has a caring and compassionate manner and is completely dedicated to helping the soulful, sad, and lovely Yan. "You must learn how to do one thing: calm yourself down and love yourself." His treatment eventually bears fruit, but not before some rather disturbing ghost encounters.

Early on, Yan notices a shuddersome silhouette in the hallway, and soon thereafter sees a twisted, emaciated ghost standing in the middle of her apartment screaming. He seems to be in considerable pain and the effect is unnerving. No low-key Shyamalan specter, this guy. Later, Yan gets politely coerced into having dinner with landlord Chu (Norman Chu), a widower whose wife and small son died in a landslide. Chu, a very nice guy who smiles a little too much, gradually reveals himself to be consumed with grief to the point of neurosis:

> It was still raining when they left, but once the rain stops they'll come back. I want them to change into dry, clean shoes when they come back. I always cook extra food so my wife can gain some weight. She's too skinny. They'll come back sooner or later. Sorry . . . sorry . . .

Chu's condition neatly parallels Yan's, reinforcing Dr. Law's theory that the belief in ghosts can play out in delusion and eventual dementia when coupled with some trauma or personal loss. Meanwhile, back in her pad, Yan is haunted by Chu's wife and kid (they're all wet and filthy from the landslide—a tastefully done, hair-raising sequence!). But Dr. Law insists it's all in Yan's head. He goes so far as to install video cameras in her place to prove in playback that there are no ghosts.

As Yan's treatment progresses, so do her feelings for Dr. Law. He seems drawn to her as well, but holds a firm line at the doctor/patient relationship, not allowing things to get romantic. Right about this time, though, we start getting little indications that Dr. Law is not all he seems. We see him popping pills from an assortment of prescription drugs in his bathroom. Also, brief, unexplained flashbacks begin to filter in, and they don't seem to be Yan's—images of a teenage couple in love, then out of love, then glimpses of the girl in a coffin. The more Dr. Law falls in love with Yan, the more these flashbacks, in fact repressed memories, plague the good doctor, ultimately manifesting into the ghost of his lost, teen love Yue. Yes, Dr. Law suffers from the same affliction that he finally managed to cure in Yan! Yue had thrown herself off a building following a breakup with young Law, and her ghost, still in school uniform, looks as she did after the fall (fairly ghastly). She also makes all manner of disgusting crunching noises when she walks. Yue's haunting of Dr. Law escalates as his condition deteriorates, culminating in a final confrontation on the same roof from which Yue threw herself all those years ago. But instead of jumping, as Yue would have it, Law comes back to his shrink-self and talks it out with the ghost, herself just a manifestation of his own unresolved grief and remorse. The ghost vanishes, Yan appears, and all is resolved.

Or is it? According to costar Waise Lee, shooting *Inner Senses* had a profound effect on Leslie Cheung, and he was never the same afterward. He sank into a deep depression and sought psychiatric help. Actors often speak of reaching a place emotionally were their own personalities intersect with their characters. Could it be that all the soul-searching Cheung went through in the role of Dr. Law triggered things within him, feelings and realizations with which he was unable to cope? Perhaps he'd broken up with his lover of twenty years, Daffy Tong Hok Tak? Maybe his psychiatrist had prescribed mood-altering drugs for his depression that affected his behavior? Whatever the reason, the fact remains that on April 1, 2003, at 6:41 P.M., Leslie Cheung, elegant in a chic tailored suit, jumped from a twenty-fourth-floor balcony of the Mandarin Oriental Hotel in Hong Kong, landing in the bustling Connaught Road below. According to a piece in *Time Asia* by Richard Corliss, Cheung had missed a scheduled meeting at the hotel with his manager Chan Suk Fan, and told her by phone from the twenty-fourth-floor gym to meet him out front, that he'd be right down. April fool gag? If so, it's a world-beater. Daffy Tong later told the press that Cheung had been depressed for as long as he'd known him and that Cheung had made another attempt with sleeping pills the previous November.

Cheung's death sent shockwaves throughout Asia, where he was an established international superstar. Mere days before his death, the Hong Kong Film Awards had announced his nomination for Best Actor for his role in *Inner Senses*. The emotional intensity of the film, its themes of depression and loss, its haunted and haunting quality will forever be associated with the sad end of this great actor. His suicide note, found in the pocket of his suit, reads,

> Depression! Many thanks to all the fans. Many thanks to Professor Felice Lieh Mak [Cheung's psychiatrist]. It has been a year of suffering. I can't stand it anymore. Many thanks to Mr. Tong. Many thanks to my family. Many thanks to Fat Sis-

ter [comic actress Lydia Shum Tin Ha]. In my life I have done nothing wrong. Why does it have to be like this?

Leslie Cheung was born Cheung Fat Chung in Kowloon in 1956, the youngest of ten children. At age thirteen, his father, a leading Hong Kong tailor, sent Cheung to a boarding school in England. Cheung went on to attend Leeds University in England, studying textile management, but dropped out and returned to Hong Kong where he pursued a singing career. By the mid-'80s, he'd become a major Cantopop idol and his appearance alongside Chow Yun Fat in John Woo's 1986 triad classic *A Better Tomorrow* put him on the map cinematically. From there, Cheung went from strength to strength, starring in celebrated Hong Kong films *A Chinese Ghost Story* (1987), *Days of Being Wild* (1991), *Farewell My Concubine* (1993, the first Chinese film to win the Palm d'Or at Cannes), *The Bride with White Hair* (1993), and *Happy Together* (1997), to name but a few. He retired from music in 1989, but returned in 1995, touring and recording throughout the remainder of the decade.

Supporting Leslie Cheung in *Inner Senses* is a fine cast that includes some familiar faces. There's Canadian-born Karena Lam, herself a former pop idol. Remember her from the chick flick/organ theft shocker *Koma* (2004)? She co-starred in that picture with Angelica Lee, the Malaysian actress who had her own "I see dead folks" turn in 2002's *The Eye.* Also on hand is veteran actor Waise Lee, who made his film debut alongside Cheung in *A Better Tomorrow.* Lee has appeared in scores of Hong Kong films and is still going strong. And speaking of veteran actors, Hong Kong cinema stalwart Norman Chu (over 100 films and counting) is on hand, giving a gentle, mournful performance as the widowed landlord Chu, a heartbreaking and pathetic character that proves this actor can do much more than just jump around and punch 'n' kick (and by now he's a little past his kung fu glory days). This author's favorite Norman Chu performance is as Agent 999 in Tsui Hark's 1980 cannibal action/comedy *We're Going to Eat You,* but whereas Chu is broad and O.T.T. in that film, here he creates a compact, layered character of squelched grief and barely contained emotional breakdown.

So, now you have numerous reasons to see *Inner Senses* if you haven't already. You can see why I had to blow the ending; with its final scene revolving around whether Leslie Cheung's character jumps to his death, one has to wonder how much it influenced his eventual demise. But I am convinced that there are scenes in this film where you can witness Leslie Cheung's crippling depression penetrating the character of Dr. Law. Screen it for yourself and see what you think. One way or the other, it's a moving and rewarding film and highly recommended.

7

While possession crops up elsewhere in this book in films where it plays a minor role, the following films are wholly devoted to what happens when an entity gets inside you and makes you do horrible things. Refreshingly, there are no devils, no Catholic priests, no holy water, and nary a painful crucifix insertion. There are, however, involuntary liver and brain removals and quite a bit of Italo-horror-inspired nastiness. And actually, come to think of it, there's one entity that might be the devil, depending on how you look at it, but you could just as well blame it on the rain. . . .

Another Heaven

Another Heaven begins with a quote from Revelations 12:12, the bit about "Woe to the inhabiters of the earth and of the sea! For the devil has come down unto you, having great wrath, because he knoweth that he hath but a short time." However if you care to open your Bible and scan down to 12:15, you'll get a more specific plot reveal (if you know how to interpret it, of course).

So, it's all about the devil coming down to earth and venting his great wrath, right? Well, maybe; this being a Japanese film, there's a certain measure of ambiguity in the way it plays out, leaving a defini-

2000

Japan

132 min.

DIRECTOR: Joji Iida

CAST: Yosuke Eguchi,
Yoshio Harada,
Miwako Ichikawa,
Yasuko Matsuyuki,
Takashi Kashiwabara,
Yukiko Okamoto,
Akira Emoto,
Haruhiko Kato

tive interpretation of the story up for grabs, even after the last frame. *Another Heaven* starts out more like an uproarious black comedy: Cops at a crime scene find a corpse with an empty skull and a pot of brain stew bubbling on the stove. This, after they'd all remarked on how delicious the smell was; the revelation sends them scattering out of the apartment to retch on the stairs. The scene is all "waughhaaaahh!" and "huaahlp!" pandemonium. The director continues to work the freak out and puke shtick as more such murders are discovered, each with a new brain recipe (spaghetti sauce, vinegared stew, etc.).

Eventually the film settles down into a more serious police procedural, focusing on the investigation led by the standard young cop/old cop team. Hunky detective Manabu Hayase (Yosuke Eguchi) is the kind of serious young man that has no problem with the ladies. Beautiful Dr. Sasamoto (Yasuko Matsuyuki) at the Police Hospital is giving him the eye and his sexy hippy chick ex-girlfriend Asako (Miwako Ichikawa) isn't about to call it a day (looking at her, one wonders why on earth he would). Manabu teams up with the crusty but benign Detective Tobitaka (samurai film veteran Yoshio Harada). Tobitaka shows up at the initial crime scene with old friend and chief coroner Dr. Akagi (Akira Emoto, who played another Dr. Akagi in Shohei Imamura's 1998 film *Dr. Akagi*). "The worst case I ever saw was a severed penis in the corpse's mouth," says grizzled old doc Akagi. "How base!" replies Tobitaka.

As the empty-headed corpses pile up, the inevitable media frenzy prompts pundits to utter the usual denouncements of violence in entertainment (presented here in a neat montage). But our intrepid detectives pay no attention, their minds obsessed on the conflicting evidence, namely whether the perp is a woman or a man. The violence of the crimes indicates a powerful male, but other evidence points to a female and, as we all know, the female of the species is more deadly than the male. Sure enough, Manabu and Tobitaka soon discover it *is* a woman, one Chizuru Kashiwagi (Yukiko Okamoto), and they manage to track her down, but not before she's twisted the neck of her eighth victim, a horny, sweaty guy who got lucky with her on his kitchen floor (she'd already started cooking . . .). The unfortunate fellow had picked up the alluring Chizuru earlier at a bar with two of his buddies, apparently unconcerned by the fact that she had blood running out of one of her eyes. Before breaking his neck, Chi-chan whispers with a maniacal grin, "I can hear your bad thoughts. It's fun to open a head. Bad thoughts change brains' color."

As it happens, Chizuru is inhabited by a malicious entity whose effect on the brain is quite damaging over time. In fact, when Manabu

Another Heaven: Dr. Akagi, Manabu, and Det. Tobitaka

and Tobitaka arrive at the scene, she stumbles into the living room and promptly dies, her own skull seemingly empty (no brainless bimbo jokes, please). "Her brains weren't gone," Dr. Akagi later tells us. "They shrank and dried up in a corner. Filled with ulcers too." So that's why she was bleeding from her eye, a sign that the current host brain is just about used up. So if she's dead, where's the "something" (as the two cops eventually take to calling it)? Let's just say that, like the evil black blob in 1987's *The Hidden*, our "something" has a lot more body-jumping to do and many, many more heinous crimes to commit.

I mention *The Hidden*, as do others who have written about *Another Heaven*, but it should be said that the Japanese film is not some derivative knockoff, as characterized by shortcut-minded critics. As gruesome as it is, *Another Heaven* is nevertheless a thoughtful, multidimensional film, one of those litmus test pictures that separate the true film observer from the facile dilettante. While *The Hidden* is an enormously enjoyable Hollywood sci-fi action romp, people actually talk to each other in *Another Heaven*, they have real discussions; there's a lot of introspection here that's normally lacking in formulaic action movies. Manabu is wracked with self-doubt, at one point asserting that he's not really a cop. "I'm not helping people . . . I'm just a crime buff . . . the evil enchanted me. So I became a cop." The most intriguing dialog is between Manabu and the "something"—the latter grows infatuated with Manabu, dedicating its slaughters to the detective in bloody kanji and kana on the walls of its crime scenes. As Manabu pursues the entity, he tries to understand its nature and what exactly it is. This line of inquiry leads him ultimately back to himself, and to something that is in all humans; "something" repeatedly asserts, "I'm human," leaving Manabu (and us) to contemplate the malevolent aspect of humanity and what the human condition is really all about.

Another Heaven features the hard-boiled Yoshio Harada, an actor whose onscreen persona is that of the compelling stoic. His ruggedly handsome features and intense, focused performances made him perfect for the samurai genre, enriching films such as *Trail of Blood* (1972), *Lady Snowblood 2: Love Song of Vengeance* (1972), *The Assassination of Ryoma*

© OMEGA/ANOTHER HEAVEN

Asako tries to stop the madness in *Another Heaven*

(1974), *Shogun's Samurai* (1978), *Hunter in the Dark* (1979), and *Roningai* (1990). Of course, he's appeared in other genres, in over 100 films to date and still going strong. Contrasting Harada's pleated visage is the boyish face of Haruhiko Kato, here playing Detective Tobitaka's number one fan, a crime buff who follows cops around in an SUV tricked out with computers, police radios, and all manner of CSI-type gadgetry. Kato, as you recall, gave a similarly wide-eyed performance the following year as Kawashima, the college student that refuses to acknowledge death (even while staring down the gob of a ghost) in Kiyoshi Kurosawa's most excellent *Pulse*. And last but not least we have the stunning Miwako Ichikawa. Ms. Ichikawa came to movies via modeling (surprise, surprise) and has also appeared in *All About Lily Chou-Chou* (2000) and *Konsento* (2001). She's perfectly cast as Asako, the quintessential Japanese hippy girl, her innocent, childlike character realized in her impossibly cute face (one that verges on the manga-esque) and lithe body, parts of which we glimpse briefly. Adding to her appeal is the fact that she's very good in *Another Heaven,* displaying a talent and range we'll hopefully see more of in the future.

According to *The Dorama Encyclopedia* by Jonathan Clements and Motoko Tamamuro, another *Another Heaven* appeared in 2000, a Japanese TV series entitled *Another Heaven: Eclipse.* Composed of a dozen or so forty-five-minute episodes, the series was penned by Joji Iida (who also directed several installments). In the TV show, the young hero is a private detective (rather than a cop) who enlists the help of a former senior cop colleague (not played by Yoshio Harada, although Harada appears elsewhere in the show). This kind of cross-pollination between TV and cinema is not uncommon in Japan; a show in one medium will often be re-worked in the other soon afterward, if not simultaneously, as in this case.

Earlier I mentioned that, this being a Japanese film, there was a

Manabu smells marinara
with a hint of brain in
Another Heaven

© OMEGA/ ANOTHER HEAVEN

certain measure of ambiguity. This is not to imply that all Japanese films are ambiguous, but ambiguity is certainly a central aspect of Japanese culture. For example, it is customary for the Japanese to keep things vague in communication, to avoid direct questions and direct answers, a convention known as *aimai*. It is perhaps for this reason that *Another Heaven*'s writer/director, Joji Iida, toys with the audience when it comes to just who and what the "something" is. At film's end, you have to pay close attention to really "get it" and even then it's something of a conundrum. Upon my first viewing of the film, I admit I was rather flummoxed; but just like *Suicide Club* (another head-scratcher), *Another Heaven* is not impenetrable. There is an internal logic to the film, but Iida isn't going to give it up just like that. In order to understand and appreciate *Another Heaven*, you have to *think* about it, a refreshing aspect common to many an Asian shocker. Hopefully, the inevitable Hollywood remake will retain some of this quality.

Body Jumper • Pob Weed Sayong

Is all this dark cinema bumming you out? Seen one too many serial killings? Fed to the teeth with cannibalism? Tired of all the torture? I've got just the thing: a Thai horror/comedy, gleefully silly and over the top, yet with enough shocks to make it into this book. Yes, it's *Body Jumper* and it's all about the Pob.

See, Pob is the legendary liver-hungry ghost of Thai folklore. Tradi-

2001

Thailand

90 min.

DIRECTOR: Haeman Chatemee

CAST: Danai Samutkochorn, Angie Grant, Chompunoot Piyapane, Chatewut Watcharakhun, Chaicharn Nimpulsawasdi, Napatsanun Thaweekitthavorn

tionally portrayed as a disgusting old hag, the premise of *Body Jumper* is, "What if old Pob possessed the body of a hot college babe?" That would certainly make it easier for the old girl to get at men's . . . livers! Later, pursued by a group of college students turned high-tech ghostbusters, Pob is forced to jump around to different bodies, hence the title. The ensemble cast are young and crazy and totally committed to delivering the laughs and screams. Let's meet them.

- Gir (Chompunoot Piyapane): She's the Pob, possessed while on a trip to Sam Kotr village, the scene of a Pob exorcism back in 1932. Gir and her friends had traveled to Sam Kotr to help improve the health of the villagers with an exercise regimen (a student outreach effort similar to that in the 2004 Thai actioner *Born to Fight*). One night the guys all go to peep at the comely Gir as she bathes by the river, and wind up falling into the old well where the Pob spirit has been languishing in a round, earthenware jug. Needless to say, the released Pob goes straight into Gir, admiring her new tits on arrival.
- Com (Danai Samutkochorn): Red-headed Com is the first to realize something's up with Gir. He finds a spooky old book in the college library and reads up on the nature of the Pob, becoming convinced that Gir is one. Of course he has a tough time convincing his friends, who all think he's nuts until they eventually see for themselves. . . .
- Fah (Angie Grant): Ostensibly Com's girlfriend, cute, feisty Fah spends most of the film bickering with her moony man, flying into jealous rages every time he looks at Gir. Eventually she realizes that his interest is less carnal than concerned about the fact that every guy Gir dates winds up bright yellow and dead as a doornail.
- Belle (Chatewut Watcharakhun): This muscle-bound drag queen is the most consistently hilarious character in the movie. Each outfit more outlandish than the next, Belle is forever mugging, fussing, sashaying, bitching, preening, and swooning over guys. She is the core of the ensemble cast, the firm, strong shaft from which the other performances shoot forth (er, or something like that . . .).
- Woo (Chaicharn Nimpulsawasdi): Like all college guys, Com's best friend Woo is a horny fellow and the only one in the group to land a date with Gir. He takes her out to a swanky restaurant where she proceeds to order sweet liver, fried chicken liver, raw liver, and duck liver noodles. While he's under the table copping a peek up Gir's dress, she's slurping up all the liver en masse with her serpen-

tine, CG tongue. Back at Woo's pad, Gir/Pob makes her intentions known and Woo just makes it out alive, albeit with bloody claw marks across his back.

- Pim (Napatsanun Thaweekitthavorn): Fah's close friend and loyal member of the gang, Pim is plagued by a pervert in a *Scream* mask and hood who keeps stealing her underwear. Will he be apprehended and his identity revealed before he becomes a liver donor? Probably not.

Additional characters include a black guy with dreadlocks named Kong, a high-tech shaman and ghostbuster supreme; a nerdy fatboy with freckles named Wisant, Pob's first victim; and Kating, a skinny guy with braces who has a morbid fear of geckos. (There's an extended gag in Sam Kotr village where Kating has to go to the outhouse that is, of course, crawling with the little lizards.) There's also a nondescript guy with a hat. As I mentioned earlier, the cast of *Body Jumper* goes all out with antic performances and exaggerated histrionics that approach the cartoonish—think *Scooby Doo* meets *The Goonies*. Yet there's a savvy edge to the film, a knowing wink and nod, that keeps things from veering into the realm of the ridiculous. Haeman Chatemee's smart direction is complimented by the work of production designer Dusit Im-Oum and cinematographer Ruengwit Ramasoota.

Body Jumper is filled with satiric film references, lampooning movies from both East and West. There are a number of cameo appearances by Thai actors as well, that will test your knowledge of Thai film. I recognized Pawalit Mongkolpisit, who played the deaf mute hit man in the Pang Brothers' *Bangkok Dangerous* (1999); Belle grabs his ass at a

Immortal Enemy (Kaew Kon Lek) **(Thailand, 2003)** Looking for a Thai vampire epic? *Immortal Enemy* seems to have it all. You've got a gorgeous location for the shoot: a fabulous mansion on a sprawling estate. You've got impressive CG effects. You've got Winai Kraibutr, star of *Nang Nak* and *Bang Rajan*, lending his presence and class to the role of the vampire. You've even got a big zombie finale featuring a cast of hundreds invading the grounds of the vampire's stately digs, all done up in gloopy makeup. And yet this turgid movie is as plodding and aimless as a zombie, full of pulpy promise, delivering nothing. I had high hopes for this feature, thinking it a great find—boy, was I wrong. Kraibutr plays the spoiled brat son of a village headman who takes a liking to a young married woman and, when his father tells him he can't have her, has his henchmen rip her face off for spite. Thankfully, he's sentenced to death, but he drinks a bubbly concoction of his own design (of course, he's got mad scientist skills), and wakes up a hundred years later a vampire. Another bratty rich kid raises him (with a cheap-looking book of Tibetan spells) and the two wreak uninteresting havoc on the local community. Yawn.

disco and immediately finds a rather large handgun in her face. There are also a couple of janitors, one of whom was in *Bang Rajan* (2000). While most of the comedy is broad and universal enough to keep any audience entertained, as I watched *Body Jumper* I was definitely aware that some of the jokes were going right over my head, and others I did get would elude viewers less knowledgeable about Asian culture. For instance, in addition to horny dude gags like erection-induced rising tables and branches and copious flows of saliva out of open mouths (universal), there was also the issue of nosebleeds. The notion of a woman so attractive that looking at her gives a man a nosebleed is uniquely Asian; in Japan, there's even a physical gesture for it, indicating a hottie in the vicinity. And there are quite a number of bloody noses in *Body Jumper.*

Another unique aspect of *Body Jumper* (in contradistinction to Hollywood) is its use of a traditional folkloric figure for its monster. While American filmmakers might turn to the gothic horror traditions of Europe or create contemporary bogeymen like Freddy and Jason, the ancient cultures of Asia come with a whole host of ghosts and ghouls that have been scaring the shit out of people for millennia. Such creatures also carry a certain cultural weight; they resonate at a deeper level, ingrained as they are in the national psyche. China has its Gyonsi (vampires), Japan its vengeful female ghosts (from the Ghost of Yotsuya all the way to *The Ring*'s Sadako), and Thailand scores big with both Nang Nak and Pob. Just the idea of a ghost that eats your liver is wild and rife with possibilities for a twenty-first-century horror film. Most of the time in *Body Jumper,* Pob uses her long claws to simply rip out the vital organ through the victim's back. But in one memorable scene in an alley behind a nightclub, the male victim, anticipating untold sexual pleasures, is positioned on all fours, and Pob proceeds to reach right up the unfortunate fellow's fundament to get what she's after. In a daring shot filmed seemingly from within the man's body cavity, we see Pob's clawed hand reaching around for the right organ, at one point coming across what looks like an egg (another culture-specific gag I didn't get?). This incident is witnessed by the gang, finally convincing them that Gir is indeed Pob.

Body Jumper was the film debut of romantic leads Danai Samutkochorn and Angie Grant. Samutkochorn had previously worked in television and went on to star in Thai jungle adventure flick *The Trek* (2003). Angie Grant worked as a model for FRM Model Management in Melbourne, Australia. Many an Asian film geek (myself included) is eagerly awaiting another film appearance from this alluring, mixed-race beauty. And if you've seen the mind-boggling Muay Thai martial arts film *Ong Bak* you may (or may not) recognize Chatewut Watcharakhun, our Miss Belle. In *Ong Bak,* Watcharakhun played the very macho gang leader who chased Tony Jaa through the backstreets of Bangkok (providing impetus for the amazing Mr. Jaa's astounding acrobatics). For those only aware of Watcharakhun in that role, his turn as Belle is the epitome of "a role that will surprise you."

Before ending, a note on language: As you know, the Thai language has its own phonetic alphabet, making for all sorts of variations when Thai words are rendered into English. Hence, the Thai title of *Body Jumper, Pop Weed Sayong*—if it's "Pop," why have I been saying "Pob" all this time? In fact, it even says "Pop" on the cover of the book Com consults while investigating Gir. Some sources even translate the title as *Porp Weed Sayong.* So which is it, Pop, Porp, or Pob? I went with Pob for two reasons: (1) That's how the subtitles spell it, and (2) if you listen, that's how all the characters pronounce the name. Looking at the Thai letters that spell Pob, you can see the third letter is different from the first; the first is sounded as "p" while the third is either "p" or "b," so I don't wanna hear any lip from anybody that I don't know how to pronounce the name of that liver-hungry ghost. Now if you'll excuse me, all this talk of liver has made me a bit peckish for organ meat. Mmm, *organ meat!*

Evil Dead Trap • Shiryo no wana

1988
Japan
102 min.
DIRECTOR: Toshiharu Ikeda

CAST: Miyuki Ono, Yuji Honma, Aya Katsuragi, Hitomi Kobayashi, Eriko Nakagawa, Masahiko Abe, Mari Shimizu

"Everything looks dead around here."
"It won't be so bad. You'll see."

You might have heard that *Evil Dead Trap* was a routine American-style '80s slasher flick, a tepid affair concerning the now-standard unstoppable killer picking off the horny and the helpless one by one. But you heard wrong. While the bare bones of the film do indeed rely on this cookie-cutter plot, do not forget that this film was made in Japan, a country far, far away from Hollywood culturally as well as geographically. Japanese filmmakers have their own ideas about how to make a horror film, as evidenced by the millennial J-horror explosion of films like *Ringu, Audition, Pulse,* and *Ju-on.* But the exquisite blood ruby that is *Evil Dead Trap,* aside from predating them all, is in fact a hyperintense hybrid of U.S., Japanese, and *Italian* horror; *giallo* master Dario Argento casts a long, dark shadow over the picture, alongside spiritual brothers John Carpenter and Sam Raimi. In the end, the film is noth-

Gag ball blues: *Evil Dead Trap*

ing short of a multicultural terror tour de force, featuring gruesome, brilliantly rendered sound and imagery that will stay with you to your last dying gasp.

The setting: a dreary, disused army base. The U.S. soldiers have long since departed, the compound now a squalid ensemble of dilapidated structures within whose decaying entrails lurks a sinister figure in camo-colored raincoat and combat boots. It's the kind of location David Fincher might fancy for a sequel to *Se7en*. Yes, it is the titular trap, but every trap needs bait, and this one is no different. It comes in the form of a videotape. Now before you J-horror dilettantes start nodding knowingly, rest assured this tape contains no spooky wells or women combing their hair. This one is straight snuff: a girl, bound, on the business end of a large knife. I won't go into the sickening details, but suffice to say the tape provides *Evil Dead Trap* with one hell of an *eye-popping* opener.

The videotape is sent to one Nami Tsuchiya (Miyuki Ono), host of the popular TV show for insomniacs, "Late Night with Nami." A segment of Nami's show regularly features tapes sent in by viewers, but the submissions haven't been very good of late, and Nami chastises her audience accordingly. Hence the snuff tape, which immediately gets her attention. She decides to investigate. Using classic, ill-advised slasher film logic, she heads for the old army base, guided by how-to-get-there footage thoughtfully included on the videotape. Could this be a trap? None of the investigative team seems to wonder. Upon arrival they split off into easily murderable units of ones and twos.

The team includes:

- Rei (Hitomi Kobayashi): Prissy and petite, she's Nami's makeup and costume person. She's been having an unsuccessful affair with assistant director Kondou (he's got performance issues) and is not very happy about having to muck about in this dirty old compound with him. "Stop talking about your penis," she chides him, "you're supposed to be working now."
- Kondou (Masahiko Abe): He's a horror movie fan and incorrigible jokester, jumping out of nowhere with his stupid plastic fangs and providing many of the cheap-shot scares at the front end of the film. Poking around the dark corners of a dirty old building turns out to be just the thing to revive his flagging sexual powers, and

soon he and Rei are having a steamy, multiposition encounter in the midst of the rubble. Hope they enjoyed it. . . .

- Masako (Aya Katsuragi): Her job is unclear. At the outset she appears to be Nami's scriptwriter; "Are you calling my script nerdy?" she asks Kondou indignantly. However she's later identified as Nami's sound engineer. Go figure. Just think of her as Victim #4. She brings her camera along, and the killer eventually gets hold of it, using it for a nice strobe effect as he attacks her in the dark.
- Rya (Eriko Nakagawa): Pretty in pink, her role on the show is not clear until the end, when she's posthumously honored as the former scriptwriter (which seems unlikely, as she's a fluffy bunny of a girl, more suited to light clerical duties and the odd errand). Her demise is not as creative as others, but is nevertheless the most Argentoesque in its swiftness and brutality.

There's also a mysterious stranger (Yuji Honma) who appears periodically to offer cryptic advice (as well as a swig from his flask). He wears a black suit and *setta* sandals and seems to know more than he's telling, particularly when it comes to his troubled brother Hideki. . . . Also present is the boyfriend (Mari Shimizu) of the snuff tape girl, now in thrall to Raincoat Guy and transformed into a homicidal rapist (a fact one of the ladies will unfortunately discover the hard way).

What sets *Evil Dead Trap* apart from the scores of U.S. slasher films made in the '80s is its revelry in Grand Guignol excess, making films like *Friday the 13th* and *Halloween* seem pedestrian by comparison. While its American cousins tended to keep people and events primarily in the realm of the real, director Toshiharu Ikeda introduces elements of the fantastic early on, like gigantic metal spikes that shoot out from the walls and floor, impaling one of the ladies. Rather than the product of some ingenious device, these imposing implements seem to spring from another dimension, infernal prongs of doom thrusting forth to skewer pathetic humans. In any case, there's no way one guy in a raincoat could manage such a maneuver, but Ikeda pulls the scene off with such swagger and cinematic bravura that one is too transfixed to quibble over such mundane concerns.

All this is not to deny the presence of standard genre tropes throughout *Evil Dead Trap*. There are the aforementioned cheap shots (scares that come from taut nerves rather than a genuine threat) and people wandering off by themselves (as well as walking backward in order to turn around suddenly into something frightful). The Big Dark House paradigm is in place of course, as is the convention of the killer whisking away the corpses of his victims, only to produce them later in some grotesque display guaranteed to scare the bejesus out of the remaining cast (and us). And there is the false ending, wherein the killer is vanquished, the danger has passed, and we can all finally relax and—oh no, he's back! (Not to be outdone, Toshiharu Ikeda appends either three or four false endings, depending how you count them, to the back end of the picture.) But the textbook aspects of the splatter film are only the starting point for *Evil Dead Trap*'s mayhem, rather than, as is the case with so many lesser offerings, the sum total of the film itself.

As with all great shockers, music makes all the difference. Tomohiko Kira's score, while played entirely on synthesizer (the '80s again), is evocative of the themes provided by Italian prog rock group Goblin for Argento's *Profondo Rosso* (1975) and *Tenebrae* (1982), particularly the creepy 7/8 melody that serves as *Evil Dead Trap*'s primary murder motif. Anyone familiar with these *giallo* classics will find the music, as well as the way in which the murders are lovingly filmed (lingering, fetishistic close-ups) and executed (sudden, graphic jolts of violence), an unmistakable homage to the great Italian master.

Evil Dead Trap screenwriter Takashi Ishii's childhood dream was to be a film director, but, due to a unique chain of events, he became a popular manga artist first. Then, as fate would have it, his Angel Guts manga series got the attention of Nikkatsu Studios; he was hired to adapt some installments for films, opening the door to a screenwriting gig. He finally got his shot at directing with 1988's *Angel Guts: Red Vertigo* and by the '90s was an established director of such uncompromising films as *A Night in the Nude* (1993), *Gonin* (1995), *The Black Angel* (1997), and *Freeze Me* (2000). Even if you didn't know that *Evil Dead Trap* was penned by Ishii, the lead character's name is a tip off. Says Ishii:

Guinea Pig: Devil's Experiment (Za ginipiggu: Akuma no jikken) (Japan, 1988) No wonder real snuff films cost so much—the fake ones are crap! *Devil's Experiment,* the first of the infamous Guinea Pig films, is a case in point. From a strict gore-hound perspective, there are only a couple of real money shots (some fingernail extraction, a punctured eyeball). The rest is padding. Not that I really need to see this sort of thing in the first place; no story, no characters, just a woman being tortured and eventually killed (?) by three guys dressed in black wearing shades (so you won't recognize them, get it?). The upshot is, for such a *notorious* film, this forty-five-minute, shot-on-video bit of deviant nastiness is, above all, just plain dull. How long can you sit and watch a woman slapped, kicked, pinched with pliers, burned with hot oil and on and on? And the "victim" is no actress. Where a real person would be screaming bloody murder, this girl mews like a frightened tree, rendering the proceedings even more tiresome. The makeup effects are good, though—hook the FX guys up with a decent writer and director and you might have something. But as it is, *Devil's Experiment* is just an unpleasant waste of time.

I used the same name—Nami—for the female character in all my scripts. There isn't any special reason for it. It's not my wife's name. The "Nami" [of my manga] resembles my wife, so it was as if I were drawing my wife. Since she died of cancer four years ago, I can't write the name down anymore. Losing my wife ended my relationship with Nami. (*Asian Cult Cinema* #47, 2005, pp. 37–38)

Special effects man Shinichi Wakasa did a lot with very little in *Evil Dead Trap,* the budget a mere 60 million yen (roughly half a million dollars U.S.). You won't be disappointed though, particularly during the mind-boggling multiple endings when we learn the true nature of Hideki (Ishii's original script had him as a junior high school kid, but by the time Ikeda got finished with him, um . . . let's just say he has a lot in common with a certain homuncular character in a certain Hollywood sci-fi film in which a certain muscular actor utters the immortal line, "Get your ass to Mars!"). Wakasa went on to become the rubber suit maker for over a dozen *kaiju-eiga* (giant monster movie) remakes throughout the '90s, including *Mothra* (1996) and *Godzilla 2000* (1999). Wakasa re-teamed with Ikeda for *Evil Dead Trap 3* (1993).

Starring as Nami, Miyuki Ono was chosen by Toshiharu Ikeda because she resembled Sigourney Weaver. Of course, she could act as well, a talent of which Ikeda was not so sure when it came to his producers' first choice for the lead, Hitomi Kobayashi (who wound up playing Rei). Ms. Kobayashi was then the reigning adult home video queen for Japan Home Video (the outfit bankrolling the picture) and the boys at JHV wanted to showcase her and Eriko Nakagawa (another hot property) in the film, hence their obligatory sex scenes. Genre purists have complained that the sex takes away from the film, making it unworthy of true classic status, a ridiculous notion. *Evil Dead Trap* is a genre-buster, transcending slasher horror conventions. And besides, sexually active young people are *always* getting murdered in such films—it's a puritanical prerequisite! Here the sex is just more explicit. Ikeda handles the steamy segments like a pro, coming as he did from Nikkatsu, where he honed his craft making the studio's signature "roman porno" (romantic pornography).

If you're into horror, Japanese cult films, or *giallo,* check out *Evil Dead Trap.* There's a unique mélange on offer here, and some may find it too rich for their palate. But for the discerning *gore-mand,* it is a feast for the senses.

8

HELLHELLHELLHELL

This is it folks: the end of the line. You started off in the questionable embrace of your family, grew to adulthood in a warped society filled with frightening technology, only to experience confinement, psychosis, and possession. And now you're going to Hell. But don't worry, you won't be alone. Not by a long shot! Hell is jam-packed with writhing moaners impaled on stakes or drowning in lakes of fire—misery loves company! Not to mention the folks inhabiting living hells involving voodoo curses, rape, torture, and a horny sex demon whose rutting has the unfortunate tendency of ripping his partners in half. Hell is where you find it, and in this chapter you'll find it just about everywhere.

Hell • Jigoku

You who are dead, this is the first great hell of fire. Here flesh is peeled, bones crushed, eyes plucked, and limbs severed. For each time you cry out you are returned to life to face the torments of hell again.

Oh, great, just what you want to hear. That's going to make getting up in the morning a special experience. And while the first hour of *Jigoku* (I prefer the Japanese title) takes place in the earthly realm (the last forty minutes comprising a gruesome grand tour of the netherworld),

1960

Japan

100 min.

DIRECTOR: Nobuo
Nakagawa

CAST: Shigeru Amachi,
Utako Mitsuya, Yoichi
Numata, Utako
Mitsuya, Torahiko
Nakamura, Fumiko
Mitaya, Akiko Ono,
Hiroshi Hayashi, Akiko
Yamashita, Jun Otomo,
Tomohiko Otomo,
Koichi Miya, Teranori
Niimiya, Hiroshi
Izumida, Kimie
Tokudaiji

one gets the distinct impression that the Earth-bound sequences aren't really playing out on Earth at all but in some remote corner of the dark plane, a nightmare funhouse mirror reflection of a life lived on Earth countless ages ago. After all, part of the whole horror of Hell is actually *going* there, so what better way to reinforce the experience than to eternally shuttle back and forth, reliving your pathetic life and then descending into the abyss again and again? Director Nobuo Nakagawa doesn't make this explicit, but there are certainly clues, such as the quote above, scenes at the outset of the protagonist actually falling into the flames, as well as the presence of an eerie, clearly demonic character who continuously pops up out of nowhere to start trouble, even after we've witnessed his death. But I'm getting ahead of myself here. . . .

I'll start again: Nobuo Nakagawa's classic film, *Jigoku,* is unlike any horror film you've ever seen. Imagine Luis Bunuel interpreting Dante by way of Hieronymus Bosch and you start to get the picture. It is a *disorienting* film. Horror master Nakagawa fully exploits the power of disorientation through sound and image (jarring noises, jump cuts, upside-down and sideways camera, bizarre lighting, O.T.T. performances) to put the audience in a vulnerable state. You're never quite sure of your footing here; in fact it's more a feeling of suspension, of your feet not touching the ground at all. And, like all great works of art, it's somewhat confounding the first time around, offering more and more with each return visit.

There are also quite a number of characters, their fates intertwined, so perhaps we should meet them now:

- Shiro Shimizu (Shigeru Amachi): The central figure, a lugubrious, perpetually frowning college student. He's depressed and wracked with guilt over the inadvertent deaths of a drunken yakuza and his own sweetheart, for which he feels responsible. But is he?
- Tamura (Yoichi Numata): A fellow student and Shiro's unwanted pal/personal demon, this obnoxious bad penny is never far from our hero, getting him into all sorts of trouble and generally making his life miserable. Tamura was driving the car that hit that drunken yakuza, Shiro merely the passenger. However, Shiro feels partly responsible and Tamura does everything to reinforce the feeling.
- Yukiko (Utako Mitsuya): Shiro's girlfriend. She meets her doom early on, in a taxi that swerves suddenly and plows into a telephone pole—death cab for cutie. But did you see that? Just for a split second the cabby became Tamura, then switched back. Hmm. . . .

- Mr. and Mrs. Yajima (Torahiko Nakamura and Fumiko Mitaya): Yukiko's parents. Dad is one of Shiro's professors at college. The couple was overjoyed in anticipation of Shiro and Yukiko's pending nuptials. Then mom lost her mind from the grief of losing Yukiko. Also, Tamura has some dirt on Prof. Yajima, an unsavory incident that occurred back in World War II.

- Yoko (Akiko Ono): Junkie ex-girlfriend of "Tiger" Kyoichi, the dead yakuza. She and Tiger's mama-san (Hiroshi Izumida) are out for revenge on Tiger's killers (mama-san witnessed the hit-and-run). After picking up the grief-stricken Shiro in a nightclub, Yoko figures out who he is—and that he's one of the men she's after. And she has a gun. . . .

- Kozo Shimizu (Hiroshi Hayashi): Shiro's dad and a real piece of work. This lowlife runs the Tenjoen Senior Citizen's Facility, a third-rate old folks home where he lives with his mistress while his wife Ito (Kimie Tokudaiji) quietly wastes away in the next room.

- Kinuko (Akiko Yamashita): She's the mistress, a goofy, flirty chatterbox who longs to return to Tokyo, hopefully with her new heartthrob, Shiro.

- Ensai Taniguchi (Jun Otomo): He's an old, drunken painter living at the Senior Citizen's Facility. He spends his days drinking and painting portraits of Hell for the local Buddhist temple. He also has a bit of a past with Shiro's mother. . . .

- Sachiko (Utako Mitsuya): Ensai's daughter and the spitting image of Yukiko (played by the same actress with a slightly different hairdo). When Shiro comes to stay at the "Facility" for a while to tend to his dying mother, he's struck by Sachiko's resemblance to

Hell (Jigoku) (Japan, 1999) Oh, dear. This piss-poor remake of Nobuo Nakagawa's netherworld classic is not the kind of tedious nonsense for which director Teruo Ishii should be remembered. God bless Ishii, he made some fine films in his day, but this ain't one of them; perhaps at seventy-five he was just pooped out. This *Jigoku* starts out OK; some trippy-looking demons have fun chopping up a child molester with a big saw. But soon the film grinds to a halt, becoming mired in an extended subplot concerning the Aum Shinrikyo cult and its sarin gas attacks of 1994 and 1995. Ishii travels well-worn tracks, offering plenty of T&A, but soon even nubile young flesh can't alleviate the boredom of dozens of underdeveloped cultist characters and their muddled machinations. By the time they finally go to Hell to be skinned alive and have their tongues ripped out, who cares? We're so bored, it's beyond anticlimactic. To add insult to injury, a cameo for Japanese film veteran Tetsuro Tamba is clumsily shoehorned in at the end of the film; he shows up in the underworld looking old as the hills in a shiny black wig, slices some demons with his sword and wanders off. Huh?

Yukiko and the two are soon falling in love. But that could be a big mistake!

- Doctor Kusama (Tomohiko Otomo): Resident quack doctor at the old folk's home, he's responsible for countless deaths due to malpractice or disregard. A real class act.
- Akigawa (Koichi Miya): He's a sleazy, one-eyed reporter whose stories have caused harm. Kozo's crony, he spends a lot of time hanging out at the old folk's home.
- Haiya (Teranori Niimiya): A corrupt cop. Like Akigawa, his professional and personal choices have resulted in the deaths of others. He's always hanging around with Akigawa, Dr. Kusama, Kozo, and the rest, a real motley assortment of scoundrels.

After a night of partying at the Senior Citizen's Facility, events suddenly conspire to the ultimate disadvantage of all involved, and soon everyone goes straight to Hell. The Great King Enma, ruler of the netherworld, shows them around the place and gets them acquainted with the various unpleasantries that await them. There is the Sanzu no Kawa (River of Death), upon whose bank (the Sai no Kawara) the spirits of children are punished for the sin of dying before their parents. They pile up stones by day, only to have the demons come around and kick them down every night. Eventually, a child's stone pile will turn into the Bodhisattva Jizo and take the kid to Heaven.

Not so lucky are the adults who are here to stay. They can look forward to being tortured by big, hairy demons with axes and clubs chopping and crushing them to bits forever. Prof. Yajima is forced to relive his dark moment back in the war, when he stole a dying fellow soldier's water. He crawls across a desert dying of thirst himself, accompanied by other thirsty souls, only to be directed to a bubbly, viscous-looking river and told by King Enma: "This is the pus wrung out of your festering carcasses and a cesspool of your foul wastes. Drink all you wish!" Elsewhere, Gozo and Kinuko are boiled, Gozo is flayed, Kinuko is beheaded, and both get their teeth bashed in by club-wielding demons. Dr. Kusama is sawn in half (great grimace and guttural scream work here from actor Tomohiko Otomo). Also, the bad policeman gets his hands chopped off and the journalist gets his good eye popped out.

Other attractions include the Lake of Blood (a nasty swim for nasty people guilty of "adultery, lust, license, and lechery"), the Field of Long Spikes (my name for it—Shiro gets a big one right through his foot), and a couple of gigantic eight-spoked Buddhist wheels (one aflame). As you may know, these wheels can symbolize the Noble Eightfold

Hell (Jigoku)

Path (which leads to enlighten-ment) or the Wheel of Birth and Death (symbolizing reincarnation). In any case, they stand as ironic reminders that the whole concept of "Buddhist Hell" is completely at odds with the teachings of the Bud-dha, just like Jesus Christ didn't go around preaching about the tor-ments of Hell—he was all about the Kingdom of Heaven. Nevertheless, every culture has its own elaborate mythology concerning the myriad tortures and eternal suffering of Hell. It keeps the peasants in line and makes for a great horror movie, so what the . . . hell!

Shigeru Amachi turns in a solid performance as the tortured Shiro, providing an emotional through-line of guilt, sadness, angst, and re-pulsion. He is the only character in the film that shows any hint of mo-rality, but even he is compromised, drawing a similarity to Dr. Germain in Henri-Georges Clouzot's 1943 masterpiece of misanthropy, *Le Cor-beau*. Samurai film fans will know Amachi as the tubercular ronin Hirate in the first Zatoichi movie, *The Tale of Zatoichi*, as well as Raizo Ichikawa's *real* father in Kenji Misumi's classic chambara *Destiny's Son* (both 1962). Nobuo Nakagawa devotees will certainly recognize Amachi from such films as *The MP and the Ghost* (1958), *The Lady Vampire* (1959), and the legendary *The Ghost of Yotsuya* (1959).

Filling in on campy villainy and hammy dementia is Yoichi Nu-mata as Tamura, Shiro's unwanted friend—or is that fiend? His face is usually lit from below in spooky blues and greens, a big indicator that he's not of this earth, or at least hasn't been for awhile. If you're good with faces, you'll recognize Numata as the old innkeeper with a dark se-cret in Hideo Nakata's original *The Ring* (*Ringu*, 1998). Here he's thirty-eight years younger, full of exuberance and wild mania, and proceeds to chew up the scenery and steal every scene. His own torments down in

PAT GALLOWAY'S PRIVATE COLLECTION

King Enma, Lord Host of the Fiery Netherworld

Jigoku are particularly memorable.

As mentioned earlier, the secret of *Jigoku*'s success is in its ability to disorient the audience. The film sustains a weird, disaffected feeling, reinforced by the odd dichotomy of Amachi's existential sullenness and Numata's antic mischief. Even before the story begins, the director has already started in on us. The first image in the movie is that of a lone coffin, then the coffin going into the crematorium. Next, however, it's as if we've been spliced into a completely different movie as the opening credit sequence presents naked girls and wild, busy jazz, along with screams, sirens, gunfire—WTF? This can be interpreted as depicting sinfulness that will be paid for later in the nether regions, but really it's just Nakagawa messing with our heads. Soon enough he's back to images of corpses and a narrator solemnizing, "Once drawn by that merciless wind, the fair youth of morning is at dusk naught but bones . . ."

Enhancing the alienated vibe of the film, sudden, irrational shifts in the action occur, subverting the narrative. Nakagawa uses this technique to keep you off guard, off balance, unsure. Then there's the way the story in the old folks' home seems to go on a bit too long, the listlessness of the atmosphere there—it's all calculated to create in the audience a sense of ennui that Nakagawa can then shatter as he plunges us down into the fiery depths. Sound is used to jarring effect, as when Shiro is walking along the silent train tracks in *geta* clogs and suddenly the scene jump-cuts to a train just missing him in mid-blare. The sudden shift from safety to narrowly avoided danger and corresponding bombast gives a shock and breaks the laws of film narrative. But breaking rules is what great art is all about.

In creating the unforgettable experience that is *Jigoku,* credit must be given to composer Chumei Watanabe for the wonderfully creepy score and production designer Haruyasu Kurosawa for Dante-esque visions of never-ending pain and woe. These two men were also instrumental in the previous year's *The Ghost of Yotsuya,* Nakagawa's other acknowledged masterpiece. For anyone who ever shuddered at the thought of eternal damnation, *Jigoku* will provide a terrifying, bone-chilling sneak peek.

Living Hell • Iki-jigoku

2000

Japan

104 min.

DIRECTOR: Shugo Fujii

CAST: Hirohito Honda, Yoshiko Shiraishi, Naoko Mori, Rumi, Kazuo Yashiro, Shugo Fujii, Hitoshi Suwabe, Noboru Mitani, Sei Hiraizumi

Couples who are fighting don't usually eat their dogs or stick bugs into eye sockets.

Thus speaks the inspector (Sei Hiraizumi) at the scene of the crime, and he's right. We know he's right because it's two-and-a-half minutes into the movie and we've just witnessed the heinous crimes of which he speaks. A married couple was done in by a feral young woman (who feasted on the poor dog) and her psychotic old granny (who held a stag beetle to the woman's eye and then did the man in with a hammer).

So begins *Living Hell.* Take Alfred Hitchcock's *Psycho,* Robert Aldrich's *What Ever Happened to Baby Jane?,* and Brian De Palma's *Sisters,* put them in a blender, add a generous dollop of J-horror (investigative reporter, generation-spanning backstory, vengeful ghost—alright, there's no vengeful ghost, but there is a ghostly, homicidal old woman), plus psychological and physical torture, and you've got the recipe for a wicked little blood feast. Director Shugo Fujii was going for a cross "between Japanese-style and American-style films. A lot of Japanese horror films are ghost stories, like *Ringu,* for instance. A lot of American horror films deal with serial killers and things like that. So I wanted to do something in between these two genres" (Rudy Joggerst, "Shugo Fujii's Own Living Hell," http://www.reel.com).

Shot in nine days (with another week for post production) for $100,000, it's a low-budget gem, shot through with creativity and verve reminiscent of Robert Rodriguez's *El Mariachi.*

It should be stated at the outset that *Living Hell* has something of a Chinese puzzle box plot, revelations coming continuously throughout the film, and while I try to never give away an ending, even discussing half the film will spoil some of the surprises, so you might want to stop reading now.

For those of you still with me, I'll start with a breakdown of the main characters:

- Yasuhito (Hirohito Honda): A neurotic young man, Yasu is wheelchair-bound, his infirmity a symptom of his chronic anxiety. He is sullen and peevish and his life is about to take a turn for the worse with the arrival of . . .
- Chiyo (Yoshiko Shiraishi): At first glance she appears to be a near-catatonic old woman in a kimono, her face deathly pale and expressionless yet somehow deeply disturbing. She's supposedly a distant relative and comes to live in Yasu's home along with . . .
- Yuki (Naoko Mori): This one is just downright freaky. Beyond skinny, she is positively skeletal, with a face like a junky punker and a ghoulish vibe that contrasts yet compliments her "grandmother" Chiyo. The two have been invited to stay with Yasu's family by . . .
- Father (Hitoshi Suwabe): We don't see much of dad through most of the movie, as he works in Osaka during the week and only comes home on weekends. But there's more to dad than meets the eye. Along with Yasu, his other children include . . .
- Mami (Rumi): She's your average pretty young Japanese girl, horrified at the news that relatives are coming to stay, as this will make her the default cook/maid/hostess. She'll be more horrified before they're through. In addition to Yasu, she has another brother . . .
- Ken (Kazuo Yashiro): Right at the outset Ken comes off as a prick. He knew about the houseguests for a week before he told Mami, one day before their arrival. However, he believes it's important to help those in need and supports his father's decision to invite Chiyo and Yuki into the household. Does he have an ulterior motive? He works with . . .
- Mitsutake (Shugo Fujii): A reporter for a tabloid magazine, he's the new guy trying to establish himself with a story about a homicidal granny who's wanted for murdering a couple with her granddaughter (hey, this is where we came in!) after escaping from a mental institution. He's got a lead on the whereabouts of her son, who happens to be named Ken, and his editor sends a senior reporter along with him who happens to be named Ken. . . .

Living Hell alternates between Mitsutake's investigation and Yasu's experience home alone with Chiyo and Yuki, who take a deadpan delight in torturing the ill-fated invalid. The two psychopaths start small, pinching him and pulling his hair, and steadily escalate the torment, em-

Old Chiyo and her trusty stun gun, *Living Hell*

ploying worms, darts, pliers, a stun gun, a mallet, hot sauce, and salt. For lunch, they serve him roaches and his own pet bird over rice (no, this film is not pet-friendly, but the dead pet props are rather fakey-looking, making these scenes less disturbing for animal lovers).

Meanwhile, Mitsutake meets with an old professor (Noboru Mitani), who fills him in on the real story behind Chiyo. It seems she had her first child at the age of forty-three, a depraved little sociopath named Ken who, at the age of nine, somehow managed to overpower a nurse and subject her to vile mutilations. Around this time, Chiyo participated in strange medical experiments conducted by a mysterious Dr. Kurando. As a result of the experiments, she gave birth to conjoined twins. Where are these twins now? They'd be twenty-two years old by now. Yasu is twenty-two. So is Yuki. Hmm. Will Mitsutake put together all the pieces and do something before poor Yasu winds up dead or hopelessly insane? Or will our intrepid reporter become a victim himself?

Living Hell features Hirohito Honda, whom you'll remember from his brief-but-memorable appearance as Boys #16 Niida, the vicious loser with the crossbow who hits on (and is subsequently emasculated by) Chiaki Kuriyama in *Battle Royale*. He acts with his mouth a bit too much in this movie—the greater his horror, the wider his gob. However, his screams are satisfyingly blood-curdling and his desperation as the vulnerable Yasu is palpable. Yoshiko Shiraishi (the director's aunt) plays Chiyo like a Unit 731 doctor: cold and methodical, bringing home the stark reality of the compassionless, blank-faced torturer, infinitely more terrifying than the gleefully sadistic variety. The same goes for Naoko Mori's Yuki, but the actress's severely emaciated body and straw-like black hair take her one step beyond into the realm of the supernatural—she is a wraith or some kind of insect spirit assisting Chiyo in her wicked work. Kazuo Yashiro's mobile facial features get a workout as he gradually morphs from staid regular guy into the *real* Ken. And be sure to keep an eye out for Sei Hiraizumi as the inspector; an experienced character actor (*Violent Cop, Postman Blues, The Eel*) and all 'round cool guy, he appeared in the film for free as a favor to the director. His two appearances bookend the film, lending gravitas and credibility.

Director Shugo Fujii spent ten years in the United States during which time he graduated from the California Institute of Arts with a film degree. Looking at his short films (which are all on the *Living Hell* DVD) one can see that he's got the goods, and, given a more generous budget, could have done a lot more with the project. For this reason, the rather ambitious revelation at the end of the picture (think *Fight Club* or *The Sixth Sense*) doesn't come off as well as it could have, and when you go back and watch it again, knowing what you know now, there are inconsistencies that a little more time and a few reshoots would have cleared up. This is no reflection on the abilities of the director; it's just what happens when you've got a shoestring budget and two weeks to make a film. That said, it's remarkable what Fujii does do with a hundred grand, hardly enough to cover the craft services in Hollywood. He does as much with his camera as possible (extreme angles, lighting tricks, dolly/zooms, montage, effects with mirrors, reflective surfaces, and beveled glass), and the synthesizer-based score has a pounding intensity, at times sounding like the dominant synth theme from Dario Argento's *giallo* classic *Tenebrae*. And the casting is brilliant. How he got such sheer creepiness out of two women standing motionless before the camera is amazing. You'll never get the image of those two frightening females out of your head.

So enjoy *Living Hell*. Come for the torture, stay for the story, grapple with the bizarre denouement, then watch it all over again. Invite grandma. On second thought, better not.

Erotic Ghost Story II • Liao zhai yan tan xu ji zhi wu tong shen

What can I say? I can't get enough of Anthony Wong, and *Erotic Ghost Story II* features one of his all-time great performances as the all-snarling, all-biting, all-fucking sex demon Wu Tung. If you only know Wong from his role as the charismatic cop in *Infernal Affairs*, this grotesque, funny, sexy little film will turn you out good and proper.

Right away you know it's a sequel (it's got that "II" in the title), but this film bears little resemblance to its predecessor. In the first film, Wu Tung was played by Tan Lap Man (another actor who, like An-

1991

Hong Kong

97 min.

DIRECTOR: Peter Ngor
Chi Kwan

CAST: Anthony Wong
Chau Sang, Charine
Chan Ka Ling, Kwok
Yiu Wah, Noelle Chik
King Man, Chang Siu
Yin

thony Wong, moonlighted as a rock musician) and had a very different MO—he spent the movie seducing a trio of fairy sisters in the guise of a humble student. This time out, Wu Tung is a full-on force of fornicating evil, ravaging women so fiercely that, at one point, he tears one in two! No matter, he keeps pumping away on the lower half. That's one horny demon! I should add that Wong is sporting a huge white wig, kabuki makeup, and big shoulder pads, giving him a decidedly late-'80s heavy metal hair band look. Turn down the volume, throw on some vintage Ratt or Cinderella and *voilà!* Instant rock video. And Wong is so deliriously hammy as Wu Tung, so completely dedicated to his role, that his shenanigans go right past verisimilitude into real porno territory. In one scene, biting the flesh of the latest virgin offered up to him by the inhabitants of the local village, you can clearly see he's not messing around; Wong is biting the hell out of that girl. In fact, the sex scenes in *Erotic Ghost Story II* are so extended and elaborate that at some point you have the thought that these people might as well be penetrating one another. Why not? How on earth *aren't* they? Were the craft services people dosing all the food with saltpeter?

When Wu Tung wants to walk around amongst the humans, he takes the form of mortal Chiu Sheng (all these name spellings are taken from the subtitles which appear to be the Mandarin forms, even though the dialog is in Cantonese; I apologize for the inconsistency). Chiu Sheng's appearance is toned way down from the fabulous camp glam of Wu Tung, but he's still got a stunning electric blue eye makeup and lipstick combo going. This seems to please lovely Yu Yin (Charine Chan), who is, in fact, the reincarnation of his lost mortal love, Hsaio Yen (the opening scene shows a head-over-heels Chiu Sheng expressing his affection by actually licking Hsaio Yen's *eyeball* to the bedroom tones of a smarmy sax). Since their love was forbidden, two fairy fox spirits were sent down to burn lovely Hsaio Yen on a cross "to prevent lust from ruining mankind." However, right as Wu Tung is running one of the lovely fairies through with a large plastic sword, the other one manages to retrieve Hsaio Yen's "spirit pill" from the incinerating body and toss it into the womb of a woman nearby. Just in time, too, as the woman was going into labor. The child, Yu Yin, is born with a glowing, purple birthmark that later turns out to be a magic talisman capable of defeating Wu Tung.

But wait, there's more. In Feng Yueh village they've been making regular offerings of virgins to Wu Tung (at first they're said to be monthly but later it shifts to yearly—I think "monthly" was a bad subtitle, yearly sounds more reasonable). They have an annual lottery and if you get the little red piece of paper with the big zero on it, that's it for your daughter. She gets stripped naked, greased up to a glistening sheen, and a topless lady shaman does a spastic, vaguely Sapphic death dance around her, all the while chanting "ya ya ya-ya-ya." Then our victim takes a ride on a sedan chair, gets dumped on the outskirts of town, and Wu Tung eventually spirits her away. Back at Wu Tung's cave, a demon lady dances around and drips hot candle wax on her breasts. This is supposed to be Wu Tung's other half, the yin to his yang or some such thing (it's a little muddled), but she seems to be more of a companion/servant. She and Wu Tung "make use of virginal humors to attain everlasting life."

So the routine is this: Wu Tung rips the virgin's clothes off with his teeth, growls, snarls, makes mouths, bites (very hard), wrinkles his nose, juts his jaw, bares his teeth, the whole bestial bit. He's got a funny tail that looks like a big dildo; it comes in handy for the inevitable three-way (the virgin in front, the demon lover around back).

Meanwhile, after twenty years or so, little Yu Yin has grown into a lovely young woman, a fact not missed by hunky fisherman Shan Ken (Kwok Yiu Wah)—one look and he's smitten. Therefore, when she's inevitably chosen for the next Wu Tung sacrifice, Shan Ken's very upset, all the more so as he's been selected as one of the sedan chair-bearers. He does his duty, but later, after much wine, he decides "to hell with this" and grabs his trusty axe. Just as Wu Tung is getting all moony looking at Yu Yin (the smoky sex sax blowing like a nauseating, anachronistic wind), Shan Ken swoops down on a bent tree, gives Wu Tung a whack, and catapults away with Yu Yin.

Shan Ken lives with his brother and sister-in-law, a couple who copulate continuously and supply a good deal of the sex scenes in the

Guts of a Virgin (Shojo no harawata) (Japan, 1986) Back in the '80s, when most slasher filmmakers were spicing up their bloody offerings with a bit of the old in-out, Kazuo Komizu aka Gaira (from the big, green meanie in *War of the Gargantuas*) was thinking just the opposite. Working at Nikkatsu, Gaira decided to up the ante on the studio's line of "roman porno" (romantic pornography) films by adding depraved carnage sequences, resulting in what he called "horror plus eros." And it worked. *Guts* [or *Entrails*] *of a Virgin*, essentially one long fuck-fest interspersed with the occasional impaling, hanging, or beheading, was a hit (although no virgin entrails are actually on offer). The story concerns the members of a photo shoot (sleazy photographer, his sleazier boss, easy models, and maltreated crew) holed up in an old house overnight (you know, it's not like you can just drive in *fog* . . .). Some kind of lust-spawned incubus is prowling around the grounds, picking off the horny group one by one (and doing some diddling of his own). It's all rather sordid and there's a definite misanthropy to the film reminiscent of Henri-Georges Clouzot (*Diabolique*), but somehow the elements click into place, making for an uncomfortable-yet-can't-look-away film experience.

film. At one point they have a ménage à trois with the demon girl, who has come to the village to charge up on sex energy so that she can use it to help heal Wu Tung. He waits recuperating in a large, spiky cocoon. It's a marathon three-way, complimented as it is by an off-camera bubble machine.

I don't want to give everything away, so I'll just say that before it's all over, Shan Ken winds up frozen naked in a block of ice, there's some business with a "soul-taking hairpin," we meet a powerful midget monk (covered in green glitter paint for some reason), the village goes berserk (one fella appears to be doing a pig) and, oh yes, there's that scene where Shan Ken's sister-in-law gets torn in half by Wu Tung. This is particularly distressing to her, as she was enjoying herself and the halving cut off all sensation. What's a girl to do? Did I mention that they were fucking in a bed filled with bubbling blood?

If you only see one film in the Erotic Ghost Story franchise, I'd recommend this one. You've got Anthony Wong, you've got a lot of hot sex, you've got . . . good lord, what haven't you got? If this film doesn't slake your lust for depraved Hong Kong cinema, you're probably a demon like Wu Tung, in which case I'd advise you to watch your tail. . . .

Go, Go Second Time Virgin • *Yuke yuke nidome no shojo*

1969
Japan
65 min.
DIRECTOR: Koji Wakamatsu
CAST: Mimi Kozakura, Michio Akiyama

Can a boy and a girl find love in a nightmare of gang rape, mass murder, and bad beatnik poetry? That's the theme of art house/pink film *Go, Go Second Time Virgin*, a triumph of style-over-budget filmmaking from the "King of the Underground," director Koji Wakamatsu. Wakamatsu's genius lay in his ability to literally make something out of nothing. No script? No budget? No location? No problem, "Waka" needed only an idea. A passionate and iconoclastic filmmaker, he had the power to manifest movies with little more than sheer will. That, and a boatload of creativity. Roughly 90 percent of *Go, Go Second Time Virgin* takes place on the roof of the apartment building where Wakamatsu lived at the time, an expansive cinematic vista compared with 1966's *The Embryo Hunts in Secret*, which took place almost entirely in his apartment. But Wakamatsu found a way to make these pictures work, using unorthodox cinematography, original storylines, plenty of sex and violence, and an emphasis on character.

Disturbingly, the first thing that happens in *Go, Go Second Time Virgin* is a gang bang. We see four youths (including a couple of hippies and a guy in a Gilligan hat) carrying a girl (Mimi Kozakura) up to the roof to have their wicked way with her. As they do so, under the Tokyo night sky, the girl screams *ie* (ee-eh, which means "no") repeatedly and then falls quiet, wincing sporadically with a far-away look in her eyes and, finally, a tear. A boy with glasses who has followed the group up to the roof (Michio Akiyama) looks on passively, not participating, then masturbates. A creepy, droning female voice sings soft and low over the proceedings.

The rapists finally leave, but the girl continues to lie on the cement roof, unable or unwilling to move. Until now the film has been shot in black and white, but the girl flashes back to a previous rape on a beach and the scene plays out through a filter of electric blue. The film shifts back to black and white as morning arrives—bells ring, a housewife hangs her laundry out to dry, and the girl is still lying in the same spot, watched by the boy with the glasses. Finally she sits up. "August 8th. Morning." She examines a puddle of blood on the pavement between her legs. "I'm still alive." She notices the boy. "Ohayo!" (Good Morning!), she says sweetly. The boy stares, catatonic. "This is the second time I've been raped," she tells him.

The boy and girl stand at the railing and look down at the world below: the cars, buildings, sidewalk scenes—the urban landscape that extends to the horizon. Their alienation is palpable. The roof is their private world. "On the morning of August 8th I was raped again. I bled. Crimson blood will dry. I sleep on that puddle of blood. Sleep . . . live . . ." Throughout the film, the girl launches into spontaneous poetic reveries, the horrendous experiences she endures affording her moments of detached transcendence.

The camera cuts to the rapists who have spent the night on the roof as well, sleeping in a janitor's station. One awakens and rapes the girl again to the haunting strains of *Summertime*. "Kill me!" she cries again and again. The punks finally leave and the boy and girl discuss suicide. The girl asks the boy to kill her. The way he stares at her, it's obvious that he's infatuated. "I guess I'll kill you," he says, "I'm an expert after all." (Is he just posturing, or does this nerdy fellow have a dark secret?)

The boy leaves but soon returns with a dress (for her) and a bottle (for them). He watches her as she showers. The girl launches into her main poem, to which she adds stanzas throughout the remainder of the film:

> Go, go second-time virgin
> The masterpiece picked by men
> Go, go second-time virgin

Take the right road, even when a detour
Go go, second-time virgin
The joy, the nitro of love.

She asks the boy, "Do you know it?" indicating she is quoting. "Are you the second-time virgin?" he asks. "Yes, a seventeen-year-old high school girl." The boy whips out a few lines as well:

Bask in the sun until you can't sweat
Get thirsty and drink up the sun
Get sleepy and open your red eyes
Hold off peeing and shitting
If you want to die.

The boy takes the girl down to his hangout in the basement. There is a large pile of paperbacks, all returned copies of a poetry book the boy had published. He grabs one and reads:

Eyes open. Eyes closed.
When open, if open
Wake up. Wake up. Wake up.
Open, nose open
Pores open, all open
Choke on air
Eyes open, eyes open
A hose opens repeatedly
Progressing into an open eye
Pick a woman and open
Open your eyes again.

The girl is taken with the boy's poetry. "You can rape me," she offers pathetically. All sex is rape to her, as rape is the only sex she's known. The boy declines but asserts that he is not impotent. At last they introduce themselves. The boy is Tsukio. The girl is Poppo.

Tsukio takes Poppo up to an apartment on the fifth floor. The film shifts to color as we view four naked corpses strewn across the floor amidst large, gooey puddles of bright red blood. "Don't think I'm crazy," says Tsukio. "I killed them, but I didn't like it." In flashback we see the four, two couples, having a wild, booze-fueled orgy and subsequently pulling the unwilling and protesting Tsukio into the midst of their fleshy indulgences. They hold him down as one of the women urinates on him. Tsukio does what anyone would do: grabs a knife and stabs them all to death. Then he puts the women's panties on the men's heads and wraps a cord around the necks of various victims, stringing them together in imitation of the recent Sharon Tate murder scene (this is the first of several references to the Manson family murders of Tate and her guests that fateful night in August 1969).

Seeing the bloody corpses causes Poppo to reconsider her death request. Tsukio suggests instead that she do what he did—get revenge by killing the rapists. They do a little stabbing practice on one of the dead bodies.

Returning to the roof, who do they find hanging out but, yes, you guessed it, the rapists, this time with a few girls in tow. The punks don't pay them much mind and proceed to have a freak out to the unmistakable sounds of "The Return of the Son of Monster Magnet," the big freak out number on Frank Zappa's debut album, *Freak Out*. Their freak out consists in running around the roof, drinking, sniffing paint thinner, and getting off with the chicks. Eventually one of the punks gets around to noticing Poppo and rapes her again, joined by one of the girls. In the midst of her defilement, she recites:

> Go, go second-time virgin
> Your prick, it gets protracted
> An empty flat without extension
> Like thin soup rising
> The incest kitchenette.
> Your swollen abdomen
> And your cycle, bicycle.
> Go, go second-time virgin
> Riding in your hand
> Like a yellow dream toward the virgin spring.
> To stash away dead birds below a window
> Like the ultimate thief.

Throughout *Go, Go Second Time Virgin*, poetry acts as a catalyst, precipitating an action or development. So it is that this, Poppo's last installment, triggers something in Tsukio, who springs into action with his knife, killing two. He'll kill more before it's over, as well as sing his song, "Mama I'm Taking Off." And love will bloom with Poppo, however brief. . . .

A note on the rape scenes in this movie: Since *Go, Go Second Time Virgin* was filmed according to '60s pink film conventions, the depictions of rape aren't terribly graphic, or even all that violent. The cast of young amateurs playing the rapists are hardly threatening and their actions toward Mimi Kozakura consist largely in lying immobile on top of her and playing with her breasts. It is the idea of what's being represented, coupled with her own desperate reactions, that convey the humiliating violation of the crime of rape.

"It doesn't matter how you shoot a movie. As long as your spirit is there, it will cut together." Thus speaks Koji Wakamatsu in an interview included on the *Go, Go Second Time Virgin* DVD. Farmer, yakuza, ex-con, filmmaker, radical, and Bob Marley fan, Wakamatsu is one of a kind, a Japanese director who went up against the system and prevailed, winning the right to make films his way. Having skipped school most of his life, and never having attended film school, he was forced to develop his own methodologies, like making storyboards out of newspaper clippings and shooting and editing purely on instinct.

Koji Wakamatsu was first exposed to the world of filmmaking as a yakuza hireling, assigned to collect payoffs from film crews who shot in his boss's territory. After a stint in prison, he left the yakuza to pursue a career in movies. By 1963, he was making films for Nikkatsu, but this didn't last long. Ever the iconoclast, by 1965 he was out on his ear over studio reaction to his film *Secret Acts Within Four Walls*. Fortunately for him, by this time he had gained enough of a name in the business to go independent. He specialized in pink films, becoming one of the genre's leading lights during the '60s and '70s. Wakamatsu was eventually approached by Shochiku, where he worked with actor Juzo Itami (who would later make films of his own like *Tampopo* and *The Funeral*). Waka even produced Nagisa Oshima's groundbreaking masterpiece of sexual obsession, *In the Realm of the Senses* (1976).

Go, Go Second Time Virgin, for all its exploitative aspects, is nevertheless a unique and well-made film. Lurid yet lyrical, purple yet poignant, it is Wakamatsu's *Romeo and Juliet* on a rooftop. Such was Wakamatsu's genius (or luck) that even the rooftop works as a perfect metaphor for the personal experience of the boy and girl: a flat, barren wasteland bordered on all sides by oblivion, yet open and limitless as the whole wide sky.

The Joy of Torture • *Tokugawa onna keibatsu-shi*

You've got to hand it to Teruo Ishii: the man didn't fuck around. Back in 1968, if you bought a ticket to see a movie called *The Joy of Torture*, Ishii-san was hell-bent and determined to give you your yen's worth. Unlike other Ishii offerings that year, like *Onsen anma geisha* (*Hot Spring*

1968

Japan

96 min.

DIRECTOR: Teruo Ishii

CAST: Teruo Yoshida, Fumio Watanabe, Yuki Kagawa, Masumi Tachibana, Asao Koike, Kichijiro Ueda

Massage Geisha) or *Tokugawa onna keizu* (*History of the Shogun's Harem*), this time there would be no campy, tongue-in-cheek aspects, no humor to take the edge off, and seldom a calm moment to recover from the attendant horrors (or joys, depending on your tastes). There are two ways to deliver an exploitation film, with a wink and a nod or dead serious. The *Joy of Torture* falls squarely in the latter category, making it one of the more disturbing pink films in the genre. Consequently, there are only two ways to enjoy a film like this; you either continually remind yourself it's only a movie, or else get in touch with your inner deviant and *get your perv on!*

Tokugawa onna Keibatsu-shi translates as "Tokugawa women's punishment" (Tokugawa referring to the period in Japanese history from 1603–1868 during which the nation was ruled with an iron fist by the Tokugawa shogunate). Alternate English titles include *Joys of Torture* and *Shogun's Joy of Torture*. It is the first in a series of eight torture films Ishii made for Toei studios from 1968 to 1973 and sets a very high bar indeed for future sequels to outstrip (and outwhip). The film is composed of three vignettes set in the early Tokugawa period exploring various prohibited acts and their subsequent sadistic punishments, as well as an opening credit sequence showing random yet gruesome tortures and/or executions (included here are a woman beheaded and halved with an sword, another burned at the stake and a third split between two oxen). Although the films in the series focus primarily on the torture of women, it should be noted that plenty of men suffer horrendously as well, usually on the behalf of (or in retribution for) the unfortunate females. Also, perhaps to even the score somewhat, Ishii made a guys-only entry, *Yakuza Punishment: Lynching!* (1969, see sidebar). Let's

Yakuza Punishment: Lynching! (Yakuza Keibatsushi: Rinchi!) (Japan, 1969) One of the better and gorier yakuza films you're ever likely to see is Teruo Ishii's *Yakuza Punishment: Lynching!* Actually there's not much lynching in the film but what the hell, there are all sorts of other heinous acts to test your mettle. The credits alone catalog a host of horrible acts and once the stories begin, eyeballs are popped out, tongues cut off, hands mangled with broken glass, arms lopped off, faces burned beyond recognition, a guy's crushed alive in a car compactor, and another is dangled out a helicopter and taken for a drag along the edge of Tokyo Bay (perhaps that was the lynching bit). Like *Shogun's Love of Torture*, *Yakuza Punishment: Lynching!* is comprised of three vignettes, but this time they span three different historical periods in the life of the yakuza, namely the Tokugawa era (topknots and long swords), the late-Taisho/early-Showa period (straw hats and short swords), and modern day (late-'60s chic and *lots* of guns). Each story is concerned with a different rule and the inevitable fate of the rule-breaker. It's a cracking film that moves at a brisk pace and provides a compact lesson in yakuza history.

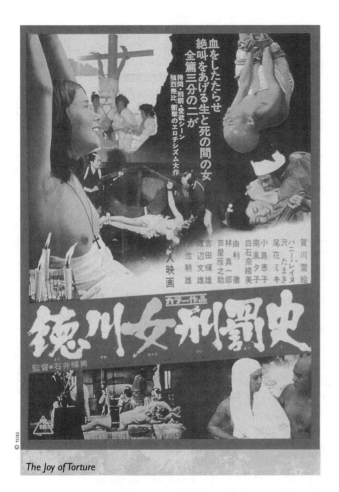

The Joy of Torture

take a look at the three stories that comprise this unparalleled anthology of agony (the titles for each are mine).

FORBIDDEN LOVE

Mitsu (Masumi Tachibana) and Shinza (Teruo Yoshida) are in love. The only problem is they're sister and brother and the authorities take a dim view of incest. The dimmest view possible, actually, as it's punishable by death. To make matters worse, lovely Mitsu has caught the fancy of corpulent old Boss Mino (Kichijiro Ueda), who'll stop at nothing (including arranging for a log to fall on Shinza's head) to have her. Paying Shinza's doctor bills, Mino seeks to exploit the obligation, finally raping Mitsu in a private room at Hisago restaurant. Mino continues to plague Mitsu, finally taking her right in front of her still-convalescing brother. It's all too much for Shinza, who stabs himself in the neck and dies. Mitsu, distraught, takes the knife from Shinza's neck and proceeds to slice Mino up a treat (although he survives and tells the authorities all about the two siblings' secret love). Since "questioning" back in the Tokugawa days involved prerequisite torture sessions (at least in Ishii's world), Mitsu is hung up and whipped for awhile, but never admits to making love with her brother. But upon final questioning by a kind official who bears a striking resemblance to her dead brother, Mitsu becomes confused yet strangely soothed by the benevolent stranger (also played by Teruo Yoshida). I won't say whether or not she confesses and is crucified upside-down in the rising tide. I will assert, though, that this piece offers the most touching incestuous love scenes I've ever seen.

HARROWING NUNSPLOITATION

"Murder case of the Abbess of Juko Temple, 1666," reads the Shinza-resembling good cop of the previous vignette as he pores over old case files. He's having a crisis of conscience, unlike his bad cop partner Nambara (Fumio Watanabe), who seems to execute his duties with a certain relish. As it happens, the young Abbess, Mother Reiho (Yuki Kagawa), was going along just fine as the "bottom" to her lesbian lover/servant Rintoku's "top" until one day when she gets a look at Shunkai, a handsome monk from the monastery next door. She spies Shunkai and Myoshin, a nun from Juko Temple, enjoying a little splendor in the grass, a beautiful and erotic scene evocative of the Garden of Eden, yet sicklied over with threatening, Hammer Film-like music, signaling impending doom. Afterward, Reiho confronts Shunkai, ordering him to pray naked under a waterfall to purify his . . . hey, wait a minute, she's stripping and joining him! He's her first man and she's in love, but he gives her the dish in no uncertain terms: he only did it on Myoshin's behalf and Reiho had better back off or he'll expose her.

Shunkai doesn't know who he's dealing with. Before you can say, "Hell hath no fury . . ." Reiho has Myoshin down in the temple dungeon (do temples have dungeons?), all trussed up like a turkey. Myoshin's put in a vat of water into which Reiho's minions release buckets of loaches (a type of eel) that immediately swim straight up her nether regions (we actually see this in an underwater close-up, in fact a clever reverse action shot). Myoshin's private area suffers further atrocities as nuns stuff it with red peppers, and finally cauterize it with a red hot poker, this ultimate indignity bringing about her death.

When Shunkai learns what happened, he loses his head, literally—Reiho hacks it off. She cradles the head and says, "You are mine now. You can't even talk back. You are my servant. I won't let you go, you belong only to me now! (laughs maniacally)" Thankfully, by now an old nun has called the police and our good cop/bad cop team are soon on the scene. As the guilty nuns are hung on crosses and skewered with spears, Good Cop again ponders whether this is really justice. Bad cop Nambara, however, is visibly aroused and enjoying every minute of it.

TORTUROUS TATTOOS

Horicho (Asao Koike) is the best tattoo artist in Edo (later Tokyo). He's showing off his latest work, an image of a woman suffering in rope bondage done on the back of a geisha named Kimicho, when Nambara happens by and starts laughing derisively. "This woman's face is a product of your imagination," he says. "You gave it a wry look. Listen

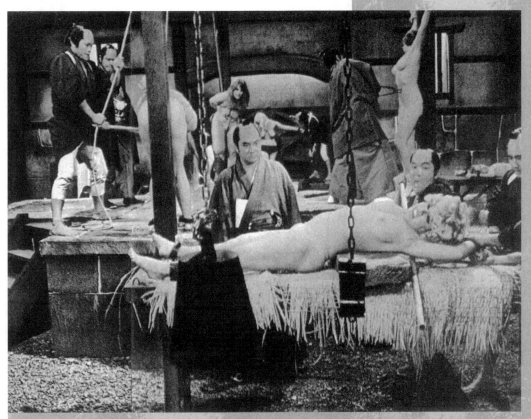

The grande finale torture sequence from *The Joy of Torture*

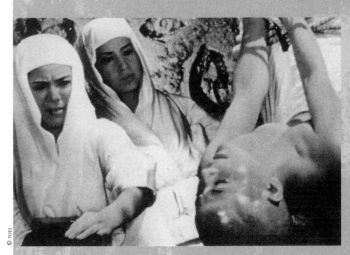

Poor Myoshin (right) suffers untold attrocities in *The Joy of Torture*

Horicho tattoos the horrors he witnesses in *The Joy of Torture*

Teruo Yoshida

carefully. An expression of real agony is not so ugly. It shows a kind of joy, a kind of pleasure, a strange sort of ecstasy." Horicho is devastated. Later he seeks out Nambara at his home and asks the official to show him some real torture to help develop his craft. Nambara is intrigued at the proposition of sadistic exhibitionism and agrees to take Horicho down to Nagasaki, where he's been doing a brisk business persecuting Christians. Meanwhile, Horicho has spied the perfect skin for his new project on a girl in a bathhouse and kidnaps her. He takes her along to Nagasaki, where Nambara has rounded up a bunch of European women. "Christianity is banned here," he tells them. "You pretended to have been shipwrecked and entered our country to propagate Christianity. The government assigned me to question you strictly. I will torture you first." Thus ensues a regular torture-palooza: whipping, crushing stones, breaking bones, fire and hot wax, water wheel, trussing and hanging, stocks and bondage, the works, all intercut with shots of the riveted Horicho tattooing away amid the screams. But something's missing. He needs a model for the wicked ogre in his tattoo, the one inflicting all the pain. He asks a flattered Nambara to pose but the egregious official just can't seem to get the right look until . . . in a flash, Horicho grabs the fiend's short sword and runs him through, getting just the right look. "Torturers must feel the pain of the tortured," Horicho declares as he twists the blade. "I don't know what hell is like, but in this world you can't torture people for fun!" Yes, we have a moral!

OK, so I blew the endings of the three vignettes; forgive me, but it would have been impossible to write a coherent review otherwise. By far the most gruesome of the three is the one with the nuns. Even though the women all wear ill-fitting bald wigs and heavy makeup, giving, the lie to them actually being nuns, still the acting, directing, lighting, and score all collude to suck you in to a vortex of nastiness that's hard to take lightly. You can also detect shades of influence on Norifumi Suzuki's corrupted cloister classic *Convent of the Sacred Beast,* particularly in the close-ups of lascivious looks on the senior nuns' faces during torments, and the way the most innocent are subjected to the greatest

That's gotta hurt: *Yakuza Punishment: Lynching!*

suffering (although here the action is set in a Buddhist nunnery, whereas it's a Christian convent in Suzuki's film). But where Suzuki opts for a dreamy, colorful *surreality* to simultaneously enhance and soften the blow of cruelty and malice (as does Junya Ito in the Female Prisoner Scorpion films), Ishii never flinches, taking you straight into the hellish black pit of the sadist's soul.

As a boy, Teruo Ishii (1924–2005) was influenced by the Japanese master of mystery and the bizarre, Edogawa Rampo (1894–1965). Rampo's pen name is actually a "Japanized" version of that of his own idol, Edgar Allen Poe, and he specialized in a form of fiction known in Japan as *ero-guro-nansenso*, short for "erotic grotesque nonsense." Ishii made *The Horror of Malformed Men* (1969) and *Blind Beast vs. Dwarf* (2001, his last film), both based on Rampo tales, and throughout his career he frequently infused his work with the ero-guro sensibilities inherited from his role model. Ishii initially worked as an assistant director at Toho and then, from 1947, at short-lived splinter studio Shin Toho, where he eventually graduated to director, making boxing pictures, superhero movies, and underworld suspense films. When Shin Toho folded in 1961, Ishii moved to Toei, and by the mid-'60s had made a name for himself, as well as burgeoning yakuza superstar Ken Takakura, with the popular Abashiri Prison film series (Takakura went on to make more films with Ishii than any other director at Toei). After ten Abashiri pictures, Ishii was ready for a change, and found a perfect vehicle for his ero-guro leanings in the Toei torture film cycle kicked off by *The Joy of Torture;* the Grand Guignol subject matter dovetailed perfectly with his own Rampo-inspired aesthetic. By the mid-'70s, Ishii found himself making karate and biker films and, bored at the prospect, retired at decade's end. Giving the '80s a miss, Ishii returned in the '90s to make independent films in his own warped way. The '90s also saw an Ishii renaissance of sorts as film festivals and retrospectives, as well as the efforts of writers like Patrick Macias and Mark Schilling, helped to boost exposure for Ishii's work, pleasing Japanese film fans around the world. Teruo Ishii died of lung cancer on August 12, 2005.

Stealing the show as the sadistic Nambara in *The Joy of Torture*

Nobody gets told twice in *Yakuza Punishment: Lynching!*

is magnificent heavy Fumio Watanabe. I've written about Watanabe elsewhere in this book, so let me just say that this is a standout performance; it's hard to imagine how he could be any more repellent, unless you made him a cannibalistic pedophile into the bargain, and even then the sheer cruelty and sadism he radiates here would tend to overshadow the impact of such tendencies. Watanabe seems to be enjoying himself to such an extent that watching him, one wonders whether he wasn't a bit of an S/M freak himself, although I prefer to put it down to professional technique and leave it at that. Masumi Tachibana, here as the sweet and incestuous Mitsu, was a pink film favorite, appearing in a number of *Joy of Torture* sequels. Look for her in the second vignette of *Yakuza Punishment: Lynching!* (see sidebar). The third vignette of *Lynching!* features Ishii regular Teruo Yoshida as a mysterious gunman who insinuates himself into a yakuza organization and winds up the last man standing. Yoshida also starred in space vampire cult classic *Goke, Body Snatcher from Hell* (yet another picture, like the Female Prisoner Scorpion films, that influenced Quentin Tarantino's Kill Bill saga). If you'd like to see Yuki Kagawa (psychotic nun Reiho) with hair, she's one of the group of escaped convicts in the second Sasori picture, *Female Prisoner Scorpion: Jailhouse 41.*

The Joy of Torture is an example of how an artist can transform a bottom-line-driven studio demand for sex and violence into something more. It isn't nice and it isn't pretty (for long), yet it's an expertly mounted, tightly packed (and budgeted), and surprisingly affecting film that will resonate long after the final kanji.

Versus

2000

Japan

119 Min.

DIRECTOR: Ryuhei Kitamura

CAST: Tak Sakaguchi, Hideo Sakaki, Chieko Misaka, Kenji Matsuda, Yuichiro Arai, Minoru Matsumoto, Kazuhito Oba, Motonari Komiya

Versus is the kind of film that should be in every household. Like food, beer, light bulbs, a phone book, and a can of WD-40—it's that essential. Once you've seen this truly magnificent hybrid of yakuza, zombie, samurai, vampire, reincarnation, martial arts, occult, comedy, and action, you'll understand and seek out your own copy. You're lucky; it's much easier to come by today than years ago when I bought mine, a Japanese import for which I paid an arm and a leg. But what the hell, with so many arms and legs flying around in this picture, I got my money's worth.

The film opens with text that reads:

There are 666 portals that connect this world to the other side. These are concealed from all human beings. Somewhere in Japan exists the 444th portal: The Forest of Resurrection.

Cut to a samurai vertically halving someone. The camera zooms in through the still-separating body to the samurai's face, then pulls back out to reveal the warrior surrounded by zombies in period costume. The synth 'n' shamisen score sets the proper mood of tension and uncertainty. The samurai makes quick work of the gory group before getting cut in two crossways by a sinister-looking priest/wizard (Hideo Sakaki). Cut to title (in flaming letters). Hell yes! Right out of the box, it's living-dead chambara, and we've still got the better part of two hours of insane splatgore to go!

The story shifts to the present day and we now observe two escaped convicts. They're headed for a rendezvous with some yakuza, ostensibly to make a getaway, or perhaps it's a setup? One of them, the hero of the piece (played by Tak Sakaguchi and whom I'll call Hero since no one has a name in the film) casually plucks a severed hand from the handcuff on his wrist and tosses it aside. He's all-cool, Mr. Sang Froid, and, although he looks like a male model, he's tough as nails and extremely self-confident. "I never lose," is his operative phrase.

On a road on the edge of a forest (the aforementioned Forest of Resurrection you think?), the two convicts hook up with five thugs: a biker with a ponytail (Yuichiro Arai), a suave psychopath in a green suit

(Kenji Matsuda), a fella with glasses that looks like a Japanese version of early Pink Floyd-era Roger Waters (Kazuhito Oba), a short, weasely guy (Minoru Matsumoto), and a dude in a leather coat that bears a striking resemblance to a young George Takei (aka Mr. Sulu). These guys also have a girl with them who they've apparently kidnapped. When Hero and Girl lock eyes, the score goes into a spooky, swoopy, synth-based across-the-winds-of-time style wash, indicating a deep but as yet unknown connection. The gangsters are waiting for some Mr. Big to show up and are under orders not to kill Hero, but Hero doesn't like the way they're treating Girl. He quickly acquires Weasel's big handgun and blows away Mr. Sulu. Cue dizzying arc shots of everybody pointing their guns at each other, until finally George Takei gets back up, now fully zombified. Much effort and firepower is expended in downing the rampaging monster-man. Afterward everyone resumes their standoff but are now somewhat perplexed as to just what is going on. Psycho Suit has an idea, and tests it by shooting the other escaped convict (Motonari Komiya). Everyone watches and waits, and yes, he jumps back up as well (to a hail of bullets). Yep, it's zombies alright. But by now Hero and Girl have hightailed it into the woods.

From here it's a balls-out zombie action free-for-all. It turns out the forest (yes, it's *that* forest) happens to be the same place the gangsters have been burying their dead enemies for quite awhile. Yes, that's right, hordes of living-dead yakuza begin to rise from their graves and, unlike your conventional zombies, these guys are *armed*. This makes for some great moments, like when Roger Waters is caught between two zombies, each with a gun to his head, and slips out just in time for them to blow each other away. Meanwhile, Weasel, his face covered in blood,

Wild Zero (Japan, 2000) Ho-hum. Some rock videos with a bunch of meandering crap in between. I'm sorry, but a Japanese rock 'n' roll zombie flick should be better than this. I won't say *Wild Zero* doesn't have its moments (namely whenever ultracool psychobilly trio Guitar Wolf is onscreen), but while it tries to make up in enthusiasm what it lacks in story, pace, or any measure of tension, as zombie films go, this one is just boring. Rock 'n' roll and zombies—how exactly does one mess that up? You've got a bizarre villain who wears multicolored Beatles wigs and skin-tight hot pants; a leggy, gun-totin' babe with an arsenal and an attitude; a Japanese version of Steve Buscemi; a pompadour-sporting rocker dude named Ace and his lady love (make that *ladyboy* love); explosions, flying saucers, plenty of undead gut-munchers, and yet it all just drags along, kicking up fewer sparks than you might expect. There's a lack of commitment here, splatgore-wise, and an over-reliance on rock music to amp up the atmosphere. Sure, zombie heads are blown to pieces, but they're fakey, CG effects—a melon on a stick with a wig would have looked better. Only recommended for Guitar Wolf fans.

gets progressively more panicked, hanging a good-luck charm from his handgun. Psycho Suit alternates between gun and butterfly knives and turns in a performance worthy of the Dennis Hopper Award for Insane Acting. There are also a couple of questionable cops in the mix, one with a missing hand and the other a pathological liar, who provide additional comedy relief. For a low-budget film, everyone does a fine acting job, even the zombies. Augmenting the atmosphere of carnage and madness, crunching heavy metal guitar riffs play throughout the zombie yakuza sequences, imparting sound and fury, *Sturm und Drang,* and a general mood of mayhem to the proceedings.

But it's not all guns and knives. There's a lot of martial arts action and good old fashioned brawling in *Versus* as well. Hero in particular likes to let his fists do the talking. That doesn't mean, however, that a moment later he won't have a gun in each hand and one in his teeth! (So gonzo was actor Tak Sakaguchi during filming that when he tried to rack the slide of the gun in his mouth with his teeth as directed, he chipped a tooth. Fortunately, one of the zombie extras was a dentist.) The kung fu action ramps up later on with the arrival of three more bad-asses: a guy with bright red Bozo hair, and two chicks. The short-haired girl and Bozo are the kung fu masters; the other girl, with longer hair, totes an impressive array of revolvers under her coat. These folks soon fall sway to the powerful influence of the priest/wizard necromancer from the opening scene. Yes, he's still alive and looking much the same as he did centuries ago. How does he manage to keep his youthful appearance? Necromancer has his own version of the Atkins Diet that he demonstrates by pulling Roger Waters's heart out of his chest and eating it.

Versus's action is balanced by great dialog and many a memorable line. A few examples:

GIRL:	You're no different from those men.
HERO:	They're bastards, I'm not.
GIRL:	I'm sorry, thanks for helping me.
HERO:	I didn't mean to help you. They just pissed me off.
PSYCHO SUIT:	Die slowly, alright? We don't want you coming back to life on us.

PSYCHO SUIT: What's going on? What are those monsters, and what about those two weirdos? What are you up to?

NECROMANCER: Something bad.

NECROMANCER: I'll give you power . . . in death.

NECROMANCER: I knew you could survive.

HERO: I don't know you. Fuck off.

NECROMANCER: Your soul does . . .

Necromancer seems almost obsessed with Hero. He entreats him, "Come with me, I'll show you the power of darkness . . . You made me wait 500 years for the girl to reincarnate, but I forgive you." They fight. Necromancer tells Hero, "I like you better as a criminal now. You used to be an awful man of justice. You really made me suffer. But you've changed. That's why I've brought you here."

The reincarnation theme is what ennobles *Versus*, imbuing it with an epic quality. The twin aspects of karma and rebirth are ripe for the dramatic picking, what with their narrative potential for eon-spanning rivalries and undying love, causing one to wonder why they aren't utilized more often in popular drama. Maybe it's just too heady, but here it's applied in just the right measure to balance the otherwise totally demented action and splatgore.

And what splatgore! *Versus* is matched in the scope and audacity of its butchery only by Peter Jackson's infamous 1992 zombie masterpiece *Dead Alive*. Blood continually gushes everywhere, including into people's faces and mouths. Severed heads go flying, at times by way of well-placed kung fu kicks. Heads are also used to head-butt assailants and catch thrown knives. A gangster's handgun inadvertently penetrates a rotten zombie chest (saved a bullet there). Zombie intestines drop and dangle and there are numerous camera shots taken through holes in people. One such moment comes as Necromancer puts his fist through Bozo's head, essentially boring a hole in it, and the camera swings around to the back to give us a close-up of Necromancer's face through the meat tunnel that was once Bozo's skull (you can even see his lower teeth). But these are just highlights; the gory gags and set pieces are too numerous to count.

Two years in the making, *Versus* was director Ryuhei Kitamura's breakout film. Needless to say this low-budget miracle and its attendant cult following put the Australian-schooled filmmaker squarely on the map, and he's since moved on to bigger and bigger projects. The manga-adapted *Azumi* (2003) proved Kitamura could make cute young girls and fey young fellows into formidable samurai warriors. In 2004, he lent his extreme directorial talents to *Godzilla: Final Wars,* becoming part of a venerated Japanese film tradition begun by Ishiro Honda fifty years before. As of this writing, he is working on the long-awaited *Versus 2.*

Ironically, for a man who made one of the greatest cult films of all time, Kitamura told *Giant Robot Magazine,* "I don't like cult movies. If you go too far, it's cult. If you stay in the safety zone, it's boring. But my style is on the extreme side." Asked to describe his taste, he replied, "Extreme. Do everything extreme." And when asked if, during the making of *Versus,* he ever thought it was too much for him, he paraphrases Hero: "No. I never give up" (Issue 36, Summer 2005).

The Seventh Curse • Yuan Zhen-Xia yu Wei Si-Li

1986

Hong Kong

81 min.

DIRECTOR: Nam Nai Choi

CAST: Chin Siu Ho, Maggie Cheung Man Yuk, Dick Wei, Chow Yun Fat, Elvis Tsui Kam Kong, Chi Sau Lai, Ken Boyle, Ni Kuang

Splatastic! When it comes to mixing high-spirited hijinks with ghastly gore, there's nothing like Hong Kong cinema of the '80s/'90s, and there's no Hong Kong film quite like *The Seventh Curse.* Clocking in at a trim eighty-one minutes, there's enough fighting, shooting, explosions, monsters, T&A, jungle adventure, brandy and cigars, human sacrifice, and spurting blood here for a whole Hollywood trilogy. There's also a blood bath (literally), battling Buddhist monks on ropes, Rambo-style raids, a treacherous witchdoctor with a deadly pet, and an ancient, unstoppable ghoul who sups with glee on the spinal cords of his victims. All this and Chow Yun Fat. Could this be heaven? If you're a Hong Kong action fan, a gore hound or both, you better believe it!

We first meet the two heroes of our tale, Dr. Yuan (or Yuen) and Wesley (or Wisley or Wei), at a party being held by real-life Hong Kong writer Ni Kuang (or I Kuang or Yi Kuang, aka Ai Hong or Ngai Hong). (I should mention that while researching *The Seventh Curse,* I came across a wealth of alternative names and spellings, so bear with me.) Under the nom de plume Ai Hong, Ni Kuang wrote numerous pulp novels featuring the exploits of his two guests, and seems particularly gratified to have them at his little soirée in fancy dress, brandy snifters and big-haired beauties in tow. Dr. Yuan is played by kung fu action man and supernatural film star Chin Siu Ho (*Ghosts Galore, Mr. Vampire*), here wearing huge '80s glasses that convey a questionable intellectuality. Dr. Yuan's friend and mentor, easygoing occult scholar Wesley, is chan-

Chin Siu Ho and Chow Yun Fat enjoy a brandy in *The Seventh Curse*

© WONG JING

neled by a young, pre-superstardom Chow Yun Fat. Ni Kuang asks his two characters to relate one of their fabulous adventures, and, with a healthy mutual slug from their snifters (freeze-frame for the title card), we're off!

Cut to a hostage crisis: Dr. Yuan is called in to defuse the situation by posing as a doctor (so far, so good). Seems one of the hostages has had a heart attack and requires medical attention. Captain Ho of the SWAT team gives Yuan a bomb (just go with it). Troublesome girl reporter Tsai-Hung (Maggie Cheung) impersonates a nurse and accompanies Yuan. Unfortunately, the terrorist/kidnappers are smart and soon have them sussed. Then all hell breaks loose: the SWAT team moves in, everyone starts shooting, and Yuan goes into full-on kung fu whoop-ass mode, all at such breakneck speed that one wonders if someone sped up the film! Tsai-Hung's ruse is exposed and she is duly chastised by Yuan: "I've never met a more frantic girl than you!" However, by now she's smitten with the good doctor and continues to plague him for the remainder of the movie.

Later, Dr. Yuan blows off some steam at an elegant, babe-laden poolside party. *Seventh Curse* producer/screenwriter Wong Jing shares a cameo appearance with prolific Hong Kong director Chu Yuan (*The Bastard, The Forbidden Past, Death Duel*); Wong regales Chu with his theory of how penis sizes vary according to latitude, leaving himself wide open for the inevitable dick joke. Dr. Yuan chats up a lovely looker, but his rap is ruined by the pesky Tsai-Hung. He heads back to his stylish bachelor pad, where another young lady is ready and waiting, but before you can say "Let's get something straight between us," some guy comes crashing in and a brawl ensues. Turns out the guy is Heh Lung (Dick Wei), a Thai fellow who's come to warn the doctor, "Your blood spell has reached one year." He urges Yuan to head for Thailand immediately and warns, "Keep away from sex or you may have a quick relapse." Of course, as soon as Heh Lung departs, the good doctor is all about gettin' it on and, sure enough, we see the effects of the aforementioned "blood curse"—veins pop out on Yuan's leg, ripples and indentations scurry up and down, and finally, with a sickening pop, a bullet-sized hole bursts open, spattering his girlfriend with blood. Talk about ruining the mood. . . .

There's only one thing for it, gotta see Wesley. He's at home, practicing on his indoor putting green, when Dr. Yuan calls. Wesley puffs meaningfully on his pipe as Yuan relates the story of his journey to Thailand the year before, taking us into an extended flashback (now two steps removed from Ni Kuang's brandy 'n' broads framing story at film's beginning). Dr. Yuan had journeyed into the jungle with a medical research team in search of therapeutic herbs for the treatment of AIDS and inadvertently got involved with the Yunnan Miao, a "worm tribe" specializing in black magic. That's when his troubles began.

Since there's far too much action and plot crammed into *The Seventh Curse* to cover here, a little shorthand is in order; I'll run through the main characters introduced in the Thai jungle flashback:

- Professor (Ken Boyle): Yes, just like on Gilligan's Island, there's a character named "Professor." He's leading the research expedition and warns Dr. Yuan and the rest of the party against any contact with the Yunnan Miao tribe. Obviously, he's the Cassandra of the piece.
- Betsy (Chui Sau Lai): Comely daughter of the ex-chief of the Yunnan Miao, Yuan spies her doing a little wet tee-shirt routine in a lake near his encampment and drops his binoculars. Little does he realize how much their mutual fates are intertwined . . . and don't ask me why a native girl is named "Betsy."
- Aquala (Elvis Tsui): The evil witchdoctor. He has taken over the tribe and rules it with an impressive array of malevolent supernatural powers. These extend to conjuration of wicked entities, raising the dead, blood worm craft, and the application of horrid goo that does all sorts of nasty things. Plus he wears a ton of pancake makeup and a stringy black wig. This is one twisted freak you don't want to mess with . . . oops, too late.
- Little Ghost: Aquala whips out this mutant baby crossed with a

worm from beneath his robes when he wants to silence someone like, for example, a protester in the crowd gathered for Human Sacrifice Night. The hapless heckler soon finds the tiny, bald-headed fiend, all red mouth, tapered tail and tiny talons, ripping through his throat. Amid gushing blood, the little creep jumps down the man's neck and exits through his stomach, *Alien*-style. Further dissent is effectively squelched.

- Male sacrifice: This young guy and Betsy are chosen as offerings to the "Old Ancestor" by Aquala's magic, glowing dagger. Betsy is rescued by Dr. Yuan, but this guy isn't so lucky.

- Old Ancestor: Aquala raises him in the inner temple with a generous slathering of blood on his tomb and a few magical incantations. Soon he is risen, a mangy green skeleton with glowing blue eyeballs. Make no mistake, though, he's plenty tough: he can mix it up kung fu–style or, if the going gets tough, transform into a giant, burly lizard man. One look at him and our young male wets himself; soon thereafter, the Old Ancestor breaks the young man's neck open and sucks out his spinal cord.

Yuan rescues Betsy from the Old Ancestor in the nick of time, but soon enough he and the Professor are taking her place, both tied to stakes in the temple. Aquala pours horrid goo on Professor, causing his face and belly to burst forth with thousands of tiny worms. Aquala jams a worm down Yuan's throat, installing a blood curse: holes will burst forth from his body, increasing in intensity until the seventh one reaches his heart, killing him. However, Betsy knows a way to forestall the curse; she takes a knife to her left breast and cuts a piece of it out, feeding it to Yuan. Now he's good for a year. End of flashback. Since all these events occurred a year ago, Wesley and Yuan decide it's time to head back to the jungle. . . .

And the film isn't even half over. The grisly, gut-wrenching roller coaster ride that is *The Seventh Curse* rolls on and on, each new scene scaling the heights of lurid invention. Before it's all over, Dr. Yuan and Heh Lung's action items include locating a giant, enchanted Buddha statue (check), freeing Tsai-Hung from the evil clutches of Aquala (check), and rescuing 100 children from liquefaction in a giant stone kid-crusher (oops, two out of three. . . .)

As mentioned at the outset, writer Ni Kuang introduces the film. It's worth noting that, in addition to creating the characters of Dr. Yuan and Wesley (in fact, that's the literal translation of the film's title, "Dr. Yuan and Wesley"), he's also the author of some 160 screenplays for Hong Kong films dating back to the '60s. A mere trawl in the copious

"My work is done."

flow of film scripts from this gifted graphomaniac yields such immortal titles as *The Flying Guillotine* (1974), *Executioners from Shaolin* (1977), *Five Deadly Venoms, Shaolin Master Killer, Enter the Fat Dragon* (1978), *Dirty Ho* (1979), and *Nine Demons* (1983).

Helming *The Seventh Curse* is director Nam Nai Choi, the man behind cult classics *Peacock King* (1989), *Saga of the Phoenix, Erotic Ghost Story* (1990), *The Story of Ricky* (aka *Riki-Oh*, 1991), and *The Cat* (1992). If you're looking for movies with mind-bending plots, generous helpings of ultraviolence and a bit of the old in-out, you can't go far wrong with Nam, truly an auteur of the insane film. One viewing of *The Seventh Curse* and you'll see what I mean.

YBIBLIOGRAPHYB

Print

Clements, Jonathan and Motoko Tamamuro. *The Dorama Encyclopedia: A Guide To Japanese TV Drama Since 1953*. Berkeley: Stone Bridge Press, 2004.

Desjardins, Chris. *Outlaw Masters of Japanese Film*. New York: I.B. Tauris, 2005.

Hammond, Stefan, and Mike Wilkins. *Sex and Zen and A Bullet in the Head*. New York: Fireside, 1996.

Leong, Anthony C.Y. *Korean Cinema: The New Hong Kong*. Victoria: Trafford, 2003.

Macias, Patrick. *Tokyoscope: The Japanese Cult Film Companion*. San Francisco: Cadence Books, 2001.

Morley, John David. *Pictures from the Water Trade: An Englishman in Japan*. London: Andre Deutsch, 1985.

Thomas, Brian. *VideoHound's Dragon: Asian Action and Cult Flicks*. Canton: Visible Ink Press, 2003.

Internet

All Movie Guide
http://www.allmovie.com/

Fortissimo Films
http://www.fortissimofilms.com/

Hong Kong Cinemagic
http://www.hkcinemagic.com/

Hong Kong Cinema—View from the Brooklyn Bridge
    http://www.brns.com/

Internet Movie Database
    http://us.imdb.com/

Kabuki 21
    http://www.kabuki21.com/

Korean Movie and Drama Database
    http://www.hancinema.net/

Kung Fu Cult Cinema
    http://www.kfccinema.com/

Thai Film Foundation
    http://thaifilm.com/

ThailandLife.com
    http://thailandlife.com/

OTHER TITLES OF INTEREST FROM STONE BRIDGE PRESS

Obtain any of these books online or from your local bookseller
sbp@stonebridge.com • www.stonebridge.com • 1-800-947-7271

Stray Dogs & Lone Wolves

The Samurai Film Handbook

PATRICK GALLOWAY

Finally, a readable book about the ever-popular genre of samurai film! *Stray Dogs & Lone Wolves* provides essential background on the samurai warrior in Japanese culture to help explain what makes these tales of loyalty, revenge, and explosive swordsmanship so watchable.

240 pp, 7 x 9", paper, 40 b&w photos, ISBN 978-1-880656-93-8, $19.95

The Yakuza Movie Book

A Guide to Japanese Gangster Films

MARK SCHILLING

Japanese gangster films, with their stoic yet explosively violent heroes, have influenced everyone from Eastwood to Jarmusch. This book features over 120 film critiques, with profiles and interviews of actors and directors like Miike, Kitano, Aikawa, and Sugawara. A distinctive reference.

380 pp, 7 x 9", 45 b&w photos, ISBN 978-1-880656-76-1, $19.95

The Midnight Eye Guide to New Japanese Film

TOM MES AND JASPER SHARP

Explore the astounding resurgence of Japanese cinema through 19 contemporary Japanese filmmakers, from the well-known (Kitano, Miike, Miyazaki) to the up-and-coming (Naomi Kawase, Satoshi Kon), with reviews of 97 of their recent films. Makes an excellent DVD rental guide!

376 pp, 7 x 9", paper, 100 b&w illustrations, ISBN 978-1-880656-89-1, $22.95

The Anime Encyclopedia, Revised & Expanded Edition

A Guide to Japanese Animation Since 1917

JONATHAN CLEMENTS AND HELEN MCCARTHY

Bigger and better! Our first edition rocked the anime world with its in-depth entries on anime famous and obscure and its superb index/film finder. Now this fantastic book is 40% larger—with all-new entries on hundreds of anime released after 2001, updates on older entries, and over 50,000 words on anime creators (like Tezuka and Otomo) and genres ("Early Anime," "Science Fiction and Robots," etc.). An absolute must-have for every anime shelf!

850 pp, 7 x 9", paper, 150 b&w illustrations, ISBN 978-1-933330-10-5, $29.95